FROM FIRED TO FREEDOM

How life after the Big Bad Boot gave me Wings

VALENTINA JANEK

RED PENGUIN Books

ISBN 978-1-949864-14-4

DEDICATION

To Joann Fiorentino Lucas, my friend and co founder of the Long Island Breakfast Club, I say thank you for being the impetus behind pushing me to start. The Long Island Breakfast Club, which has grown tremendously since your passing.

Not a meeting goes by without someone mentioning something about you. You were a consummate authentic passionate woman advocate who touched the lives of everyone you met. You never gave up. You took the time to educate everyone who came down your path to help them personally, professionally, and socially. Your most important gift and legacy was the mark you left on myself and many others on Long Island. You had faith, tenacity, strength, courage, discipline and determination, and you possessed the wisdom to be satisfied every day, one day at a time. Personal experience was what drove Fiorentino to

encourage everyone who came down her path. You had faith in yourself, my passion to create this club, and the members in our community.

Thanks for giving me the drive to write my first novella and keep going forward to develop more memories and strategies for individuals and businesses and entrepreneurs and write this book.

One of the last words you spoke to me and the members and our peers in the community was "If you sit back and let the game pass you by, that is how your life will be".

Thank you, Joann. I listened!! I know you are looking down from up there in heaven and smiling from ear to ear with how far your wisdom has taken me.

In dedication to my dear sister Maria who was a sister member of the Long Island Breakfast Club, supporting every special event with her charm, caring, humor and love, touching all who she met. Her creativity and spark will never be forgotten!

One of her favorite mottos when giving advice to members was always, "What goes around ~ comes around. You get what you give, so be kind."

CONTENTS

FOREWORD

I first met Valentina Janek because of Snapple in 1995 - she was selected as my "look-a-like", and we became fast friends. Snapple brought us together! Traveling together to different events, I loved being around Valentina—she loves people, and ALWAYS has a positive outlook—NEVER wallowing in self-pity. She has inspired me in so many ways, and she really 'talks the talk' and 'walks the walk'. Tina is a ray of sunshine in the bleakness of today, as she refuses to get depressed, and will NOT hear the word NO! (Trust me - don't try to say "NO" to her!)

This book is Valentina—and her take and tips on "life after loss" in the job market. When you lose a job, it's the fear that hits—and nothing is worse than living a life of fear. But you are NOT your job! Separate your job from your person—because life goes in different directions. Depending upon the stage of your life, life is fluid, and we need to be fluid with it. People change jobs an average of 7 times in their lives—7 TIMES! Companies of today have ZERO loyalty, so we need to be loyal to ourselves—keeping focused on OUR future, keeping our eyes on the PRIZE. It's YOUR time to shine, so do what you want, recognize windows of opportunity, and WALK RIGHT IN!

Valentina is a one-woman networking phenomenon, and I have been fascinated and empowered watching her journey for the past 25 years. She has gone through months of meeting people—never really knowing where the journey will lead. She knows her strengths and keeps it real—not getting lost in fantasy but pushing forward in reality. Losing a job later in life can be scary, but you also get a whole new view on what matters. Who knows—downsizing could be the right opportunity to become an independent contractor or start your own business if you have what it takes. Many times, what people are missing is the routine—not the task—and job loss can be the beginning and not the end. Valentina knows—from herself, and from the people she walks beside. Read the stories, learn from the tips, and glow in the sunshine that is Valentina—you'll be glad that you did!

Wendy Kaufman

The former "Snapple Lady"

INTRODUCTION

DOWNSIZED! KA CHOONG!
IT'S A BUSINESS DECISION!
YOUR POSITION HAS BEEN ELIMINATED!

Downsized—that horrible word that everyone uses. Why don't they just say it—"You're Fired" . . . ."The Donald" says it all the time!!!

Who would have thought the phrase "You're Fired" would become so popular? The greatest angst for anyone who has received those words face-to-face usually comes to them by surprise. No matter the whys or hows—if you have been part of, as they call it, the "Pink Slip", remember you can and you will recover.

Most importantly, you must MOVE ON, but that does not happen easily. There is a satisfying world out there, and I am here to tell you what my life was like **After The Big Bad Boot!**

Confucius said, "Choose a job you love and you will never have to work a day in your life." That might be fortune cookie wisdom, buts it's pretty good advice when it comes to looking forward to going to work every day.

Losing my job gave me the time to stop sitting back and let the game pass me by.

If you sit back and let the game pass you buy, that is how your life will be. To make things happen you have to persevere and never take "no" for an answer. "Well-behaved" I was not for the last few years, but well behaved women rarely make history.

It was Thanksgiving weekend . . . I was called to the President's Office, and I was hopeful the reason was a promotion, and a pat on the back for the hard work I had done for ten consecutive years. I had just finished working on a plan to save the company thousands on a potential project change. Ka Choong!!!! Was I on another planet! Not only was that not the case, I was—as they put it so kindly in the corporate world—downsized. "Your Position Has Been Eliminated" were the exact words. "It's a business decision." At the time, although shocked, I realized the time I spent in the last ten years putting all of my eggs into one basket was probably the biggest mistake I could have made in my business career.

Being a spirited, committed employee in the corporate world, and having changed positions in my career only twice in twenty years, I thought stability and longevity were considered great things, at least that's what Mamma used to tell me. Today, I have a different attitude regarding that ancient rule of thumb. I believe that you should give 100% to your current job, but have learned that giving 150% can cause you pain and no gain.

So there I was, 53 years old, trying to figure out what had happened. Because of my longevity in the organization, I felt shocked, angry, and ticked off. Never did I think in this great big world of expense downsizing that my project to save the company money would be a negative. But then again, I was asked to do a particular project, after a quick change in a management reporting structure, working for a bonehead who happened to be a very insecure male. One management change can alter your career. Up until this change, I worked for two very secure individuals who happened to be male as well, obviously not insecure boneheads! The project work completely proved I would have the results to save thousands of dollars ensuring a return on investment to the bottom line.

You would have thought that was a good thing, but another lesson learned.

I guess by reading between the lines, you can realize the underlying facts regarding the savings to the company were not pretty details.

Never think doing the *right* thing measures up to a *good* thing. Go figure. I exited on a quiet note through a rear door, and realized very quickly that the best day of the rest of my life was the day I quietly left like a bird flies away. Getting the big bad boot gave me wings to fly!

Since that time, although broke, I opened up my world in many ways. I have many stories to tell about my year of interviewing, consulting, and breaking out in the world!

Life is good when you live from your roots. Your values are a great source of energy, enthusiasm and direction. Optimism changes you if you keep it. I started to meet other women who were in the same spot as myself and we never ran out of conversation.

As I kept thinking of the funny stories that happened to me on interviews, I thought to myself, if I have these funny and uplifting experiences, others probably have more obnoxious experiences— and may want to share them. I can't be the only woman who has had these unique experiences on interviews, could I be? After thinking about this more, I went to my local radio station, and asked a friend to help me put together a voice audio to reach out to others, to email me some of their horror stories about being unemployed in this great big market of downsizing. The audio actually came out pretty well and I was charged by it—and quickly formulated a group of wise men and women who were experiencing the effects of losing their jobs. We kept each other going for a year with positivity and laughter. Optimism makes friends. And I believe that giving back could actually find you work and likely land you in a good company.

I believe that at the end of the day, your most important gift is your openness to changing the life of an individual as well as your own.

I guess in a way, my downsizing was an extension of a midlife crisis which I had already experienced, and I came out of it feeling very differently about many things. Change is usually good; sometimes it takes a while to realize the change is good.

I choose to be optimistic most of the time. I find it energizes and sustains me and hopefully has positioned me for success.

Did I get discouraged? Yes, those days were all about Baskin Robbins Peanut Butter and Chocolate ice cream cones with sprinkles while driving in the car alone, like a yoyo, just to keep going on a bad day. Or a Cosmo or two at Paparazzi's for a snack! Crying in the car was a once-a-month drama! Did you know one of the best places to cry is in the car, and in my case I never got caught because I had dark-tinted windows? I even took a laughter class, which I found interesting and invigorating. You should try it, it's fun and it's energizing, and you laugh a lot!

Virtually every midlife woman out of work has moments or months when she really feels maybe she just can't cut it, and it's "time to make the donuts," but perseverance and female friendships help lifestyle changes like losing a job. Commiseration, compassion, sharing experiences and good old- fashioned laughter get you through. All of the women I met faced age bias and lost opportunities. I am in the real word, just like you, and I have faced age bias and lost opportunities because of it. Women count on each other for the natural abilities to help one another as coaches. There is a big comfort level in having others around you with similar experiences when seeking new employment. They offered a whole lot more than going to agencies and hearing the negative responses like, "You're overqualified."

The fact is that seven out of ten business people who interview you never get back to you or follow up–as a matter of fact, very few do. It must be because there has been so much downsizing there isn't a need to be polite any longer and communicate.

Most of the women in our group are a good twenty years from retirement. Some may want to retire by 62, yet they cannot seem to re-land in competitive salaried positions.

The truth of the matter is that corporate America is not ready for mature individuals who can walk into a role with experience. Volunteering can escalate your career even higher, which eventually can pay off in a new role.

The facts are that older workers are the best employees—the "cream of the crop"—who will give more than the usual 100%.

Welcome to my world of experiencing a truly wacky few years! I was lucky enough to have had a husband who supported me through a time of financial hell, but it also proved to be very insightful and eye-opening. In my case, the interviews which I had became a string of days that I will never forget. Now the fun begins!

Chapter One
INTERVIEWS GONE WILD

Failure is the best lesson you can get to get to the next level of your career.
~Valentina Janek

BAD BOSSES - BAD EMPLOYEES - IT'S A MIXED BAG

Finally! I had a job interview. Well, at least that's what they called it before I got there. I'm not mentioning names or locations, so this can apply to anyone. There are bad bosses, ones that are so controlling that they feel all others are idiots. Ones that don't take the time to train, explain or even talk to you. I'm not talking large corporations here but small enterprises under 30 employees. What do you do if you walk into a place for an interview and its in the center of the current staff who are sitting around staring into space. There he is, the BOSS. He has 3 phones pressed to his face, while calling his staff lazy idiots. He asks his bookkeeper to cut a check then stops her 30 seconds later with instructions to do something else. Frustration and confusion are the only facial features I witnessed. He complained to me for nearly 2 hours, begging for help to "FIX" his sick company. When pressed for job details, I got a good salary offer, oh, that would be if the position were for 40 hours, but it was for 60 hours. Now that makes it more like minimum wage. But he says he loves my skills. Of course, I knew that, while standing at attention in the middle of the business version of "Hoarders!" What a fiasco. There's more! When asked about training, he states that there is no training, if you don't know what to do, then you're an idiot and shouldn't work there. He is correct. I cannot work there. I wouldn't work there. He called the next day to see if I were still interested. One of his 4 office staff had quit. No wonder, he called the man a lazy idiot right in front of me. I was embarrassed for him. Wouldn't you be? And no, I can't work in that kind of environment. It's bad for my health.

Yes, there are Bad Bosses out there. How about Bad employees? Plenty of them, too!

Elise Negrin

OH SAY CAN YOU SEE? POLITICALLY INCORRECT....

After being in an interview with a professional board of directors for a management position, the interviewer popped up with the question—I see you received an award from a municipal official in the county? What is your political party and are you involved? This one ticked Joann off. She had interviewed people for twenty years in a management position she held. She knew indeed that this kind of question was unprofessional and illegal. How poor of that executive to ask such a ridiculous question in the world of today where you have to be very specific and careful when discussing employment. She answered politely and quickly ran the hell out of there.

Joann Fiorentino Lucas

NEATNESS COUNTS

I had an interview with a subpoena service organization in the legal field. A very small eight-person office. The owner interviewed me at length and said that he was very concerned with neatness. After a not-so-interesting interview, he asked me what the inside and the trunk of my car looked like. I thought this to be a weird question. I quickly stated it was clean, and my trunk was big enough to fit a body if I had to. As he shook my hand upon my exit, he asked me if I would mind if he could come out to the car, and look in my trunk. I said, "Go for it, come right along!"

I chuckled on the way to the parking lot, and thought maybe my neatness in the car was going to get me this job. Wrong!!!! Although he did see my car was clean, I never heard from him again.

While I understand the importance of neatness, I'm not sure why or when the look of my car should be a factor.

Valentina

A PARROT FROM HELL

I once interviewed with an equipment firm on L.I. As I walked in to meet my interviewer, I heard some very strange and loud noises coming from his office. As the door opened, a large parrot flew out of the office, landed on the resume I was holding—and took a dump. "Wa, wa, wa!" shouted the parrot, and followed this greeting with a string of X-rated curses that would make any longshoreman blush.

There are those who might see the parrot—and his dump—as a good luck omen. I'm not one of them!

Anonymous

MAKING A SPLASH

I t was a very bad snowstorm in the middle of winter, and I had scheduled an interview to meet with the XYZ Fence company on Long Island. Wearing high heels, I somehow managed to get down some steps without falling on the ice and had to practically bang the door down to get a response. My knocking was answered by a man, quite short, wearing a hat covered in sawdust. Here I was, by contrast, in a classic business suit, when all of a sudden, the man was joined by a golden retriever, barking incessantly also covered in sawdust.

The interviewer kindly said, "Oh, I guess you should meet Splash. He is the watchdog, office manager and all around Gal Friday. You must like him to even be considered for this job." Huge water bowls and bubble wrap lined the hallway which led to the office where I would sit and share the space with Splash if I were offered the job. "Splash is kind of like your supervisor. He is my best friend, and will be yours too." I realized that such a small company really didn't need a full-time marketing manager, so I mentioned working possibly part time, in my desperate attempt to leave. The boss said, "Oh no, part of the position is to babysit Splash as well, as I am out In the field during the day. He needs an hour of play time daily. Do you see that bubble wrap? Once a day he plays with about 2 feet of it! It's part of his regimen." I thought to myself, could this man be for real? I left very mortified, annoyed, bewildered and disenchanted, vowing never to return to hang out and be a buddy to Splash.

Valentina (who is allergic and afraid of dogs)

CINDERELLA LOSING HER SHOES AT THE CASTLE!

Oheka Castle is a magnificent mansion on the Gold Coast of Long Island, boasting 32 luxurious guest rooms, where guests can sleep like royalty. Huge. Lavish. Excellent and refined in every way.

On this day I was lucky enough to break bread with the legendary Mr. Gary Melius, who actually grew up in West Hempstead, my hometown. He gracefully granted me an interview immediately with the hiring manager.

I arrived at the castle for an interview, and it was overwhelming, I thought, "Wow, how neat could that be to work in a castle?" What I did not realize was that in a castle, there are "no shortcuts to the top"—literally. It is not easy to climb stairs and stairs and stairs in a gorgeous castle when you are physically out of shape, which happens to describe me.

By the time I made it upstairs to the library interview room, which was exquisite, I was out of breath, stressed and in need of time to rejuvenate! As I was climbing each stairway with a serious cultured gentleman—the interviewer—in front of me, I was thinking this must be a physical endurance test. Needless to say I failed that test. When the interview started, my brain was on freeze, my voice was not pitched, and the chemistry of that interview went down to zero. After being interviewed by a very cultured Frenchman, I realized not only was I not qualified for this position, but I was intimidated as their market was going to be the Rich and the Famous from Europe. What the heck did I know about that market? I babbled through the interview and knew everything that I said was dumb and dumber. It was like a "Seinfeld" episode, and one I won't forget. The kind, cultured gentleman explained to me his vision for the people he was planning to hire, and believe me, I was not in that vision, especially when my shoe slipped off of my foot and fell all the way down the massive staircase! I kid you not this happened and what an embarrassing moment. I knew it, and he knew it immediately, Cinderella I was not!

I quickly left this castle knowing the next time I would be there for an exclusive party, I probably would need to be invited by a queen or a king. Not a great day. As I drove home, I thought I blew this one big time, for sure it was not meant to be. I may not have gotten the job, but I gained a page in my memory book and a great contact and friend with Gary Melius when launching the new West Hempstead Library in OUR hometown together, a wordly, wise individual who opened his doors to me and to the Long Island Breakfast Club.

Valentina

OH MY, A NEWS ANCHOR! I DOUBT IT!

I received a phone call one day from Richard Rose, the News Anchor from WLNY, Channel 10. I recognized his name immediately and was quite interested in meeting him. I knew I was not qualified enough for an assignment editor position, but was curious about the station and still believed that with every interview, you meet someone new who could possibly lead you to another position. Part of me was thinking, in my optimistic world, that I could be asked to do a demo and start reporting. I always thought about being a reporter, I could do it! So, off I went to my interview and was quite delighted.

My interviewer was very personable, and honest and explained to me how my competition would probably be applicants with television experience. I realized that going into the interview, but thought "why not try it"? He asked if I liked to write and I explained I could write—but specifically for the things that were passionate to me. I told him about this book that I was compiling at the time of the interview, and he chuckled and asked me if he was going to be put in the book. "Of course," I answered, "you are. It's not often you meet a high roller from TV news and get to talk about it." He asked me to send him a sampling of my writing, and I hesitated the next day to send a copy. I changed the sampling several times, but then decided to "go for it" and sent it.

At the end of my note I thanked him and suggested if I ever self-publish this story, he might want to interview me on his station. He kindly asked me to call him in a week to discuss the position. He was a charmer and a very likable person. I did hear back from the news anchor three weeks later, to let me know the station hired an individual with more TV experience. I was very impressed that he got back to me. Many interviewers do not respond.

It proved to me that reporters are really very decent people. I asked him that evening if he read my short clip on *"Life after the Big Bad Boot"*, and if I made him crack up laughing. Of course he said yes. Who knows? Maybe he was just being kind, but maybe he actually did laugh.

Valentina

"ARE MANHOLE COVERS ROUND?" AND OTHER RIDICULOUS INTERVIEW QUESTIONS

I was fortunate enough to get an interview with a great organization...and I only got the interview because I personally knew one of the board members. Now, usually I don't get my hopes up because I have been on enough "courtesy" interviews. What is a courtesy interview you ask? That is when they have absolutely no interest in hiring you, but someone, who knows someone, has recommended you for this position, so they are obligated to meet with you. You can pretty much guess which are the "courtesy" interviews. They are the ones that when you arrive, they make you wait— after all, interviewing you is keeping them from, oh I don't know, thinking about where they want to go for dinner or something equally important. Then when they finally decide to see you, the receptionist shows you in with such fanfare you just know she is in on it too. Anyway, eventually you make it to inner sanctum and then the questions begin. They are silly, inane and you can tell from the person's posture, that he or she is hoping the end will come soon. After a few general questions, "Why do you want to work here?" (because i need a job, duh, i thought that was obvious!) and the all time favorite: "Why did you leave your last job?" (duh, because they asked me too!) he or she rises and dismisses you with a small handshake. Now, because we have been well-trained, we write the necessary thank you notes. You never hear from them again, not so much as an email telling you that while you were qualified, they received so many applications, they couldn't go further because they found the perfect candidate. Sometimes the only satisfaction in a case like this, is when you hear through the grapevine that the candidate was a mess and was fired in record time. While it doesn't pay the bills, satisfaction is not without merits.

Oh yes, back to the questions. So, here I am dressed to the nines and every inch the lady. I make it inside and the interview appears to be going well. I think I really might have a shot with this one.

Then, just as I'm about to make a clean getaway, I'm stopped in my tracks with the phrase I have come to hate: "Just one more thing before you go…" and, get ready for it, here it comes…"Why are manhole covers round?" I panic, thinking, *can this be for real, or have I drifted off somewhere?*…but no, they are looking at me for an answer. I rack my brain, manhole covers, what do I know about them? Only what my mother told me, "Always be careful where you walk so you don't fall in one." That and "Beware of outside cellar doors" were my mothers words of wisdom. So, now I have to think what I know about holes…which is nothing. Aren't they all round? Hence, the expression, "square peg in a round hole."? No, that would be too easy and struggling not to appear to be a smart ass (which is ironic because at this point I'm thinking he is a dumb ass) but, since I do want this job, I come up with what I think is a reasonable answer—if the covers were made to fit the holes, and the holes are round, wouldn't it follow that covers would be as well? I breathe easy, it's a genius answer if I do say so myself. But, not good enough I fear. I leave and go on my way, equipped with cocktail party conversation for the next year…and it should be noted, that only my friends in the construction industry, actually know why manhole covers are round. (I could tell you but it would be too easy, ask around.) It has been 4 months and the position is not filled…maybe they really want a construction worker.

Another question I got was, "Why would you want this job, it seems like such a comedown."—I kid you not. This was another job that I was so overqualified for, if I didn't need a job so badly at that point, I would never have applied. I get the interview, which I now realize was another courtesy interview, with the big boss—some "kid" they just hired. I say "kid" because he looked like he just started wearing long pants that day because he somehow knew he was interviewing a grown up. Needless to say, my answer, in difference to his question, was politically correct—I think it will be interesting and I've been involved for years with the organization anyway. I really wanted to say that he looked like the type who provided nicely for his family and my family had kind of gotten used to eating daily as well. Not the right answer and the job went to someone else. By the by, he soon left for bigger and better things himself.

Anonymous

I DON'T DO WINDOWS!

In one interview I had with a small firm, I remember the interviewer asking me some questions about doing "personal work for a manager". This raised a red flag for me. I answered quickly, "I don't do windows". I knew that this job was definitely not for me. The words exactly were "you may have to do some <u>very</u> personal tasks for the management staff!" That did not sound kosher to me, especially the "*very*" part. I quickly ran the hell out of there to the car thinking—and chuckling—why me? I have all the stories; some day I will log these.

Valentina

THE STRIKE OUT WITH THE DIMAGGIOS

I received a referral from a friend that Joe DiMaggio's son was looking for a part time assistant to help him with administrative tasks. I thought, could it really be Joe DiMaggio's son? I quickly took the phone number, called, and received a return phone call from Chris DiMaggio. It turns out he was the son of the late Joe DiMaggio. He asked me to meet him at a local studio on Long Island—one which I never knew existed. It looks like a storefront but is actually a studio where tv talk shows are filmed for a cable channel. Who knew? I walked from the parking lot, flooded with snow, into a freezing cold building where I was escorted into a small coffee room with a large screen TV. In walked a regular nice-looking man named Chris who said to me, "Meet me on the set and we will talk". When I got to the set, we didn't talk; he handed me a set of cue cards and asked me to stand by the camera and work on the set, and we would talk later. I thought it would be an interesting experience. It happened to be a show that helps people affected by spousal abuse, individuals whose spouses had bled them dry of their money, homes and dignity. In walked a scary-looking man with a hood over his head. He was to be interviewed but did not want to be identified. I am standing in the background thinking, "What in the world am I doing here?" Maybe this man with the black hood on was a murderer! But then again, I was committed to getting a job, so I said "Ya never know." Joe DiMaggio's son, maybe he can help me land, and hopefully not on Mars! What a nightmare and a mess! I had to stand for two hours, on my arthritic knees, and I was exhausted. After the show, I gave Chris my resume, and he abruptly asked me if I was interested in being a volunteer! I gracefully told him that I was really looking for paid employment and already had several pro bono volunteer gigs at other agencies on Long Island. The good news is that I know now how to utilize a studio with cable access for public service announcements. The people I met were very nice, but a little weird. I was happy to leave, get a cup of coffee and go home. The man with the hood was a little scary, but really harmless. It was really a "do good" television show from a non-profit group that helps the innocent guy or gal who gets shafted because of unfair legal settlements in divorce proceedings. The focus is on mediation services . . . far from murderers, don't ya think!

Valentina

LONG ISLAND'S BEST KEPT SECRET

I received a call for an interview from the Office for Emergency Management for Nassau County, New York. When scheduling the appointment, the interviewer told me the meeting would be in the Nassau County Jail building. I thought this was odd, but went on the interview. When arriving at the jail, I was required to provide identification, and was escorted through very high secure walls to meet with the interviewer.

After discussing the position, which was in emergency management for disaster resources, I was informed that this was a project working in conjunction with Homeland Security which kind of intimidated me. There I sat, the lone woman in the conference room talking to very serious men and discovered they worked very closely with security disasters and top secret missions. Even the interviewers were one of Long Island's best kept secret. I felt like I was being interviewed by the FBI.

How I got this interview baffled me, but, of course I was interested and willing to learn. They kindly explained that there is not a system in place and this person would be part of the cartel which will be putting together systems, organization and planning booklets for procedures for disasters, but I did find out about Long Island's top secret location.

I quickly learned that at the time of this interview the counties did not have a standardized systems in place for emergencies, and this position was going to be formulated in this top secret location. Who would have thought that this project would be handled in the basement of the Nassau County Jailhouse on Long Island.

Valentina

CUTIE PATOOTIES AT THE MERCHANT MARINE ACADEMY

This interview was at the Merchant Marine Academy in Kings Point, another place I have never been to after living my whole life on Long Island. To think it took being downsized for me to travel all over Long Island and see some of these places I never knew about.

These men were cutie patooties, handsome and friendly. The offices were old and barracks-like, but the benefits were to die for. It was like a government job, and one I would have been happy to have conquered. Another rejection!

Valentina

IT'S MYYKEE

The next charity function I was planning was directly involving a sick little girl on Long Island. I believed that everywhere I turned, I was being directed to people who needed help and support. It didn't pay the bills, but I enjoyed the work, and it was getting me through the frustration of interviews and rejection. My friend and I were working hard in getting press coverage for the child, and managed to work with the local newspapers to receive press and political attention. As a result of the press, I received a phone call on my cell from a total stranger who we will call Myykee. Myykee explained to me, after reading the article about the little girl that he wanted to help.

Because of my inquisitive behavior, I felt the need to meet up with this gentleman. He too was a trip on the LIE, a highway I never drove on until being unemployed. He asked me to meet him at his factory and offered to donate bottles of perfume to be sold for the child. Again, I kept meeting kind people who wanted to help others; this had to be positive. He said if I met him on the highway, he would meet me at the exit and give me some perfume to sell for the function. There I was speeding on the LIE to meet this stranger. Myykee became a good friend as well, and has helped me for every event I plan that aids children and women on Long Island.

This experience led me to self publishing my very first short story about the triangle friendship which was an experience of life. Mykee, well, he was the owner of a perfume distributor who was so very very kind. As a gesture of my appreciation, I bought him a breakfast cake, and he said, "I don't eat" in a very funny way! I said, "You don't eat, that's a sacrilege in the ears of an Italian mama. My mama would say you have to eat. It's the law in my house."

Valentina

A MONTH OF CAFÉ CAPPUCCINO AT STARBUCKS

Because I was unemployed I decided to increase my networking to continue to meet good people who could lead me to more contacts and interviews. I also volunteered to help some political candidates in my hometown. One day while I was volunteering for a politician, he asked if I was looking for part-time work. I was open to the discussion, and he asked me to meet him at his home on Long Island. The appointment was set, and I didn't think anything of interviewing with him at his home. Many executives work from home. When I arrived, I was greeted by a large grey cat, which scared me to death. I then waited in his kitchen for a few minutes, before beginning a conversation which was not as easy as I would have liked. He started to ask me political questions about the townships of the county. I had no idea of the answers, so what did I do?

Mamma always said tell the truth! So I bluntly stated that I never worked in politics, and would not know the answers to these very hard questions, but if he gave me some information I would study it and do a good job. He then started acting like a man with power does and scared the crap out of me. Rather than display my fright, I raised the volume of my voice to match his. He asked me rather loudly, "What are you, a moron?" I answered "No," and said, "I can walk the walk and talk the talk. If you think you can make me cry, you won't, as

I worked for tough people throughout my career. If you want me to do the assignment, you won't be disappointed." It was the weirdest interview I have ever had. He disappeared to the basement, came back and gave me some very quick instructions while sending me on my way with a meeting to attend! As I left, he yelled to me "Remember, when you deal with this group, think like a moron!" He then handed me business cards for consulting which said "vice president of marketing" and arranged for a meeting with ten politicians in the area. I arrived at the meeting looking very professional with a black attaché case, not really knowing what I was doing there. He said I was to be as supportive as I could be for the new candidates who were running in the party for 2004. I figured, how hard could it be to be supportive? That was something that was natural to me. Never in a million years would I have ever thought I would have the chutzpah to do this.

I guess I viewed unemployment as a new experience. The worst that could happen was I would get fired and be asked to leave. The opposite happened. There were ten candidates at the meeting who were kind, appreciative and asking me for my advice. Although I never had experience in assisting in a campaign, I just used my common sense attitudes and gave ideas of what I would look for in picking a candidate and why. After the first meeting, arrangements were made to meet each candidate on a different morning at Starbucks. I quickly realized that all candidates go to Starbucks every morning, and eat the same thing—a chocolate chip muffin cake and a cup of coffee.

So—not a bad gig, I had Starbucks breakfast every day for a month or so. I worked with professionals, learned how to assist with a political campaign, and attended parties and usually wound up near the press reporters from the media. I was extremely happy with the post for a month, and then was invited to the victory parties and inaugurating ceremonies. A great gig, which gave me some more confidence as well as some eye opening experiences into the political powers that be. When I told my friends about this experience, again they said, "you are nuts!" The original interview, although very intimidating, gave me an experience that was fun, overwhelming and memorable.

Valentina

A DAY WITH THE PRINCE OF ROCK AND ROLL

I remember the day I was asked to meet an executive from a radio station at the Plainview Diner in Plainview, New York. I didn't think anything of it and arrived right on time. In walked a nice looking older man who seemed to know everyone in the diner—he was known as Mickey "B". Mickey "B" obviously was a popular radio announcer, and he was known as the "King of Rock and Roll." Everyone in the diner knew him, and I quickly realized that his photo was plastered all over the walls of the diner. Besides being the "King of Rock and Roll" he was also considered the "King of the Diners" on Long Island. He convinced me to follow him on the Long Island Expressway to his office in Hauppauge where I met two very mature older Italian women who ran his offices. There were pictures of him with every rock and roll idol from the 50's and I realized he was a genuine radio personality, not a joke! Mickey B encouraged me to take a position with him for commission only and sell radio space. It was not the type of thing I was used to, but agreed to try it and to train with him for a day or two. We spoke for two days and he expressed he had big plans for me, but I was not ready to work on commission only. We became friends and I was a talk show guest on his radio show, advocating for charity events. He has donated a sizable number of rock and roll tickets to many of my endeavors ever since then. Although my interview met neither of our needs at the time, I was lucky to meet this crackerjack. I speak to Mickey B a few times a year and when I visit any diner on Long Island, his smiling face on huge posters stares me in the face. When I enter a diner and see his poster, I chuckle and think "He is the King of Nice!"

Valentina

A LITTLE LESS ILLEGALITY, A LITTLE MORE HONESTY

S tory of a crazy, but successful interview I had: How I overcame illegal questions asked of me during my interview

Back in 1989, I was looking to find a job on Long Island, enabling my return home after nearly a decade in Chicago. It would give me the chance I was looking for to put thousands of miles between myself and my soon-to-be ex, while also giving me the ability to be with my family, which I had missed seeing very much for all those years.

I found a very promising job by answering a Newsday employment ad that my parents brought to my attention. It was such a great fit that the prospective employer paid to fly me in after the phone interview went well. It also didn't hurt that salaries were lower in Illinois than New York, so I would be getting quite an increase over my former pay if I took the job.

One of the interviewers—the head of the Information Technology Department—bore an uncanny resemblance to Archie Bunker (Carroll O'Connor). Though he was Italian, not Irish (like Carroll was), his way of expressing himself and even his voice made me do quite a double take. I resisted asking him if he had ever been mistaken for Archie, figuring it would not help me get the job.

Savvy job applicants and interviewers know there are certain questions that are legal to ask…and those that are not. The latter questions tend to be about your personal life if that has no bearing on the job itself. For example, they are not supposed to ask you about your marital status or about your spouse's employment. When you're being interviewed, it can be rather touchy not to answer. However, refusing to respond or calling them out on the illegality of their questioning can also cost you the job. It's your word against theirs if you choose to make an issue of it, plus that won't help you fall into their good graces if you do.

On the other side of the coin, answering those illegal, inappropriate questions can open the door to further questions along those lines as it kind of gives them permission to explore your personal life in greater depth. Usually, it's better to deflect, if you can, refocusing the interviewer on job-related questions.

In my case, the interview was going quite smoothly until the guy had the nerve to ask me, point blank, "What does your husband think of you applying for a job in New York when he's in Chicago?" Keeping my cool as best as I could, I replied that he was okay with that. The interviewer pressed me further, asking, "That sounds naïve. What will he do if you accept the job? We want to ensure that if we make an offer and you accept it, it will not fall through due to this."

After pausing for a moment, I responded, "I can guarantee you that he will have absolutely no problem whatsoever if I take this job." I figured that would be enough to satisfy him, without having to resort to telling a white lie, which I don't like doing. However, the interviewer was not satisfied with my answer. He continued to prod me about this, asking "Where will he work if you move here? Does he have a job lined up?"

Now, I was in the uncomfortable position of having to either share that I was in the middle of a divorce—which I feared would not help my chances—or tell him something else. I chose to respond as follows: "He works for a government agency in Chicago (which I named) and they have an office in New York City as well."

That was a true statement (not that my ex was going to ever leave Illinois). It seemed to, finally and thoroughly, satisfy his stated concerns.

Much to my delight, I was offered the job on the spot! He mentioned how I had an advantage over the applicants from the area as the stock market had recently eliminated a lot of jobs for those doing Information Technology work related to the brokerage industry. He spoke of how he preferred "importing" me from the Midwest, rather than take a chance on the highly paid local New Yorkers, who would likely return to jobs in their highly lucrative industry once the stock market rebounded.

The company wanted me so badly that, as part of the offer, they said they would cover my moving costs, as well as my final flight back to New York. At the time, I had only a few of my personal effects in boxes, which I'd already shipped home. Everything else I owned was tied up, pending the divorce settlement, which was to take another year and a half due to my ex's stubbornness and greed in negotiating. The only other thing I had was the car, which I really wasn't looking forward to driving cross country in the winter. I decided to take my new employers up on their generous offer to cover the cost of a moving van and had my car shipped in it. That was both for my convenience and also to avoid raising eyebrows if I had claimed I had nothing to ship.

Over the next couple of weeks, I worried about how I would break the news to my new employer that I was getting divorced. From a legal perspective, the IT director had really crossed the line when he probed my personal life so vehemently. However, from a practical perspective, I was so happy to be coming home to Long Island for good that I was willing to do what was necessary to make this possible. I had felt that, had I refused to answer or made any comments about the illegality of the question, I would have been ruled out as a viable prospect. Still, here I was, stressed from the big move, the divorce, and a new job, so it did not please me to be in this delicate situation. I spoke about how to handle this at length with my family, looking for the best way to address this matter. I planned to tell them soon after starting my new job that I had initiated divorce proceedings, thereby putting the issue to rest. I wasn't even going to wear my wedding ring, so as not to give off the impression to others that I was happily married.

Flash forward to my first day on the job. I was very nervous but reassured upon seeing a fresh arrangement of tulips and other, colorful flowers on my desk. I was disenchanted, however, when I saw the company-wide memo that was circulated, asking all of the other employees to "welcome new employee Ilene, who has moved back to New York with her husband, who was starting a new job himself at the New York office of his company!" (They even shared his name and the place where he was supposedly going to work after being transferred!)

Soon after seeing the memo, the IT Director visited me at my new office to personally welcome me. He said, "So happy to have you here from Chicago! How did things go for your hubby?" I took a second to compose myself and answered, "He's not making the trip. We decided to get a divorce." The look on the manager's face was priceless. It was a combination of shock, sorrow that perhaps this job had been the reason for the break-up of our marriage and wonder at the whole situation. All he could muster was, "I'm so sorry. I hope we didn't cause this through your new job." I assured him that coming back to New York was my own decision, something I was planning to do in any event. I felt badly about the whole set of circumstances, including the mistrust or disappointment now out there about me as a direct result of all those inappropriate, illegal questions I had been asked on my interview. I never regretted answering them the way that I did. The end result, for me, was a job that lasted several years and taught me many skills, developed my professional and technical skills and, of course, brought me home to my family at last!

Ilene Schuss

MEDICAL BILLING NIGHTMARE

I am a medical biller and I found myself out of work during the economic nightmare in mid-to-late 2008. One day I went to a doctor's office in North Babylon after responding to an online advertisement. The ad said to come to the office to fill out an application.

When I entered the office I was met by a receptionist named "Eunice." Well for a receptionist she was just a little too involved in my application process. She kept telling me not to leave anything blank because "she" (I assume the person who does the interviewing) doesn't like it. There was a sheet for references and I said I had my own so she took it and then told me if the almighty "she" saw a blank page she wouldn't even look at the application. I really wanted to walk out and say I don't want to work for the crazy "she," but I went along and filled out the paper.

Then Eunice, who I remind you is a receptionist, asked me what kind of money I was looking for! Are you kidding me Euny? So I explained I would rather discuss that with the person doing the interviewing.

Eunice took my application and said the only time available was October 3rd at 3:00 PM. So I said I would make it work and left the crazy place. Truthfully, bad economy or not, I had no intention of working there, but now I was so curious to meet this crazy "she" and find out if there was anyone else on the staff other than Eunice.

I returned to the office on October 3rd at 3 PM. only to discover that the "interview" was a group interview. The office was packed with about 30 people applying for 2 openings. Eunice was there with another woman who she did not introduce. Eunice handed out blank pieces of paper to each one of us. She then asked us to write down our personal information on the sheet and to make sure we printed and wrote very neatly because "penmanship counts on this test." She then told us that she will call out some medical conditions and we were to write the corresponding medical codes on the sheet. Half way through "the test" she mentioned again how important penmanship was at this job, so of course someone finally asked why it is so important (it was just a matter of time) and Eunice explained that all medical billing is done on paper; there are no computers.

NO COMPUTERS! Are we in the Stone Age? A mass exodus took place (including myself) and Eunice was left there stammering over and over again: "But, we're thinking of getting a computer soon…"

Anonymous

AN INTERVIEW WITH THE SNAPPLE LADY

Many years ago, when working in corporate America, Snapple, yes, the drink Snapple was a very big item. It still is today, but way back then, I did love the drink and we purchased it always for the employees where I ran the show at Compaq Computer. For many years, ten to be exact, my co workers always told me I looked like the commercial actress Wendy who promoted the Snapple brand.

When losing that corporate job within the tech company, I was devastated enough to send a letter to Wendy, the "Snapple Lady." I am not kidding I really did, I sent her a photo, I sent her a letter. Hell, I think I even sent her a box of candy, with a bunch of Snapple bottle caps for effect.

Well, one day I received a call from this wonderful lady, and made an appointment to go to Snapple headquarters in East Meadow, Long Island. Was I totally excited! I put on my best dressed suit, scarf, pearls —and off I went. The headquarters were very impressive and she was a riot, yes, a riot. Here I thought I was going to get interviewed for a job, it got better than that. This wonderful woman was kind, funny, and believed in helping people while selling and promoting the brand.

When I got there, we toured the plant, and then a limo arrived and we went driving around Long Island and had lunch. Even though it was not an actual interview, it was a blast. I still have the original letter in my interview files where I requested an interview and stated I was a Snapple look-alike and could stand in when needed.

Although I did not land a job that day, I landed a great friend who mentored me and sent me every kind of Snapple wish for many years. I have known this wonderful woman now for twenty years. I did go on a TV show with her way back when, on the "Ricki Lake Show," where they made us total look-alikes. I have the photos to prove it.

Soon after, I was invited to the NYC Snapple Parade where I met a few special people including Connie Chung and Ed McMahon I was also in a Snapple Look-Alike Conference at the first Snapple Convention at Hofstra University in Hempstead, Long Island. Back in those days, Pepsi had Cindy Crawford, Coke had Wayne Gretzky and Snapple had the star from the mailroom, Wendy Kaufman. She is still in touch with me, and we still meet for breakfast from time to time. This interview was one I will never forget and I have made a friend for life. She is upbeat, she is still a mentor and she is loved by many. She had a natural talent and still does. She mentored me and taught me, and gifted me with Snapple products for many, many years.

Life is funny, but think about this: Go out of your comfort zone when you are seeking a new job or a new endeavor. You never know what may happen. Anything is possible. You may be very surprised!

Valentina

ACT ONE SCENE ONE

Here it is: my 24th interview in three years. Yes, I did say 24. I heard about a job in a very esteemed hospital on Long Island—a position called a "Standardized Patient Actor". After doing some research, I realized there are many of these jobs all over the United States. A Standardized Patient Actor can be viewed as a patient advocate, a patient educator, a professional patient, a surrogate patient and other generic terms. So what did I do? I decided this would be easy. I called a few colleagues in the medical field, and I landed an interview with two very professional leaders in a very large university hospital on Long Island. Little did I know this position existed right under my nose where I lived. I thought and thought about this, spoke to some friends, and kept repeating "this is a great little job. I can do this." I started to think about demonstrating when I had pain, a cold, a headache, and I then started watching TV commercials before the interview. It became a little comical. My family and friends were, of course, cracking up. So off I went in the morning to my interview with quite a sense of humor, feeling pretty confident. After meeting the interviewers, and learning about the specifics of the job, it occurred to me that this would be a cinch to get. Well, I learned that there are different ways to cough and perform it, there are different ways to experience abdominal pain and perform it, and there was even one where you had to be in withdrawal from DWI and lie about it. I thought of the scene from "Seinfeld" when this happened on the show. The performances had to be as good as it gets for the doctor in training to know how to handle either the irate patient or the patient from hell with care and concern. Also, the performer had to undergo physical examinations that showed other symptoms. All of this would be given to perform in a script and the performer would have to be a good communicator for this job. The last part would be the feedback after each acting segment. There would be a training period for this job that was extensive and quite difficult. The hours were great, the facility even better, and the actor would be working with a diverse group of students and residents in the training programs. The hired candidate would work with a mandatory set of rules regarding administration and must have energy, memorization, discipline, concentration and excellent communication skills. I was very interested, and I knew I had this job for sure after the two interviews. I sat quietly in the waiting room with the other candidates who I thought did not seem appropriate. Go figure. Nothing today is easy when you are over 50 and seeking that job from heaven!

I considered this interview actually enlightening, educational, and very interesting. Did I get the job? Absolutely not, but what I did get was a greater understanding of what training programs there are in place these days for the medical industry, as well as knowing that these positions exist in many top quality hospitals.

I left there with the hope that this was only Act One Scene One. But it was a pretty interesting experience. Every time you have an interview, treat it like it's an experience that might be great—or not so great.

Have a sense of humor all the time, and it will get you through!

No Acting For Me. Not this time, but maybe another time!

Valentina

UP IN THE AIR, FEET ON THE GROUND

I went into Manhattan today to interview for a project manager job with a company called Genesis Networks. It couldn't have gone much better (well, it could have been better if they had offered me the job, but more on that later). I had done my research on their business, reading their website and other info on the web. I also read an article written by their CEO and founder, Paul Dujardin. As I sat in their waiting area that morning, a mature gentleman walked by (on his way to a meeting), and introduced himself. It was the CEO, and we started talking....I told him I read his article (he looked a little embarrassed and impressed), and we started chatting. I thanked him for the article advice. He was a nice man, and some of our past experiences were similar at ATT, Bell System, etc. We talk about his product (Video over IP), and I let him know how interesting I thought it was (sincerely).

The interview part went well, too. The interviewer was a "regular guy" and a "paisan" to boot. He even had a pony tail. I was dressed up (black suit, white shirt...suspenders even) which was good, because this isn't a business casual place. Both of us felt a bit awkward at the beginning, but became comfortable pretty quickly. He mentioned it would be an easy commute for me, that the hours were a very reasonable 9 to 5-5:30, there would be a second interview down the line, and he offered me a tour of his operations center and other areas. All things I felt were positive—you don't say those things to a candidate you've written off. He didn't feel comfortable talking salary and he didn't want to insult me with a low offer, as I told him how much I made at Verizon, that I was making less now, and would be willing to negotiate for the right position (which took the pressure off him). He mentioned a possible range (just between us, he said) and I said that would be fine.

The boss, the chief sales guy (who also introduced himself), the office manager who had called to set this up, and the interviewer...all were nice people I'd be happy to work with. I said that to the interviewer. He's done six or so interviews already, and was planning some more (they had over 1,000 resumes sent in for this one position) with decisions sometime after New Year's.

Finally leaving, during my tour, I mentioned something I had found online—another website with their company name, selling a slightly similar service. The interviewer and one of his web people looked it up and were surprised to see what I found, so I left feeling I had helped out a bit already.

I called and thanked the office manager the next day, and got the interviewer's email address for a thank you memo to him. Even if there were a lot of other applicants, I still feel like I have a chance.

Joe Iudice

DON'T EAT LUNCH IN THE DARK

This will be a different kind of job interview story. This is one that takes a lesson from our childhood—I was always told, and I'm sure you were, if you didn't have anything nice to say, say nothing. Sage advice, but I wasn't smart enough to practice it.

I was young, that's no excuse, but sometimes we mistake youth for a cape and feel we are invincible. At least I did.

I wanted to work in the hotel industry, and my family was well-connected, so it should come as no surprise that an interview was set up within a short amount of time. So I put on my best suit and went, prepared to conquer the world. The person I interviewed with was eating her lunch, wait—it gets better—in the dark. Yes, the dark, she said the lights gave her a headache. Anyway, she continued to eat. I said nothing.

In the dark, there was still daylight and it was enough for me to look around her office. She apparently collected things. McDonald's beanie babies! Who did she think she was—Rosie O'Donnell? Her freaking office was a mess and I was beginning to get the heebie-jeebies from staring at the faces of those beanie babies. I found myself wondering who she knew that put her in such a position of power? She couldn't even carry on a decent conversation.

As it went on I realized I didn't want this job, but had to ace this interview; it was, after all, with friends of my father. But finally, at a certain point, I couldn't help myself. The questions were getting insane. She asked what were my strongest points, and I said I was personable and professional. She asked what my worst trait was, and here is when I blew it as surely as if I had literally shot myself in the foot. My response? My abhorrence of stupidity.

Well, by the end of the interview two things were apparent—she had finally finished her lunch, and I was not working in the hotel industry.

I realize that I should have had better self-control, but over the years when I think back on this interview I laugh out loud...the joke is on me as she is still there is a well-respected position with standing in the community.

Go figure.

Stephanie Jeffery Carlino

Chapter Two

LEARNING ABOUT YOURSELF

Even if you are on the right track, if you simply stand still, you are going to get hit by that train.
When we question everything we free ourselves to think, and when we think we allow ourselves to act.
~Valentina Janek

"FIRING" MYSELF

September 11, 2001 was the day that I began the process of "firing" myself. We all know where we were that morning. I was getting ready to head to my job in Jericho, Long Island at an insurance adjusting company where I had worked for 8 years. It was only my third job since graduating high school in 1977. For some context, 1977 was the year that "Saturday Night Fever" came out in movie theaters, the Son of Sam was terrorizing the city and on a hot steamy night in July, a blackout plunged New York City into chaotic darkness. In 1977 I did what most of my friends did after graduation. I got a job. A few of my classmates went on to college, but most of us found jobs and looked forward to getting married and settling down. Being an Italian American woman born in 1959, I knew that my life would revolve around home and family.

Fast forward to September 11, 2001, when I, along with the rest of the world, became transfixed by the unfathomable events unfolding before us. As the World Trade Center towers collapsed in a cloud of dust and despair, I knew at that moment everyone inside was gone. Their lives snuffed out, disintegrated in an instant. Ordinary lives, just like mine. As the dust settled, both figuratively and literally, stories of heroism, bravery, resolution, and sacrifice came to light. The realization seeped into my soul that life, at least my life, had to mean more, be more, than my 25-minute daily commute and my monthly work routine, a routine from which I never deviated. It suddenly felt like I was riding on a sad merry-go-round consisting of transcribing reports and billing clients, over and over, month after month, year after year.

I spoke to a dear friend who was a court officer in the Bronx. She was working 12-hour shifts after the terrorist attack, protecting the courthouse. A year earlier she jumped off her own "merry-go-round". You see, she was a pediatric nurse at a children's hospital. When she told me that she was taking a job in law enforcement to become a court officer, I was shocked. I remember asking her, "Why? What about nursing?" Her answer was simple. She said she just could not watch another child die. I told her I wished I could do something different, something more meaningful. A few days later she called to tell me that the civil service exam for New York State Court Officer was coming up again and she encouraged me to take it. I said that I was too old for a job in law enforcement, however, she informed me that there was no age limit. With no excuses left, in December 2001, I took the exam and did well. Over the next few years, I went through the extensive and exhausting background checks, physical ability and psychological testing and finally received my appointment to the New York State Court Officer Academy. The day I received the call I did not hesitate to "fire" myself. I said my goodbyes after what now was 13 years in insurance and left the safety of my routine for a totally new and unknown world. I was 47 years old. Before I knew it, I was reporting for duty at the New York State Court Officer Academy in lower Manhattan, wearing my mandated "business attire." I was standing in line with 109 other "recruits," one-third of whom were women. As we stood in line, at attention, waiting to get into the facility I could hear loud voices, which I now know was by design. My trepidation increased, and when I finally made it further up the line I could see that the voices were those of four sergeants who were yelling simultaneously at the recruits ahead of me. I could make out something about facial hair, ties or no ties, shoes, sneakers, and various other infractions, the details of which escape me now. When it was my turn I got the once over and was directed forward. Thank God, no yelling about my appearance. I made it into the room and was handed or rather, tossed a huge bagful of things including workout clothes, a book on defensive tactics, handcuffs, and a strange little black stick. That's when I realized what I had actually signed up for...IT WAS BOOT CAMP! It was also too late to run.

That first day was a blur of paperwork, medical forms, locker assignments, and rules and regulations that were barked at us. It seemed that the sergeants' voices only had one volume—LOUD. At some point in the day, I found myself on a smelly carpet, belly-down, doing what seemed like hundreds of push-ups to a cadence counted out by the sergeants. Then sit-ups, then something called mountain climbers. My once crisp and snappy black suit was drenched in sweat and whatever was on the carpet. Through the din of the sergeants counting and yelling about how pathetic we all were, I could hear the grunting and vomiting of other recruits. I just kept doing push-ups. Out of 110 recruits, only 99 made it to graduation. Some never came back after the first day, others quit at various times during the four months of grueling training and one was terminated the day before graduation. At the end of my first day I crawled up the stairs to my bedroom and told my husband that I didn't think I could do it, but he said that I could and I would and I did.

After graduating I was assigned to Bronx Supreme Court Criminal Division and have been there ever since. I have seen evidence of every depraved thing that one human being can do to another. I have seen the truly horrific, I've seen the good, the bad, the ugly, the crazy, the greedy, the funny and all aspects of crime and criminal behavior. No two days are ever the same, there is no routine in the routine. I work with people from all different backgrounds, levels of education, races, religions, cultures, and walks of life. I have seen first-hand how our system of justice works. I've seen its flaws and its amazing ability to balance justice with fairness. I've seen its limitations and its latitude and I believe in it. I have forged friendships with people I would have otherwise never met and I have found understanding and compassion for those in society who commit crimes of varying severity for a variety of reasons, for their families and their victims. I have felt anger, rage, pity, and sorrow all at once and I would not trade it for any other career.

When I decided to make such a profound change in my life all those years ago I really worried about what my mother would think of my unconventional choice. However, of all the reactions my decision invoked the most surprising were those of my mother and her friends. They encouraged me and were curious about the job and my experiences. They gave me that "You Go, Girl!" kind of praise. I realized by their reactions that they, too, must have, at some point in their lives wished to break free from the shackles of their traditional roles and get off their personal merry-go-rounds to take a leap of faith onto that daunting roller coaster ride.

Elaine D'Arrigo

HOLLY AND THE PACK LEADER

When you become unemployed in mid-life, you reassess your skills, think about your future and for some, do quirky things. That's ME!

The quirky animal lover in me came out when one club member mentioned his problem with his very scary 100-pound dog. Holly barks at everyone, she scares people but she is really a sweet dog. Me being me, I went into action and visited him. I found a dog that barked and snarled at me, with her tail between her legs. She's scared, I said. He told me the mailman is coming soon and the dog will go berserk. I began to make friends, walked her around (he said she would drag me down to the ground, but she did not!) and asked her to obey me. I'm a good pack leader. I'm assertive and I lead, not follow.

There he was! The dreaded mailman was delivering across the street about 10 houses down. I knew Holly saw him, she perked up. The owner asked me to tie her up to the deck rail but I was reluctant. All in all, the mailman came right up to the deck and delivered the mail to Owner and Holly. Well, she sat nice and quiet and never budged. Holly is fine, but his Owner admits he's a weak pack leader. Now I will add 'dog consultant' to my resume. Job well done!

Elise Negrin

NEW SALES JOB

I started another sales job at 35. In the beginning, it was going well. It was in that six-month mark that I became disgusted with what I was doing, working for a company that I didn't believe in. I put on a good deal of weight sitting at my desk the majority of the day. My attitude at work sucked and it wasn't much better in my personal life as well. I couldn't sleep, and it was so bad that I had to go to a sleep clinic. The results from the sleep clinic were hysterical to me. The doctor took me in her office and she said, "You don't have sleep apnea. You need to stop thinking." I looked at her in disbelief. A couple of more weeks went by at work and I was called into the office on a Friday. The woman from Human Resources was letting me go. I wasn't really surprised.

I felt many different things during that year that I was unemployed. I felt at times that I wasn't wanted or needed. I felt as though I wasn't a productive member of society. I asked myself if they would take me back. I remembered something my mother said to me and I think she was mostly right. She said keeping a job was easier than looking for one, especially when you don't have one. Thanks a lot, mom. That makes me feel so much better.

Over the course of four years, I had different sales jobs which I didn't particularly care for. At the age of 40, I took a three-day workshop about real estate and started investing. I also became an ambassador for the company and traveled for four years as a testimonial for the company. I started networking with people at a real estate investment meeting on Long Island and started invested in apartment buildings and hard money lending. One of the things that I learned is to not have your money be lazy, and to learn about it because no one cares about your money more than you. I'm better off financially now then I was at 35 but don't have enough money to retire.

At the age of 44, I moved from Long Island, New York to Tampa, Florida. I never lived anywhere else. It's now 2018 and the economy has been good for 8 years overall. I believe another recession is coming and we all need to be prepared.

I think the whole moral of my story is that we all have a limited time on the earth and money comes and goes. The key is to be happy and passionate about what you're doing or you won't be successful. There's no such thing as work-life balance. It's a circle.

Nicole Slater

CARNIE GIRL

"Carnie Girl" I call myself…and proudly. Working as a ticket taker in a local Carnival I'm no place I ever thought I'd be. Hell, on a good day I wouldn't even go to a local carnival! After all, when I was away at finishing school, I was up nights thinking where I was going to board my horses, NOT that if I played my cards right, I'd be selling tickets to a circus where people would pay to watch horses! That never even crossed my mind. But, because of my circumstances, that is exactly where I found myself for 6 long weekends, and there I was asking "How many tickets would you like?" The discount coupon was only good until 7 pm. "The dancing elephant (who knew elephants could dance???) starts in 15 minutes."

These are phrases I repeated hundreds of times over the Fourth of July weekend—I repeated this phrase whether they understood it or not, and I know I have to learn Spanish for next year! It was humbling, especially this weekend, when in the past I used to host my party for a cast of thousands, complete with DJ and fireworks, at a modest cost of $5,000. So, instead, I swallowed my pride, gave up a family weekend of fun and worked 49 hours as "carnie girl"—but came home exhausted, proud and $490 richer!

In the past, that windfall, however modest, would have gone towards a splurge—Gucci shoes or Chanel sunglasses—this year, it went toward a car payment!

Stephanie Jeffery Carlino

A SERIOUS ENDEAVOR

T hen there was my mission work. I volunteered with a private police non-profit organization to help keep kids safe on the internet. I met with a few volunteers weekly and it quickly became a mission for me to learn about all the safety measures to help kids.

This experience brought me to network television, videos and radio talk shows. Who would have thought? I have been in local newspaper print, or local television and radio talks shows, and have had a great experience, which has given me courage and strength. This led to a TV appearance on "The God Squad." I became very inspired by being on a few shows with Monsignor Tom Hartman who is the "God of Long Island"—a Gentle Giant. I kept telling my girlfriends, maybe I am destined to be a nun now! I was enjoying the work, but believe me, I am far from being a nun! Here I was, inexperienced with television and radio, and had experienced three talk shows, as well as radio spots realizing that there are no limits to what you can do when you put yourself out there. It was the most tumultuous time of my life and a big learning experience. I wouldn't change a thing. How did I get to this point? I always treated people the same. To give is to get and although I was not getting paid well, I was learning more lessons that I thought I ever could have this year. The way you treat people speaks volumes about your chances for opportunities in life.

Valentina (We miss you so, Fr. Tom!)

SNIFFING SIPPING AND SWIRLING WITH THE EXPERTS
SSSSSSSSSSSSS..........

S oon after that, I started thinking about wine when I saw an ad for wine tasting, and thought it might be fun! The next interview I had was with a winemaker, and I took on a gig learning how to do wine tasting. It lasted for two months, I had a great time, but quickly realized, it was not the job for me. I learned how to do the tastings, sip, sniff, and swirl.

It was called "Swirling with the Experts!" Another fun gig, but it did not pay the bills. If anyone would have said that one day I would be doing wine tastings, I would have sworn on a stack of Bibles I wouldn't have. I was a professional always behind the desk doing the usual things in the workplace. Although it was fun, I learned many things about the wine industry. It's nuts, but I found it invigorating. I guess it was possible that opening up my world with an open mind was bringing me into situations I had never experienced. Call it crazy, but I was having fun!

Valentina

I BECAME THE MODERN VERSION OF PERRY MASON

During my 35 years of practicing law, I had a general law practice which evolved into a more specialized successful personal injury, medical malpractice, nursing home negligence, and defective medical device litigation law practice. I had many highly satisfying "Perry Mason" moments in court when I was able to able to get the witness/wrongdoer to break down and tell the truth.

However, I was dissatisfied with my business model, closed my law practice, obtained insurance licenses, developed an expertise in Elder Law, made thousands of new connections, started an internet TV and radio show, and have reinvented myself. Most trial lawyers don't do elder law, and most elder lawyers don't do trial law, but I view myself as "The Elder Law Perry Mason."

Now, I plan estates, draft wills, trusts, and related documents, find clients appropriate insurance policies, and provide clients with skilled representation in court, if necessary.

Andrew Rosner

HOW I FIRED MYSELF AND FOUND MYSELF

As the saying goes, "Man plans. God laughs." After a lifetime spent denying I even had a mental illness, to myself as well as others, my life took a turn when I took on a job, became overwhelmed, and decided to "exit stage left." In the wake of that negative event, I ended up finding myself.

The year was 2013. After several months of unemployment, I'd finally landed a new job with a former employer. I was thrilled to be back with an organization where I'd previously thrived. These people knew me, I knew them and I would essentially be doing a job (After School Program Director) almost identical to the one I'd held 9 years before. On paper, the stars had aligned.

Almost from the beginning, I could sense things were not going to go smoothly. My office at the school was not equipped with a computer or working phone, my Assistant Director had health issues and could not report until several weeks later, and my current supervisor had his hands full wearing several hats at the parent agency making it difficult for him to offer me his full support.

That being said, I forged ahead. I'd been out of work for several months. I did not want to disappoint my wife, my former employer and of course myself. Meanwhile, the problems were not getting resolved, and then one day my boss tells me I have to go to a mandatory meeting in Manhattan having to do with our AmeriCorps volunteers. OK. A change of scenery. I'd worked in the big city before, I knew the subway system. So far, so good.

I arrived early at the designated office. There was another Director of an After School program there, too.

The woman we were to meet with ushered us into her office and proceeded to hand us a huge binder and launched into an hour-long briefing on the reporting requirements for this federally-funded program. In my head, I was saying "OMG! I have to do all of this for just two members of my team. Yikes!"

I had supervised AmeriCorps volunteers in the past and never dealt with this, so I was kinda blind-sided. After the meeting concluded, the other Director and I picked up our binders and headed downstairs in the elevator together. Both of us were shaking our heads and I said aloud, "How am I supposed to do all of this in addition to everything else I have to do to run my program??" I returned to the parent agency and told my supervisor I didn't know if this job was going to work out for me. He tried to encourage me to stick with it, said things would get better and he would try to find more time to resolve the problems I was encountering. I did not have much confidence that was going to happen anytime soon, esp. since I knew he would be leaving soon for a two-week vacation at Disney. I told him I didn't feel well and needed to go home. On the way home, I stopped at a pharmacy, obtained a couple of boxes of sleeping pills and went home to take a very long nap.

Suffice it to say, I was found and my life was saved so I'm here to tell my tale. This is what the folks in the field call a "critical incident."

Alarm bells were ringing in my head as I lay in the hospital bed. I couldn't dodge this one. I was basically forced to sign myself in for treatment at the hospital's Psych Ward. Naturally, we called my boss, informed him of the situation and told him I could not return to the job. What seemed like an awful turn of events at the time ultimately led me to acknowledging my illness and the need to seek help, feeling better, and eventually I returned to the workforce.

Has the stigma around mental illness disappeared? Nope. However, I no longer feel like I have to hide in the shadows for fear of negative perceptions or discrimination. Now, I check off that box on the job application where it says "Do you have a disability that may require accommodations?" I don't have to say what my disability is, but at least I have been up front, put my fears behind me, and laid the groundwork should I experience a crisis or need some sort of adjustments from my employer.

Last year, thanks to inspiration from Mike Veny, a respected speaker and author on Mental Wellness, I began a telling my story in public forums. By dispelling myths and informing the public and the business community, I hope to be a catalyst for change so the stigma around mental illness no longer has the same power it has today. That's how I fired myself and found myself.

Frank Pomata

I REALLY MISS NEW YORK

I had great work making lots of money and going along smoothly, then the bottom fell out from under me and I couldn't find work either. I was working at the mall for $6 an hour and working at anything I could find. I finally found a job at an old restaurant that I worked at ten years ago when I first moved to Denver. I was promoted to manager and did that for a year or so. It was fun and I love the restaurant business, but knew it would not last because of the long hours and the money wasn't great.

I then decided I needed to try this little furniture business. I opened it two years ago and I have been making a go of it. I have finally started getting recognition in the city and I keep getting written up. I've become a queen of marketing. It's a neat store and I'm looking forward to continuing its growth. I am the acting president of the neighborhood association and have been getting everyone together to start advertising and promoting the area. It's been a challenge and I hope it turns soon. It really is a neat area. I don't sell online as of yet but, I am looking into it because that's what I need to do.

. . .

It's interesting how life changes. I look in the mirror and see the change in my face but the spirit is still alive and thriving. I'm onto new and bigger things, however it's all different now.

Francis Peonia

MY MOMENT OF CLARITY

At the time that I had my "Moment of Career Clarity," I had already accumulated 10 years of fundraising experience and had accomplished a great many valuable things that had positively changed people's lives as well as the future of several charities. By design, I did not remain at any one job for an extended period of time because I perceived myself as being a "sponge" who wanted to learn from a variety of different people. I wanted to be taught by the best in my field to hone my skills and knowledge while "on the job" instead of attending the classes that they taught. So, I applied to jobs where these people held the position of Director of Development and where I could work directly for them.

I felt that I was at a high point in my fundraising career, and I interviewed and received offers from a major hospital system, an established Jewish organization, and a well-known nursing facility. At that time. my goal was to solicit and attract enough money to add a wing to a healthcare facility as a means of helping the community and making a difference. I did my due diligence, researched my potential employment venues and spoke with many people. I accepted the offer from the healthcare facility because my ultimate fundraising career objective was to learn about securing "major gifts" from a highly-regarded individual in the field.

A short time later, the woman who became my new supervisor called me into her office, informed me that this job was "not a good match" for me and fired me. I was really devastated but decided that I would make the best of the new situation. (Years later, I bumped into a co-worker from that job who informed me that "my" lady supervisor didn't like me because I was "young, too bubbly, happy, warm, creative, tech-savvy and made connections very easily," unlike herself.)

At that time, I was crushed. But looking back, I now realize that this situation was the best thing that could possibly have happened to me. Instead of searching for a new job, I decided to start my own organization. I soon found myself planning events for three different networking groups, and my company began to be hired to plan events in both the United States and Canada. Today, I am proud to share the news that my company, Infinity Relations, Inc., is a registered New York State Certified Woman-Owned Business (WBE) and that we are celebrating our 17th year in business in 2019.

Cindy Mardenfeld

THERE IS NO FREE LUNCH

It was 2008 and I was about to be interviewed for a superintendent position with a major construction company in New York City. It was about the same time the United States was plunged into the subprime mortgage crisis. Due to the crisis, the real estate development company I was presently working for did not have any new construction projects planned, so I knew I would be laid off as soon as the current project was completed.

At that time, the construction project I supervised was a block away from the New York Stock Exchange, so I routinely ran into financial managers and bankers whose careers were on the line. Their prognosis was bleak.

Soon, I was told by my prospective employer that the company was no longer hiring, and in fact, was bringing workers back to New York from Las Vegas, as construction projects there came to a halt.

Now, while I had worked in the 9 to 5 world for many years, I had also been a professional singer, working on weekends. Singing was and is my passion. In 2009 Chazz Palminteri asked if he could use my voice in his one-man play on Broadway, "A Bronx Tale". In the play, my voice would be heard singing Sinatra's "Fly Me to the Moon" in place of Sinatra's, since my voice is very similar. At the same time, a French music organization contacted me to see if I would front their big band for some concerts in France. Of course, I said…YES!

Eventually, in 2009, I was laid off and soon was on my way to France to sing. It was a great experience and I wished that I would never have to go back to working 9 to 5 and just sing for a living.

The prospects of finding a new job in the construction industry were not good in 2009 and continued into 2010, so I relied on singing at a restaurant and at weddings to get by. As I picked up more and more gigs, I became able to work solely as a singer. My wife works as well, so together we get by.

Singing is not only my passion, but it is also therapeutic. It allows me to express myself fully. It transports me to a place, a zone, of complete satisfaction. I am happiest when I am singing for an audience.

As they say: "There's no free lunch." Making a living as a singer is not easy. Sometimes you trade off money for the chance to do what you love. I do what I love to do…sing.

Jim Altamore

NEVER GIVE UP ON ANYTHING!

Ok, so I'm 66 years old and wondering where my life went and how I ended up in a dead end job. Looking back on my career, I peaked early and it's been downhill ever since. But, I am more fortunate than those who can't find jobs, so there is that "make lemonade out of lemons" thought process (side note: does anyone care that I can't stand lemonade? Lemons are actually better, you can put them in water, you can squeeze them on food – lemonade provides only one option, drinking it. Ponder that for a few minutes).

As I'm locked in my mundane job it should come as no surprise that to keep my sanity, I daydream.

I daydream about the past—clothes that no longer fit, shoes that are out of style, and my non-existent social life. (Now that I see it in writing, it's more like a nightmare than a daydream.) But I still push on.

One person keeps circling in my thoughts...the one that got away. Well, not exactly, but sort of. He relocated to another state to open his own business. More power to him, and I was supportive as I wanted the best for him. We each kept plodding along, he growing his business and me just plugging along. Every so many years, for whatever reason, we communicated. Not sure why or how, but we did.

He called with exciting news—he bought a condo on Marco Island… yeah him (seriously?) and bought a Corvette (mid-life crisis or just an ass and I never saw it before) I started to dread his calls and eventually stopped responding. That didn't last long, and once again we were back in touch.

I learned something about myself on this job—at the beginning, it was horrific. People were hired and fired with such regularity that at first I wrote down their names on a list, and then I eventually switched to stick figures. The office was chaos—screaming, yelling and sometimes you were ducking for fear of being hit on the head by flying objects. This was a feeding ground for insanity. But I needed the job so once I accepted the fact that I couldn't change the job, I changed my view of the job. I no longer looked at it as a career, but rather as a place to wait out the years till retirement. I told myself I had the big jobs, big salaries, and staff. And with that came responsibility. I could leave here at 5:15 and if the place burned down to the ground, so be it. No one was calling me to put the fire out. That subtle change in my behavior made all the difference.

Fast forward to 4 years later and we are happily "committed to the commitment" (that's what people say when they are staying together without getting married), and he is retired and I am still in my dead-end job until the end of the year. Then I'm going to retire and we are going to do what we should have done 30 years ago—enjoy life, together.

Moral of the story—never give up on anything as Nietzsche said: "the formula for happiness is a goal and a straight line." Well, I eventually got it right; don't give up and you will, too.

Stephanie Jeffery Carlino

THE BOOT OF ALL BOOTS

BEEN THERE DONE THAT: Advertising Copywriter ... columnist/assistant editor local press ... freelance writer, local publications ... 39-year Executive Director, local Chamber of Commerce

FIRST DAY ON THE JOB FOR THE LOCAL CHAMBER OF COMMERCE: Having been hired on my past credentials, on January 1, 1977, I began my new job as executive director of our local chamber of commerce. I had been directed and expected by the Chamber Board of Directors to pull the Chamber up by its bootstraps and to serve as the Chamber's chief spokesperson.

I had learned at the onset that I was to inherit a publication to put in order and expand, to develop a newsletter, coordinate all Chamber activities and events, create a village holiday parade and coordinate the tree lighting and handle all publicity and marketing efforts. Over the years, these were to include more than one hundred 20-page full-color news bulletins and media articles, 38 community guide publications and agendas for all board meetings and events plus publicity for 115 Chamber honorees throughout my tenure.

In the late 1980s, I was to serve on a "blue ribbon committee" to secure a permanent home for our Chamber following five temporary locations over a 40-year period. In 1989, I was a major player in joint efforts to move a historic house from its original site to Village-owned property. The move was publicized throughout Long Island and had been accomplished through loans from 12 local banks. Now, finally, a permanent home for the Chamber! I was ensconced in a large second story office for 28 years along with an assistant director and part-time bookkeeper who shared the main level. Along with my other functions, I had been responsible for handling all arrangements and monthly payments on the 12 different bank loans.

The Chamber president who hired me back in 1977 and had followed my 39-year career, had recently stated that "(She) is the heartbeat of the Chamber and maintains it as the largest and most respected Chamber on Long Island, and furthermore, in the tri-state area. She has tripled membership from 125 in 1977 to nearly 400 in 2015.

RECOGNITIONS: Throughout my tenure with the Chamber, I had racked up a few: 1992 Chamber of Commerce "Community Achievement Award' ... 2002 Zonta Club of LI "Woman of the Year" ... 2005 Nassau County Council of Chamber's "Business Person of the Year", 2012 named for Excellence in Business Education Scholarship, 2015 local Republican Club "Community Service Award", 2016 Village Government recognition for "Community Service", 2016 Local Rotary Club's "Community Service Award", two Rotary Paul Harris Fellow Awards, Rotary's highest honor, and 2018 Award for Community Service, local property owners' association.

WHY THEN, AND HOW, DID I GET MY DESPICABLE BOOT? Traditionally, the Chamber Board did not meet during July and August. However, I felt the need to meet with the president to discuss some critical issues, and we met on July 15, 2015. Before sharing it with the officers, out of courtesy, I thought it appropriate to tell him of my plan to retire at the close of 2016. Although I faced the date I'd set with trepidation, I felt it the most appropriate time to retire since I would reach two meaningful milestones: 40 years in my Chamber position and at age 85. The president was a bit startled, asking whether I had anyone in mind to replace me. I gave him one possible name to pursue. We closed our meeting amicably. The next day, under the guise that we were to meet to discuss the issues I had brought before the president, he called asking that I set up and prepare the agenda for an emergency executive committee meeting (officers and myself). Having set it up, I arrived, cheerfully distributing the agendas.

THEN THE AXE FELL! The president told me that before we started the meeting, he wished to inform me that I was to be relieved of my position at the close of the year. I was told that I had been replaced by a former town trustee and past member of our Board and that he was to take over my position in two weeks. I was to be paid through December 2015, to move downstairs to share space with my assistant director (leaving all my files and records in my former office.)

I was expected to continue my functions while breaking in my replacement. When asked for the reasoning, I was told the Board wished to "go in another direction," but was thanked profusely for my 39 years of hard work and dedication. I asked whether the full Board knew of this executive decision and was told they did not. When asked whether it was because of my advanced age, the president said he would deny that. His retort to my question as to why he had not told me of this decision when we had met the previous week, he said he was "waiting for this." I refused his humiliating offer to remain through December and said instead, that I would vacate my office by August 16. I then left the meeting devastated and in a nightmarish trance. I drove around for 20 minutes before coming home to confront my husband with my devastating news.

THE CLINCHER: The next day I received an email from a labor law firm with a "Release Agreement" (RA) attached. Unbelievably, it had been signed two days prior to my firing. The document directed me to sign a many page document stating that going forth, I was in no way to use the names of the officers or place blame on the Chamber for my dismissal. My being paid through December hinged on my signing the RA. Following several revisions, and knowing that I had refused to stay on the job through December, I was told if I left in two weeks I would receive a severance of $15,000—but only if I signed the papers. I was stunned to think the officers (only three were the culprits), with our tight budget, wished to be rid of me so badly they would go to this expense.

I discussed the wisdom of signing the RA with my husband and secured his agreement not to sign it. In my heart of hearts, my integrity and pride of legacy meant more to me than the $15,000, so I opted to receive nothing! I had called our family lawyer who felt I had a solid claims case. Having taken notes at my firing, I had provided him with a complete chronology of the meeting. However, as time went by, my attorney was too busy to pursue it so I lost out.

Meanwhile, I had so many friends and associates on the Chamber Board with whom I had worked for so many years, I wrote to seven of them asking for contacts I might pursue on my new job hunt. I heard from only one director who said he would "keep his eyes/ears open." Once they learned of my firing by the officers, the directors were instructed not to speak with me and this included my former assistant of nine years who had also been my good friend.

FIRED TO FREEDOM! I didn't get a job, that is to say, one for which I am compensated.

Rather, I delved deeper into volunteer work for my nonprofit organizations and continued to do what I love—public relations, publicity, editing a weekly press column and volunteering for whatever falls my way. The really nice thing about it is that I AM FREE to do whatever I do on my time and schedule. I can throw in a load of laundry, prepare a dinner course or text one of my eight grandkids between paragraphs and phone calls. It's taken me nearly three years to transition from FIRED TO FREEDOM … and I love it!

Anonymous

STICKING TO MY ROOTS DESPITE THE BOOT

My name is Adriana Sotomayor, but here in the States it is Adriana Vitacco. I came to Long Island on vacation 3 years ago and met my husband Bobby Vitacco. We got married within months and we're really happy, although the process of becoming a resident was very long and tedious. I had to be in my country, Ecuador, so it was hard to keep a relationship like that, but we worked it out. I finally became a resident after a lot of money in fees and trips and, after a year of waiting, got my social security card and started applying to jobs.

I am a well-educated person from Ecuador, grew up in the city, always close to my family, and I have great values and manners. I have a Bachelor's degree in Business Administration given by Excelsior College in Albany, New York. I actually went to Nassau Community College in 2012 with a student visa, for 3 semesters and after that, I went back to Ecuador to finish my degree and finally obtained it through Excelsior College since they have an alliance with my American College in Ecuador.

I got a job within two months of applying as a teller at Capital One. I accepted it even though I wasn't too happy about the position knowing

I'm capable of a lot more, but since I had just moved here I had to start somewhere, you know?

That job was completely different than what I expected. Although I did like helping customers, I enjoyed that closeness and helped all of them in the best way possible, and I always gave 150%.

My branch was not well-managed, and I just didn't like the people I worked with, their ethics and lack of professionalism. It was hard because here I was making no money at a job I didn't like, working with people who did not appreciate my work and didn't treat me right. The truth is, I had no choice because my family needed the health insurance. This problem came as a complete surprise to me.

There were no rewards for me even though I well-versed in Spanish and 60% of our customers were Hispanic. As a matter of fact, my boss told me I didn't HAVE to speak Spanish—that it was completely up to me, and that if somebody who doesn't speak English comes to our bank, a translator would be brought in. Well, this was just the beginning, and needless to say I was unfairly fired. There is not much more to say about this unpleasant journey except I deserved better.

Now I'm starting a little business of handmade clothing and accessories from my country with REAL materials and fair prices. I'm also a professional jazz dancer and would love to start giving classes next year at a dance school as a hobby. I've done a lot in my short 26 years and I'm proud of it. I was a pre-K English teacher in Ecuador, dance instructor and more. Now I do social media management, website building, and am trying to focus on my little shop.

I have a 10-month-old baby who I'm in love with and want to show him that dreams can come true. My current dream? Honestly, I like stability, I'm happy with living with my family, I'm comfortable in every way, I don't want to be rich and I have wealth in my love of my family. I want to reach a point where I don't have to worry about finances. But doesn't everyone want that?

What makes me happy? Teaching. I love kids and love that they're so open to learning new things every day. In the near future I hope I can get an ESL certification since I speak Spanish. I would love to help my Hispanic community in every way I can. For now, I'm going to focus on my family and my shop. After all, this is the country of opportunities, right? I won't give up.

Adriana Sotomayor

HAPPINESS

I was a receptionist for the corporate office of a medical company and for two years, I went above and beyond for them. I was always trying to better myself by asking for more projects from other departments than just administration. Everybody noticed my hard work and dedication to the company but when it was time for raises, I never received what I should have received. It was always disappointing to me but I still worked as hard as I could and had numerous meetings with the HR department discussing a salary increase, but they always found reasons, unfair reasons, to not push me up in the company because they felt I was great where I was. They were "afraid" they wouldn't find someone like me for replacement. When I got pregnant, I knew in my heart that I didn't want to go back because I was not going anywhere with this company, and as much as that scared me knowing that I would have no income, I took the plunge. I went on maternity leave and sent HR the email that I was not returning. Knowing I wasn't going back to a company that used me and tried to squeeze every work ethic out of me without the proper salary increase made me feel so free and so alive, although having a new baby and only one income, which was my husband's salary, scared the heck out of me. But somehow we have made it work and we are ok. And the best part, I felt so much happier. I ended up taking some jobs on the side that I was able to do from home while taking care of my baby. I am so grateful for my toddler and my life now. I have been there for every milestone.

Of course, I'm very lucky to have the option to resign from that very nasty place. Not everyone is able to make a choice like this, but remember, do not accept unfair treatment.

Think of those experiences as having ants in your pockets. Those ancillary negative thoughts—those ants in your pockets—can give you the absolute experience of knowing what you will not do on your journey of life.

Christina Box

A 180-CAREER CHANGE BEFORE THE AGE OF 25

I hadn't received anything below an A-minus on a paper yet—nor had I confused the different spellings of their, there and they're, or it's and its, or any other words that were introduced into the English language for the sole intention of drawing red lines on students papers.

So when my professor stood at the front of the room threatening an automatic C on any submission that confused the meanings of the above grammatical adversaries. I thought, "About time these guys learn how to differentiate."

One week later I accepted my paper, pompously prepared for an A, when instead, sitting in its place, there was a big red C and a note that said, "See me."

It was the first big blunder in my writing career—and at that point, I was an accounting major. For the next three and a half years I was an accounting major. I actually transferred to a college with a stronger business program because I was an accounting major. Analyzing numbers till my eyes crossed was my calling, or so I had decided.

As an accounting major, I was taught to chase the "Big 4," which I did, successfully landing myself an internship with Pricewaterhouse

Coopers (PwC). This turned into a job offer that I accepted half-heartedly—standing in the rain in front of the mailbox staring at the envelope reminding myself that "a lot of other people would kill for this opportunity," while my best friend sat in the car shouting, "Just mail it already, they are going to pay you a lot of money." And they did, for the whole year I worked there.

When I voiced my discontent, everyone suggested that I consider another aspect of accounting—surely it was the only audit that I disliked. I agreed that audit was my least favorite aspect of the industry, but was pretty confident that any position that handcuffed me to Microsoft Excel would bore me to tears. Although I was there—physically working—for a year and a week to be exact, my spirit disappeared about four months in. I began printing out graduate school applications about six months in.

But what was it I wanted to do with the rest of my life? (Or for the next year, as my friends and family liked to tease.)

I thought back to my university days. Although numbers had been my game, freshman year kept me writing—the required composition class where I made that first error; the mandatory English lecture that I slept through at 8:15 in the morning; the creative writing seminar I signed up for with the same bastard that gave me the C. (He wrote "see me" because he felt wrong giving me such a low grade when it would have been an A paper otherwise, so I ended up with a B+ and a new-found admiration for the cynical, miserable guy who approached teaching college students as if it were a prison sentence.)

During my senior year, I had to write advertising proposals and business plans. I took a women's studies class that asked me to analyze gender inequalities in the workforce. I even submitted an article about my study abroad experience to the British Council. After many semesters of debits and credits, I was writing again, it was fun and, apparently, I was good at it since my study abroad article was published in the British Council's internationally distributed educational newsletter.

The answer was easy. I enrolled in a Masters course for Journalism at Nottingham Trent University. I wrote; I edited; I graduated. And then I spent the next year trying to explain my reasons for making such a drastic career change so early in my life—and why I don't want to write for an accounting magazine.

This industry was tough. While Binghamton University's School of Management had dedicated a lot of time to teach me to win over—and evidently conform to—the accounting world, I was now applying to the same writing, editing, reporting, proofing and assisting job positions as 1,000 other candidates—all just as desperate to get their foot in the door.

I started with mass-producing a general fill-in-the-blank cover letter. But this proved hopeless after 90 applications in a three-month period landed me only one interview. I tried personally tailoring each; I tried including anecdotes about my experience; and eventually, I tried cynical, self-ridiculing humor hoping that if someone with the right personality just took a half-second glance, I might be in.

I wasn't in.

But I am optimistic, or so I like to think, and knew my day would come. And it did when a high school friend emailed me an advertisement for an assistant editor position at a trade magazine for the dancewear industry. Who knew they had one? Having spent my childhood, a portion of college and a lot of my adult free time in a dance studio wearing dance clothes, this was right up my alley. The experience required not only someone who could write and edit to par but a candidate with a strong understanding of the business and financial issues that independent retail shops need advice on.

I didn't know at the time of my interviews that my soon-to-be editor (I am still tickled over being able to use the phrase "my editor") was as keen on my experience as I was to prove I could live up to my only slightly exaggerated resume.

I was in.

Now, on the best of days, I feel excited and positive about going to work and on the worst, perfectly content. No more do I sneak into the bathroom to cry or worry about working on the weekends. I found my calling. And I am proud to say that in the last eight months of my role, only once did my brain's eagle-eye spell check allow one of my grammatical adversaries to sneak by and scar me with the equivalent of a big red C.

Elizabeth Louise Hatt

BROKEN IN FIVE PLACES, HEALED NONETHELESS

The career path I'm on now was not always it— owning a dance-exercise studio—but I've come full circle from wanting to "be" a dancer. Dancing was never encouraged by my parents; in fact, they refused to help with college finances if I pursued it, but said that they would assist me only for something "steady", like nursing or teaching. Both of my parents were quite modern and liberal for their generation and this was incongruent.

So after getting my degree in Education, traveling with my college sweetheart and getting married, being a stay-at-home mom and deciding not to go back to the elementary school classroom (which I had done for a few years), I opened "Eileen's Dance & Exercise Studio" in our renovated basement level with ballet bars and mirror! I included childcare in my den—as I felt going to adult classes while my daughters were babies with great childcare onsite "saved" my life. All was going wonderfully, including my "Mommy & Me" classes! On a fateful day, while scurrying across a local avenue to the post office, a van made a sneaky move on his way to the left turn lane—and ran over my right foot in a sandal. I fell down—and thought I was dying. Luckily it was only my foot—my spine and head were OK. A lovely angel lady on the sidewalk came over and swooped me up to the sidewalk where emergency services with buckets of ice were arriving.

My "new-age" friends said that this "right-foot forward run-over" meant that it was time to begin something new and head on another path. I turned a deaf ear at first and was wallowing in self-pity for weeks, even with a psychotherapist making house calls. Soon enough, a few positive things occurred by my own actions—as I couldn't deal with all the bickering with my husband and daughters, who understood, but also only up to a point. I decided to talk to a friend who was (and still is) a successful biofeedback therapist, and at the time president of the New York State Biofeedback Society. She encouraged me to go for training to be a practitioner. I asked for and received family support and my husband drove me into the city for training each weekend. Sometimes I stayed over at my friend's place. The education and relaxation techniques involved in this mind-body modality truly helped me heal fast!

Additionally, during this period while my cast was on I was so grateful that it was only my foot (broken in 5 places), summer in New York, and I had a newly built deck to relax on! Subsequently learning about gratefulness, I know this attitude really help keep my spirits up.

Then another wonderful event occurred: A local physician called me whom I'd met networking. He didn't know my condition and thought I still owned the Studio, and asked me to write and teach— including Hatha Yoga, a Stress Reduction course for his patients based on the new work of Dr. Jon Kabat-Zinn of UMass. Medical Center, who was passionate about teaching and "prescribing" Mindfulness-Based Stress Reduction for outpatients at UMass. Medical Center. When I stated my situation, he simply said that I'll be fine when we'll start in October, and to read "Full Catastrophe Living", by Kabat-Zinn and call him when I completed the large book which mostly documented the medical success stories of patients who were already in his program. Well, it all came to pass! I read this amazing book, helped write the curriculum for our course, and healed quickly and fully. I attended

Kabat-Zinn's week-long training for "practitioners" and worked with the doctor in three locations for two years until he needed to close the course. I took on an adjunct position at Hofstra University's Health & Physical Education Department which included teaching Hatha Yoga and Stress Management and went on to receive business and life coaching training certification, and later Anger Management and EFT (Emotional Freedom Techniques). Early in my Hofstra career, I decided not to pursue Biofeedback (even though I know it truly has its place in reversing many conditions and diseases) as I found people could truly heal mind-body with the guidance of a skilled practitioner without machines, when they have a strong intention to do that.

Eileen Lichtenstein

THE "DURING" IS THE JOURNEY

My mother was diagnosed with breast cancer when I was thirteen years old. At thirteen I had no idea what breast cancer meant. In an instant, I came to know the three parts that my life had just been broken up into: before cancer, during cancer, and after cancer. I have learned that I can't change the before because that was already over. I learned from my mom that I could in some way change the "during". She taught me to stay positive, never give up, stay focused, have faith, be kind, appreciate the little things and so much more. My biggest struggles in all of this were coping and dealing and learning to live after the loss.

I lost my mother when I was 21 years old. It was just the beginning for us. The start of a beautiful mother-daughter relationship. A friendship. The time when I began to see her as a friend and not just a mom who told me what to do. I began to value her opinion and see her point of view. Then, in the blink of an eye, three months after my twenty-first birthday, she was gone. My excitement for us, and all that was going to be, was completely shattered.

After you are dealt such a great loss in your life, sometimes all you are left with are memories, the "what ifs", the "could have beens." You struggle with all that is to come in life without your loved one by your side. You think about how different and more beautiful life would be with her still here.

Some people find it easier to shut out all of the feelings because then you don't have to feel. Others use the loss as a guiding light in their life. I have chosen not to forget. I won't forget her smile, her laugh, her touch, her mannerisms. I won't forget all the good moments filled with laughter and love. I choose not to forget the tough moments where obstacles were overcome.

Although a loved one may be gone it is your job to keep her alive. I believe loss is a two-way street. You can't just sit there and count on a ghostly figure appearing to give you a sign. You have to have faith, you have to believe, you have to talk to them, talk about them, remember them, picture them in this life, smile and carry them with you wherever you go and in all you do.

Some moments are harder than others. Some moments unbearable, unthinkable, unimaginable, but I choose each time to continue on. I find ways to keep my mother alive. I find ways to bring her along on their bittersweet journey. I find ways to connect with her through this veil I cannot see through. I know she is here.

It isn't easy, but everyone who lost a loved one should try to find comfort in the smallest of things. Remember the old times but take a dream, a sign, a song, a light flicker, a penny, a sound, a butterfly, a number, or just anything that made you stop for a brief moment and think of them as a new memory for you to hold.

Today and every day I am grateful for where I am in life. Life hasn't been easy. Big moments, small moments and every moment in between are all bittersweet. There is always going to be something missing from my life. I think that the most beautiful thing is when you find the good in a bad situation. When you are able to smile through the pain. When you find purpose again. When you enjoy life anyway. That even after a loss, such a huge loss, life can still be wonderful, beautiful, incredible and happy. It's all what you make it. We only have one life. I know I live every day for the ones that can't.

Allissa Pietrowski

THE WRITING ON THE WALL

I worked for a not-for-profit about 10 years, and I started to see the writing on the wall. At some point every organization becomes greedy, and you can see how it begins changing policies. As I watched this happening and I was nearing retirement age I chose to leave my position and begin my own business. My business partner and I made a decision to reach for the stars and started our own training organization. Although my decision caused me to lose a small pension, I made the best decision possible. I love being an owner of a business and I love sharing my knowledge with my students. Being in business keeps me moving every day and keeps me young. It's never too late to start something new and change careers.

Liz Box

FLYING ON MY OWN

I wasn't fired. I decided to fly away myself in 2015 from a job I loved for almost 22 years.

I had a great run and saw changes coming afoot, like with everywhere else, and decided to join my husband in retirement. He had already retired nine years before, and though I loved coming home to a clean house, a well-stocked cupboard and fridge, wine and dinner on the table waiting for me, I felt it was time. I left on a high note and the office gave me a wonderful sendoff.

I was a career counselor in the Town of Hempstead's Department of Occupational Resources—HempsteadWorks—helping people from all walks of life, from laid-off executives to disadvantaged youth and public assistance recipients one-on-one with their training and employment needs. It was a very satisfying role, one in which I pulled strings sometimes, schmoozed with other institutions and generally cut a wide swath in the community, obtaining resources and information that could aid my customers. I became my customers' advocate because I soon realized that people don't just come to agencies like mine for a job, and some aren't even ready to get a job. They bring a variety of life problems to the table along with urgent basic needs. Consequently, I tried to do more for them. With a telephone in hand, I helped some save homes with mortgages they couldn't pay; helped a laid-off gentleman successfully appeal a large medical bill when his insurance refused to pay for treatment; found community resources for heart and diabetes medications and no-cost physical therapy for others. A sixth-grade honors graduate went on his end-of-year class trip because I remembered schools have petty cash for students in need and I called the principal. His mom was receiving public assistance and just couldn't afford it. I felt, if not me, who else might do this for them? I had the knowledge and the capability and used them. If I helped ease their burdens, they might succeed at school and job searches with my help. I helped them to respect the "system" by surprising them that they were not just bodies or "numbers" when they sat at my desk.

Senior magazines, adult education, and other classes suggest you have a plan. Don't retire to nothing. Have a purpose. I have to tell you that certain things I thought I would do, fell apart. Either opportunities ended or fizzled, and two dear friends died, with whom I would have enjoyed spending more time. While I enjoyed my hubby's company tremendously and we planned to travel extensively with tour groups, I wanted everyday life to matter beyond looking forward to seeing Judge Judy on television and blowing dust balls around the house. I did not want to be busy just for the sake of being busy! While I was happy not to have to be somewhere every day at a certain time, I still wanted activities to sink my teeth into.

People feel the need to stay active today—or even work part-time. Some have to continue working. It's all in the attitude. My job was therapeutic after one of my grown sons died. I could have left much earlier than I did, but after some time off, decided one morning to sit up in bed and then put my feet on the floor. I knew if I didn't do that, I'd never return. I wound up staying another ten years and I'm glad I did. The old job still has my testimonial letters on their website and I continued to plod on, helping people in crisis. It also helped me to forget my own and move forward from the profound blow of losing a child.

My "plan" for retirement is still evolving. Because I loved my work, I continued it on my own terms as an adult education instructor for a course called, "Finding Your New Job." I continued to stay in touch with my LinkedIn network, which consisted mostly of former customers who sought me out to invite me during the economic crash of 2008. You can continue doing your work as a consultant in a different capacity than sitting at a desk all day long.

Most surprisingly, along the way, I found passions I never, ever knew I had! I discovered I loved horses, after having met Triple Crown champion American Pharoah on a road trip. My husband and I now volunteer for HorseAbility, in Old Westbury on Long Island, New York, an equine-assisted therapy program for children and seniors.

Additionally, I began writing plays by dusting off unpublished short stories from years ago, that were forgotten during my full-time working years. A former customer inspired me. I soon found a black box theatre in New York City and have produced three plays there! It's creative and cathartic because you express what you know and what you feel about your life. It comes alive right in front of your eyes. Who knew? I have officially stretched out of my comfort zones. It takes a while to feel comfortable with that. But it beats boredom, self-pity, and the ho-hum status quo.

The one thing I found about retirement is that you have lots and lots of time on your hands but it is just as easy to wind up with no time or fill that time with only busy chores because you no longer have the daily structure of a 9-to-5 schedule and commute. AARP has "encore" career advice and lots of ideas for working into retirement and even a self-assessment quiz.

My advice is to give yourself time to discover a new you. It is a process that evolves but don't stress out if you don't immediately find what it is you like. Some people are happy to spend time with grandchildren and some babysit while their adult working children go to their jobs. It may be quite enough if that gives you immense joy and purpose. Others are content to grow and tend to gardens and home. Some are content to travel occasionally. Without having grandchildren, the decision was easy for me: I had to find something else to fill the long day in a meaningful way.

Just live your life open to ideas. You'll know when something clicks.

Leaving a full-time job after so many years might feel a little strange at first. You might be glad on bad winter days. There are pros and cons in every lifestyle, working or not. I like to consider myself still working. I've flown the coup of an office and am working on ME.

Gloria Schramm

VERY MISUNDERSTOOD TO VERY UNDERSTOOD

I t's 2010 and I am totally bombing on interviews. I went on fifteen job interviews and I could not get a job. Was it my hair, my body, my vocabulary (which is broken English)? Is it my attitude, or is it just not my turn? I started to become depressed, unkind, and not very happy with myself. My self-esteem was in a very low place. I started to believe that I was not employable. I went out in the evenings to a tavern in New York City and it became a habit for me. I started to meet up with some individuals who were not so normal - at least that's what I thought. They were very kind-hearted, very friendly, but there was just something not so normal about them. Because of their personalities, I started to enjoy my evening visits to the tavern.

I found myself intrigued by a brand new group of people who always talked about the job they had and how it was a family environment, and something different. I saw Mike, Julie, Jasper and Theresa every other night.

I would take the train into the city as this group of individuals intrigued me, but I wasn't sure why. Maybe it was because I was lost, broke, feeling no work was coming. But they were happy, loving their jobs. Finally one evening I asked if they could get me an interview with their boss. They were happy to get it for me and gave me an appointment, address, and directions. When I entered the building, to meet Mr. V, it was dark and dingy. It had a bit of a weird odor but I figured it was an old building. I interviewed and they gave me a job in video but did not give me a specific role. Needless to say, I was very scared. It looked weird. Weird it was, but I was drawn in. I wanted to try it. First, there were the introductions in a reception area of other workers who were extremely happy, but dressed in very black outfits. At first, I thought, "This is weird, let me get out of here." But then, I met one beautiful woman—elderly—who was quite interesting to me. She spoke about the clients in a way that was enticing. She said "We are all here for a reason, helping others to get through their issues one day at a time." Without any further documents, I took the job and was given a new black uniform to wear. As I unhinged the plastic from the uniform, I realized it was something out of a magazine and it was not *Woman's Day* apparel. I tried it on, looked in the mirror, and I looked pretty awesome. From there, I was trained in a very unique atmosphere that seemed like a house of horrors.

The other employees entered in similar apparel and started to introduce themselves to me. Remember being unemployed for several years, I would be willing to try anything to get paid. They gave examples of client services which were odd, but not horrible. It seemed to me that the clients all had special needs. They explained that their clients were special and needed specialty types of attention. I soon realized I may be over my head but I still stuck with it. After a week of training, watching other employees in a weird setting, I was given my first client. I realized that each client was eccentric (the word I would use) however, they all needed assurance that they would be treated with the best appreciation of their issues. Realizing each of them had a specific health issue, I started to see that even though the treatments I was giving were weirder than I could have thought, they were very needed by clients. I call them my patients now.

Let's take Earl. He had some health issues and could not bear to accept them, so he came to the gripper station location to release his frustration and emotions which were deeply seeded from his experiences as a child. Each client had a different problem but were all there for the same reason. Lack of support at home, lack of friendship, and feeling of being alone. Due to these types of feelings, they needed a different kind of support. Well, I started to feel like I was helping the clients tremendously and I was given my first raise. I realized after starting this totally unheard of job which is called a "dominatrix" that I liked it. I started to save money and started to feel that in this company the other workers became my family. We were all there for a reason of need as were the clients.

In the past, I thought of a domination as an ugly regimented exercise, but I soon realized that the clients were all coming there with a specific need, whether it be needing a mom like figure to hug them, a stroke of kindness, a person to talk to or just plain company to sit in a room with. The work attire was weird but it was what the client needed. I became very intrigued and very much a part of this family. I had never had a job like this, but I would never tell my family, I always said, and still say, I am in medical sales. I am very happy. I moved into an apartment in the city, I work every day and I enjoy my clients who are very needy. Up until I did get this job, I always thought of this type of service to be ugly, nasty, and unheard of. But what most people do not know, there are different degrees of stimulation for positivity for others. I was not involved in any sexual performance at all, it was all emotional support. I felt like maybe this job was similar to a shrink, but no specific degrees needed and a vocabulary that is pristine. The outfit just enhanced the client in feeling special. I cannot tell you how very special it is and was for me. It opened up a new world of wonderful people, steady employment, and a learning ability of my own that every single client has a special need as well as a special type of support. It made me realize that these clients were normal but they had some medical issues that they had a hard time handling, as a result of an unforgiving illness or surgery. All in all, I love my job, I am quite requested now and I have a family of people at work who are individuals who get it. I never would have said that I would be working in this type of environment but I am and learning every day that every single person that comes through that door is normal in many ways. I also feel that I am filling the needs of people who do not have support and cannot discuss their issues with their friends and family. I remember when I was unemployed and felt the same way, but never addressed it to get the help that would soothe my ego and my mental attitude. Now, I sit pretty with no demands at work for anything but support, individual attention and kindness to others. Either way, I guess the word dominatrix was always a bad and ugly word to me, but in the end, it isn't and it has taught me a new line of work, not exactly a career, but self-sustaining. Believe me, it was a surprise to me, but I never knew it would be good for me. I would not change things now at all, but I keep it under wraps. For all intents and purposes, I'm in sales. In the past, if anyone told me about this type of job, I would have stayed clear of it because I thought the job duties were out of the question, however I learned quickly, that there was no sexual innuendo; it was just playing the role of a mother, sister, grandmother or aunt. Go figure. You never know.

Today I am happy to say I have a great job with great people.

Anonymous

FINDING MYSELF AFTER BEING RAISED BY A STRANGER

September 14th, 1994, a date with no meaning perhaps to most. It was, however, a night changing everything about who I thought I was and introducing me to a person I was never prepared to meet.

Growing up with depression/anxiety, a bad side effect was the fear of night and falling asleep. I was only ten at the time and my father became the only remedy to my illness and I grew attached to the comfort of his presence when night broke. He held me and promised me that he would always protect our family; that no one would ever harm us. According to him, I had nothing to be scared about, nothing to cry about. He always knew just the right words to speak to ease my fears brought on by the vulnerable state nighttime caused me to endure.

This night started out like every other, watching late night movies until I finally grew tired in my father's arms. When it got really late he would carry me to bed, and any worries or tears cried were washed away by his reassurance and love. Before he would leave my room he would brush hair out of my eyes to kiss my forehead goodnight. Closing my bedroom door halfway allowed some hallway light shine in and he stuck his head in and asked, "How much do you love Papa?"

in which I whispered in Italian, "I would die for you!" Those were the last words spoken to my papa.

I took one last look around the room and closed my eyes. I told myself I would be okay, I was a fighter just like my father said. Within seconds my eyes were reopened by a startling knock on our front door. It was so loud that it appeared unfeasible that it came from a human hand. Quickly jumping out of bed thinking the worst possible, I ran into my mother in our hallway, also running to make sense of the noise. We watched as the man I once recognized as my father became a stranger, moving lifelessly towards the door ignoring my mother's screams to know who was behind the door. Within seconds our small living room was crowded with multiplying amounts of FBI agents wearing bullet-proof vests and shotguns in hand.

The words "drug smuggler", "money laundering" and "mob relations" were used multiple times during the three-hour long house search. Among the many different emotions we felt and horrifying things we saw, we all agreed that my father's arrest was a horrible mistake; a tragedy falling upon the wrong family. Before the FBI left, they reassured us that not only did they have the right man but that they three years worth of surveillance tapes to back up how well he hid his double life from us. September 14th left me without my father, a family unit and my sense of self. I no longer knew who I was or what was unfolding before my eyes. If my father wasn't the man I thought he was then who was I? How could the one man I turned to to ease my depression be the one to also worsen it? The only thing I did know was that my life would never be the same, nothing was what it seemed.

The following day the story broke in all local, national and international news medias. My father's Manhattan pizzeria was used as a meetup point for what was penned the "second pizza connection". My hero was anything but, according to everyone else. David Letterman did a skit mocking my father and the hidden business he ran. News reporters joked that he was serving much more than pepperoni with his pizza and my heartache became a public comedy skit which I prayed would be over soon. Any hope that school would be an outlet from the hell at home was erased when a classmate did current events on the story. School became an overwhelming interrogation from classmates who felt it was their right to know details of the poverty, heartache, and incarceration that my father and family endured. Many children teased as they so often do and they made it very clear that my sister and I were not wanted in the wealthy predominantly Jewish Hewlett, New York school district. Trying to be strong and ignore the taunts and teases I struggled to complete school but became homeschooled when it got to be too much.

Family members stopped bringing my cousins around, friends stopped calling and I started to feel as though I were diseased. My father's mistakes were now reflecting upon my sister and me, and we were viewed poorly because of them. I believed that maybe I wasn't worth that much because everyone around me told me so. My depression got worse and I eventually never got out of bed and did things other teenagers did. I had no energy to survive and overate to fill the void and emptiness inside of me. I reached a very dark place and ballooned well over 200 lbs by my 15th birthday. I couldn't even look in the mirror; I had become the disgusting mess everyone told me I was. I awaited my sixteenth birthday to legally drop out of school and prayed for my death. In my eyes, there was no hope and no future for me.

My sister took me aside one day and painted my future for me if I continued on the road I was on. She helped me see that, yes, we had a tragedy, but that we could still triumph by holding on tightly to one another. We had a wonderful mother who sacrificed everything she had to keep us fed, a grandmother who was also working with us to keep us stable, and most of all we had unconditional love for one another. Those who walked out of our life so easily were never meant to maybe be there and my sister helped me to see that that was okay. My father made a horrible mistake with a debt we were paying for but we didn't have room for failure, that's what everyone wanted. We had to be stronger and I wanted to be—for her and my mother. I admired her strength to not give up and I wanted to prove to everyone that I could make something positive with my life and that I deserved it also, despite my name being labeled "dirty". So I sat and I thought what I needed to do to make this possible.

Going to therapy to work on my illness, heartache and to build upon my lack of self-esteem was the first step. I doubled up on all my classes during my senior year of high school in order to graduate on time. I kept my head down while walking in public and ignored any ridicule classmates sent my way. I focused mainly on the goal of succeeding in life and getting my family out of the mess my father left us in. Working out and eating healthy helped me to shed over 80 lbs. When I got accepted into C.W. Post Long Island University I took that as an invitation to finally discover who I was and what I wanted people to know me as. I needed to let others see I was much more than the daughter of a criminal. With the weight loss and a chance at a future, all the ugliness painted on me inside out began to slowly fade away. My depression was still a daily struggle but the more goals I accomplished the more confident I got and the higher I set the next ones.

I studied Journalism with a bigger purpose than learning the art of reporting in mind. I sat in class taking notes on students also in the room with me. I wanted to know every in and out of how a reporter comes to be. How some become so ruthless for the sake of a story. I needed to understand what makes another human being leave ethics behind in order to fully recognize the humility I had faced a decade earlier. My story, my heartache was the biggest story at the time and thus made headlines. After taking classes, my publicized story was no longer a personal attack from society and I accepted it as what it was: news.

With a degree in hand and a new relationship with my father in the works, I have now taken back my name Katherina Ambrosio. I'm not the little girl scared and lost with no future. I'm not the daughter of a convicted criminal. Everything I have in my life I worked hard and fought for. I'm a college graduate who carefully covered a wound needing to be healed. If it wasn't for the people especially awaiting my failure, I could never have found the strength to do as much as I have. There is nothing like being face to face with someone who doubted you, them not recognizing the new you and you putting out your hand.

Katherina Ambrosio

EXTRA! EXTRA! 'PAPERBOY' LOSES JOB

I secured my first "real" indoor job in the Summer of 1969 after completing my second year of college. During previous summers, I had worked outdoors at a local park and a town swimming pool, visited some of my dad's accounting clients to do their end-of-the-month bookkeeping chores and umpired many more Little League baseball games than I care to remember.

So, after finishing my sophomore year at Syracuse University as a newspaper journalism major, I told myself that it was time for me to get a "Big Boy" job. My target was a summer position at my community's weekly newspaper—the Valley Stream Mail Leader on Long Island. But first, I knew I needed to put together a compelling resume and come up with a list of reasons why they should hire a complete stranger with no formal experience in the field to do jobs they didn't know that they needed to be done—and then pay him as well.

Bright and early on an early June Monday morning. I walked into the paper's small building near the center of the village without an appointment and was greeted by an older woman sitting at a reception desk. After I told her the reason for my visit, she advised me that I had to talk to the owner of the paper, Sam Tenzer (the Tenzer name was familiar to me since a "Herbert Tenzer" had just retired as a

Congressman from that district), and that she would go into the back room and get him.

She quickly returned with a tall, well-dressed, gray-haired man in his 70s who she introduced to me as Mr. Tenzer. After a couple of awkward comments, he offered me a seat at a second desk in the front office and sat down across from me. He glanced at my resume and asked me why I was there. Without wasting a moment, I pointed outlines on the sheet of paper in his hand that I thought would be of interest to him—that I was a lifelong resident of Valley Stream, that I was attending the #1 ranked communications school in the country and was majoring in newspaper journalism there and that I wrote articles regularly for the school's daily newspaper and weekly newsmagazine. I also threw a few creative ideas at him, but I'm not so sure he ever caught them.

I must have been pretty convincing because the very gruff and curmudgeon-like Mr. Tenzer (who confirmed that Rep. Herbert Tenzer was his brother) said that he would hire me to work there three days a week for about $3 or $4 an hour. (The minimum wage back then was $1.60 an hour, so his offer didn't seem so unreasonable to me at the time.) I accepted his offer and he said that I should start the next day. I showed up at 9 a.m. the next day to begin a job that would turn out to be very educational and challenging on the one hand—and quite frightening on the other.

Over the next several weeks, one of my most important responsibilities was reviewing all press releases and unsolicited story suggestions that arrived in the office mail from political and governmental sources, civic and religious groups, sports organizations, stores and restaurants, loyal readers and lots of other information suppliers and deciding which ones should appear in our next issue and which ones should end up in my "circular file."

I got to edit all of the releases, write headlines for the stories, compose captions for the photos, lay out all of the pages and even redesign the front page to include a "That Was Then...This is Now" feature which involved a historic picture of a Valley Stream landmark from 25 or more years earlier... and underneath it a shot of the same venue in the present. I also answered phones, re-organized their outdated subscription card system, proofread the Legal Notices every week with Mr. Tenzer, schlepped the old postage meter to the post office once a week to be "refilled" and even wrote a couple of stories as well as the paper's editorial after that summer's moon landing.

But after a few weeks, things started to get tense at work for me. I learned that Mr. Tenzer had a collection of subscription renewal receipt books in the office which had no basis in fact. I ignored them—until the day he came to the table where I worked, plopped a new receipt book and a pile of old subscription order cards in front of me and ordered me to write out bogus renewal receipts that he could use as the basis for the advertising rates that he was charging clients.

I told Mr. Tenzer that I did not feel right about committing fraud under any circumstance and that I did not feel comfortable following his request. He told me that if I didn't do what he asked, my services would no longer be welcome there. Very reluctantly, I allowed my gratification from the other elements of my job and my need for money to get the better of me, and I became a criminal for the first and last time in my life.

Fast forward a few days. It all started innocently enough when the office phone rang on a quiet Friday morning and I answered it. There was a very excited woman on the line who said that she was a long-time reader of our paper and that she was calling from a pay phone near the railroad station where an accident had just occurred on the elevated tracks right above her. I grabbed a pen and sheet of paper and started jotting down the details of the accident from the eyewitness's point of view. The call lasted about 15 to 20 minutes.

When I hung up the phone, Mr. Tenzer, who had been hovering over me for most of the call, asked me what the call was all about. After I told him, he literally exploded at me. He lambasted me for wasting my time and his paper's time by taking down the details of a Friday morning train accident when his paper's next issue would not be coming out again until the following Thursday. I argued that we had no idea what the story would turn out to be and, of equal importance, I didn't want to be rude to a loyal reader who honestly felt she was doing a good deed for us by cutting her short and hanging up on her.

I was shocked at Mr. Tenzer's reaction. He stared at me with piercing eyes and sternly told me to "Get your coat and hat and leave–and never come back." I had been fired! I got up, mumbled that it was the middle of summer and I didn't have a coat or hat that day and left.

On the short drive home, I played the last half hour of my life over and over again in my mind. Should I have hung up on the caller? No. Should I have not taken notes? No. Should I have not stood up for my choices? Of course not.

After I was home for about an hour the phone rang. It was Mr. Howe, also an elderly gentleman who stopped by the Mail Leader office every Friday to drop off his humor column for the following week's issue. He asked me "What happened?" I told him my side of the story and he asked me to hold on for a moment. He came back on the line a minute or so later and reported that he had just talked with Mr. Tenzer and that I could have my job back. I mulled the offer over in my mind and rolled the dice: "I'll come back," I replied, "but only if I get a $3 an hour raise."

I took a shot that they needed me more than I needed them. Again, Mr. Howe asked me to "hold" for a moment. He came back on the line after a minute or so and told me that Mr. Tenzer said ok. I thanked Mr. Howe for all of his help and told him that I would be back in the office on the following Monday morning–still probably without a coat or hat.

I finished out that memorable summer (remember that in addition to landing men on the moon, we also saw the Mets on their way to their first World Championship and the Woodstock Festival change the culture of America during those months) without further strife.

What I took away from that job was confidence in myself that I could work in almost any type of newspaper office under almost any kind of boss. But on a bigger level, I learned that if I stood up for my beliefs, even if they were not particularly popular, good things will probably happen.

Ira H. Silverman

PURSUE IT! I DID

Seek and pursue. That's a good thing to do. Think about it. When I lost my job, I felt the door open up. Why? I guess because I never jumped out of my comfort zone when working for a great company with a culture to die for. A wonderful culture of family and business values.

Did I long to do some "out of the box" things when having this terrific job? Sure, but I would not put them to the test at the job as it was a great place. I wanted to retire there, but life does not work that way. To pursue when you are out of work requires action to be done. I started to read much more because I had the time. I would look at a magazine and a photo cut out the photo and start to think about the colors. We did that with the publisher when producing magazines. I would then show it to some friends and ask "What colors do you see?"

Do you see white and gold in the photo (when it was clearly those colors) and some people answered that they saw black and blue?

Weird answers. Curiosity makes you think when asking others for opinions. Crazy as it sounds some people saw the black and blue when it really was white and gold. Was this a paradox of errors. In hindsight, some people see things differently and agree to disagree. Why? Is there a truth that comes out during this experiment? I guess you can say if you believe in your thought, then it's the right answer for you—whatever works for you

When looking for a job, I realized what I thought I knew, and what I really wanted may actually not be what I really wanted! The change, and the idea of making the new change in your work life, just happens in a moment. It's very important to explore the questions like "Where am I going?" "What am I doing?" "What makes me happy?" "What do I want to do that I can do well and enjoy my job?" These are very simple questions to ponder. I did. I explored and I tried some new types of things which made me explore the truths of "What am I going to do now?" The answer takes time; it just did not happen overnight. I experienced that exploring for the truth was a huge project, but it will decide your destiny for your work and personal life. "Really," I thought, "Am I really absolutely truthful and I knew I wasn't there yet?" It's a process. I realized that getting to the truth, the real truth, of what I wanted at that moment was undecided. But knowing that was the truth to be undecided, it set me free. Free to do what? Free to be open, wide open, to try some new things to explore with some confidence. Why? Because there would be no boss or manager saying, "It's not in your plan." Having the ability to say and do whatever you want is empowering during your job loss if you have the right attitude. Truth be told, for anyone curious to ask the questions of yourself regarding who, what, and what you want down the line, it can be challenging, scary, and confusing. With that in mind, when thinking about your new path, ask yourself the questions and be absolutely honest. Explore the questions honestly. An opportunity may be right outside your comfort zone.

I pursued many things which I never did before. It made me stronger, it gave me strength, and it helped me to learn new things and be more open to trying the new wave of putting yourself out there one day at a time.

Try it. Pursue, and you will have success. Ask the Questions. Say "Yes" to an idea you have never done before. You may surprise yourself. I did! The truth sets you free for sure.

Valentina

FORCED OUT–IDENTITY CRISIS FOLLOWS

I n 1999, I had the incredible opportunity to join a newly created non-profit, the Long Island Works Coalition, that had recently been established through the Long Island Association under the direction of its president, Matthew Crosson. I created my new position, Director of Marketing, and joined the organization ready to launch this exciting and worthwhile cause of maintaining our young workforce here on Long Island. I joined a small staff of 2—an executive director and an executive assistant. At the time, and on my first day of work, my Mom underwent a triple bypass and I began the position working from home. I was given lots of flexibility and I appreciated the understanding of my personal life challenges. I was in for an amazing and gratifying 11 years!

As time passed, I created a very thorough marketing program for our small non-profit. I created a newsletter, press releases, marketing materials for our events, and programs and fliers. After a year, I created a new position, Director of Community Relations, and the organization agreed to hire another marketing manager. In this new position, I became the voice and face of the organization. I began to create presentations to business organizations throughout Long Island—chambers, rotaries, Kiwanis and Lions Clubs. I also begin working closely with Long Island school districts, creating and supporting advisory boards, and helping to create events. The job was always flexible and more than a 40-hour, 9-5 work day.

My last position in the organization was Director of Educational Programs, which fit all of the activities and day-to-day planning in which I was involved.

During this time period, my husband was diagnosed with pancreatic cancer, and again the organization was flexible with my personal needs. I was trained by the Ford Motor Company Fund to run Career Academies, and after 3 out-of-state training opportunities, I brought back the program and training materials to several Long Island schools.

In addition, our small staff of 4 was involved with our annual internship fair every January, attracting hundreds of high school and college students, in addition to Long Island companies seeking interns for the summer.

I attended all Board of Directors meetings and submitted minutes of the discussions. We continued to be a popular non-profit, offering programs for students and interns for companies. We were the bridge filling the gap between industry and education on Long Island. However, in the 11 years at LI Works Coalition, we had a very limited plan for raising money and maintaining our organization's fiscal health. At one point, we partnered with Goodwill Industries, but that fell apart after one year. After my husband's passing in 2009, I became even more committed since I had even more time to spend working. By 2011, the organization was floundering, trying to figure out sources of funding to keep it alive. On March 1, 2011, we closed our doors and said good-bye to LI Works.

As a result, and due to the identity that I had had for so many years, I felt like Superman. What else could I be? Everyone knew me from this organization. I had done so much networking. My LinkedIn database was huge and when I went to any networking meetings, everyone always said, "I know you from LI Works Coalition." I was lost! I felt that I had lost another loved one. First my Mom in 2000, then my husband in 2009 and then LI Works in 2011. It was very hard for me. I didn't know what job would be best suited for me after this one. I wasn't even sure what I would enjoy or be good at. So, I tried a number of them. First, I tried a home-based business based on a marketing approach. Then I tried a software company that worked with non-profits. Then I worked at a career school. Then I worked at a non-profit that worked with international students. Then I worked at a profit-making company that worked with the school districts bringing career programs for all students, especially those with special needs. Now I am working part-time for a not-for-profit foundation that provides financial literacy and education to people of all stages—from youth through retirement.

I have a long job history. I have owned 3 companies, have worked for 5 non-profits, and have worked in several different industries. However, if I were to look back on my record, the most traumatic event happened when I was no longer part of the LI Works Coalition. My takeaway from this is the knowledge that you always have to be open to change and be flexible about what may happen to you in your professional life. I still go to places who remember me from this organization, but now I am okay with it and it helps open up doors for me. I happily think back over the years and reminisce about the wonderful opportunities I was given to grow the organization and develop my own cadre of skills. I still miss the important work we did and the cause for which I fought so hard! But it is like any other death—you learn to move on. It is always part of you, but you are not defined by it anymore.

Lisa Strahs-Lorenc

WHO WOULD'VE THOUGHT!

As soon as I graduated college in 1967, I immediately started working part time for Eastern Airlines. I was more than content in their reservation department and when the Director of Sales asked me to join his sales team full time in Manhattan, I was ecstatic. I was in Sales at both LaGuardia, and back then, Idewild Airport.

I was single, traveling all over the world, and even when I got married in 1971, I continued the same life until my son was born in 1974 and then my daughter in 1975.

We moved to Long Island and continued to work but the commute to Manhattan and taking care of two children was too much. I knew I had to quit my job of 17 years to stay home and take care of the family. However, my husband insisted I continue working and wanted me to start my own travel agency. Even though he found me an agency to buy in 1985, I didn't want to do it—it would be too much work and responsibility, and it was no longer a 9-5 job.

At that time it was a small mom and pop office with only a staff of three. My husband insisted I go into my own business even though I explicitly told him it would be too too much for me. At this point, I was class mom at the school my children attended. I enjoyed my life as a mother with my children.

Right from the beginning, my husband was very negative about the agency amounting to anything. He said this was just pocket change so I won't get bored because the children had started school. With much refusal, I signed the contract and I now owned my own travel agency.

With my expertise in travel and my knowledge of sales, I started getting many business contacts. I actually started to enjoy the perks, free weekend cruises, free airline tickets all over the world, and meeting CEOs of large companies.

Knowing myself as headstrong, I wanted this business to grow. When my husband saw me actually enjoying this new venture, he keep telling me: "Better enjoy it while you can, you will never last!"

This statement made me want to prove to him and myself I WILL NOT FAIL. The agency grew to a staff of twenty and we had twenty big business corporations as clients.

I went to schools, churches, temples and joined every club in my area. I was away with groups almost every month.

After 30 years as an owner, I can proudly say I am a very successful businesswoman and owner and enjoying a great life and a business to boot.

I guess I have to thank my husband (who is now my ex) for insisting I purchase the business, for I never would have become the woman I am today.

All I can say, Peter, is "Thank you very much for thinking I would fail —I proved you wrong."

To all the women out there whose husbands put you down, you have the power to succeed and change your life and be happy. Don't ever stop dreaming, for dreams do come true!

Anonymous

KINGDOM COME, KINGDOM WENT, BETTER THINGS TO COME

My bed was my dominion, my kingdom, my throne. I would curl up in robes of feathers, caressing the silk of my skin. Every thread kissed me softly and I'd lay my crown atop a field of down, as I dreamed of coin and gems—emeralds, rubies, sapphires—the earth, the sun, the sea. I used to be a king—the leader of my land. I could come and go as I pleased, and that is what I was: pleased. I ate supper in the dining hall, and worked my way around the land and its people, smiling as I passed and they smiled back at me: the king! My robes dragged behind me in the dirt, and I pointed my golden scepter at the stars and I sang:

"I'll be there one day with you all! Among the stars and across the sky! I will be there one day, mark my words, one day soon, I will be there with you."

Every day I would go into the kingdom, and collect my coin, and every night, I would see the stars—their white shine like teeth and tile. Every night I would return to my bed, to my throne, to my domain, and I would rest again. One night I dreamed of men—thousands of men with pitchforks and fire, dirty and ridden with bugs, covered in dirty sacks and rags brown like mud, ripped and torn to pieces. They came for my coin. they came for my throne and my crown and my gems.

They came for the earth, and the sun, and the sea. They came and they came and they came and they did not stop until I, the king, became as torn and poor as they. And then I woke, covered in sweat and fear, the night still black and blue outside my castle window. A star shot across the sky, and in the distance, across the land, the faint flicker of orange and yellow. I felt the heat from my bed, and I knew it was no longer a dream. My kingdom had been, and my kingdom lived no more.

And now my bed is my sarcophagus, my coffin, my end. I am mummified now, penniless and covered in wraps filthy with dirt and sand. My skin is rotting and mushy, cold and moist to the touch. My scent is sour as if my body was out in the sun I once loved for too long, but the room is pitch dark—a tomb for my heart that breaks with each passing day. I can't get out of this casket. For dinner I eat spoiled meat and infested produce, slobbering on their flesh, scattering the pieces across the crypts.

I want to leave, I really do, but I am trapped—I'm trapped in this hole in the dirt, and I try to scratch at the walls but my fingers are raw and the skin is falling off, and the hole gets deeper and darker the more I claw. If I listen closely I can hear the voices, so soft and sweet, I bet they taste like candy. I try to yell, yell at them, but the chamber echoes a deep drone and no one can hear me. Nobody comes to my aid. Can they not hear me suffering? Can they not hear my wails and my cries?

I have nothing to my name, no money, no love, no escape—just these wraps and these scraps and this empty grave all to myself. My anxieties disguise themselves as tiny scuttling bugs that nibble and crawl underneath my skin and skull. I wonder some days if there is any way out if there is an end to this suffering. I am trapped in my bed and my head and I can't get out, so the only thing I can do is sleep, but I have not dreamed in months. Some days are better than others, but when night falls, I still lie here in this pit, alone and filled with a blackening void that I cannot help but succumb to. So I close my eyes every night and hope to dream again.

And then one day I did.

It came to me in a flash: a bolt of lightning or a shooting star, I could not tell which, but my body and my soul came to life. And I saw once more, the earth, the sun, and the sea. I flew with the stars in the night, no longer holding a golden scepter, or clad in royal garb or a crown. I donned no dirty wraps or rags. I was just my flesh and my soul, careening through the universe filled with light and life, golden aura beaming from my chest.

In this dream I smiled—I smiled for what felt like the first time in eternities, for however long I was locked up in that wicked tomb. I looked down from the sky and saw the blues and greens of the ocean, so I decided to dive in because I could. I let myself swim around like an underwater missile, waving at the whales and the barnacles wrapped in seaweed. I tasted the salt on my lips and let it wash away the impurities I once thought I owned in my soul and on my skin. The sun beamed in through the layers of ocean water, crystallizing light on impact, shining and shining brighter. So I flew up there, crashing through the waves, up. up, up!

I charged toward the sun with might and hunger, reaching for the light I had forgotten about for so long. I kept going. I kept going because I let myself keep going. I rode farther into the massive yellow orb, punching a hole through it until it burst, sharing its light upon the rest of the universe. And then I woke. No longer a king, no longer a mummy, no longer a god flying through space and time—I was me. And I knew, finally, that I could continue forward and catch that light that shines even when I could not see it. And so I will.

Benny Varotta

OF AURORAS AND SNOWY OWLS

I was talking to some photographer friends in October, two years after my retirement as a newspaper chain's executive editor. We were discussing the most memorable pictures we've taken, and I said that I loved the Northern Lights shots I took on my trips to Iceland and the snowy owl photos I made on a weekday visit to Jones Beach. One of the photographers said how proud and thrilled I must be to have captured both of these "trophy" images. "You know, most of us live our whole lives hoping we'd be able to get even just one of those, and you have multiples of both."

That unexpected comment suddenly crystalized my joy at being retired, being finally free from the time-eating, energy-sapping, anxiety-provoking, positivity-destroying, managerial-tip-toeing, daily-deadline-driven life of an editor and journalist.

The advice you always hear given to retirees is to "keep busy." I offer something different: You should be as busy as you want to be, but the challenge is to be selective, to realize that you (to the extent your health enables) are in control—at last—of what you want to be busy with.

I have never felt as free to live my best life as I do now. Sure, with age comes more doctors' appointments, more MRIs, more pains and aches, less income, a little less physical mobility. But age also brings more wisdom, more maturity and, best of all, discernment, calmness and appreciation for what one can do.

So I can head off to Iceland on the hunt for auroras. I can lie in the sand in winter on a Tuesday clicking the shutter at a rare bird. I can write what I want. I can nap. I can cook. I can help others. I can be more of myself. I can learn what I want, not just what I must.

Of course, I didn't wait until retirement to start taking pictures, or writing, or being myself, or learning. These are activities people do their whole lives.

And most of the many thousands of people I have interviewed for jobs in 43 years of management, and hired and fired, were seeking to do what was best for them. It may sound crazy, but some of the best conversations I've had at work were with folks I had just fired or who were in my office to resign. Because in those situations, they had—unwillingly or willingly—realized that the jobs they were in weren't the jobs they should be in. And that's wonderful.

"To thine own self be true," the Bard wrote. Losing or leaving a job, changing careers, moving away or moving home are all daunting prospects, emotional catastrophes. But they can also be brilliant opportunities to learn lessons, practice resilience, sharpen skills, do more interesting things, simplify, meet new people, and appreciate the cleansing focus that hunger brings. Getting fired is a temporary disaster—no doubt! But it can lead to a permanently better you, a happier you, a stronger you.

. . .

When I decided to retire it was because the income no longer mattered to me as much as my time. Not that I like the idea of having less money; it's just that at a certain age, a different age for each person, you start worrying that you'll run out of time before you run out of money, and it's easy to decide which one is more indispensable.

For those who quit or get fired before it's time to retire, I say GOOD FOR YOU! What happens next is up to you. You can revel in the misery, linger too long in self-pity, or go learn something more about who you are and start doing who you are. Best wishes to you.

John O'Connell

John O'Connell spent 20-something years in corporate Human Resources Management, and then another 20-something years as a reporter, editor and executive editor for a constantly award-winning Long Island weekly newspaper chain. He retired in 2016 and is semi-self-employed as a columnist, editor and event photographer.

Chapter Three

IT AIN'T EASY BEING "MATURE"

*No matter how old we are, life offers us constant opportunities to
create and experience new paths for the future.*
~Valentina Janek

AM I INVISIBLE?

As a recent laid off worker, or as we now call it on Long Island —"downsized"—as a midlife to senior jobseeker, there are four words which needs to be communicated to corporate America. "I am not Invisible!" In retrospective of what has happened here on Long Island in the past ten years, I had a very overwhelming feeling that being out of work, over fifty, and experienced made me invisible. Yes invisible, that's right!

It felt lonely, even though I was amidst several others in the same scenarios who had received the pink slip. Many people would say, "Oh just get yourself back in the groove," easier said than done at this age, especially when most interviews were given by very, very young recruiters who made you feel that your experience was a negative. "You will be bored," were the words coming out of the recruiter's tone, even though as the jobseeker you would communicate, "I am looking for stability, benefits, and doing a good job." Your confidence flew out the windows after each and every interview of being told the same answers, at least they were honest, however it added to your very negative attitude. Maybe I should have just gone to work in an old folks home where I would be the youngest jobseeker!

Then there were the ideas of benefitting the community by being unemployed, by volunteering in a company, non-profit, school or some type of project based positive role. When you volunteer, everyone will love you, they will also have you placed at times within a circle of influence of familiarity with people who want to be in this environment, therefore you will meet people who may even help you with a job lead, a new idea for yourself, of even give you another adventure that may be of interest to you.

Community on Long Island in many forms is the glue that holds this great landscape together. What happens is somehow, somewhere we are finding ourselves around others that have either experienced tragedy or loss, and within a circle are very happy to be a part of a group reaping the benefits of a community force. In these instances, you forget the pain, the heartache and the experiences that made you go with this connection, as we long for the past. But somehow, others wind up becoming a piece of our future, and we also find that we have left a mark on some others. A new adventure may be in the works based on the positives that the previous gig brought to you. Most of the time these experiences are healthy, and teach us the amazing benefits that come from being in a community environment, which will infuse your resume and career with more happiness, integrity and respect. Think about it, try it, I am sure you will be surprised!

Anonymously, a Volunteer Addict

TOUGH FOR SOME...

At 55, I found myself unemployed, wallowing in a world of no jobs due to the economy. I had already been downsized from a six figure income (2007) to less than $50K, which is tough to live on on Long Island. First the car went, replaced by a used, less expensive car. Then all the perks went, such as gardening help, housekeeping, etc. That job lasted 15 months, again downsized due to the banking industry. Seeking a job was futile. All my connections in the financial world were not doing well. After 93 weeks of unemployment (2011), I liquidated as much as I could, rented my home and left for Florida hoping for better. In six years, I had four jobs. Only one lasted more than three months and believe me, they were low-paying. One lasted three days; poor management I could not tolerate. Most jobs I qualified for, I was told I was overqualified. Yes, I was told that and one even said he did not want to relinquish his job to me!

Fast forward, I struggled without benefit of pension (first employer committed pension fraud—another story) for eligibility of Social Security. Without going into detail, I lived off my savings and whatever else I had. Today, 2018, I have been on Social Security for two years, and that is it. No more savings, nothing. When they say history repeats itself, I have to agree because I feel I am back to my young years when posters served as wall art. And sadly, I have to use the food pantry to supplement my own pantry.

Many people have fared better because they had severance, a pension or something else. That pension loss was, for me, a gigantic slap in the face for giving my former employer 24 years I cannot recoup. For the past two and a half years I stopped seeking employment. Maybe I will qualify to be a Walmart Greeter—probably not.

Anonymous

MY HIGHS AND LOWS

After being unemployed for two years, a feeling of anger, sadness and comfort stirs inside of me. There is comfort only to learn there are other people confronting the same stereotyping as I am.

I am in my early 50's and have been operating in the corporate world for over 20 years. I am a high achiever, worked 24/7, believed in the corporate mission, never out sick, and strived to be the best I could be. As I climbed the corporate ladder, so did the age. The company was changing and I knew it was time to move on. I learned a new manager would be assuming the responsibilities of my department. A young cocky woman who had no respect for people or experience. She squeezed me out. It was music to my ears to learn she was asked to leave 4 years later.

I have been on so many interviews and keep track of them by writing articles.

Contacts were made, resumes were sent out and yet—nothing. I get offers at less than half of my previous salary. I, too, have filed applications at Costco, Walmart, and Home Depot. Something must be done. There are too many people riding in this seat who are victims of this treatment.

I once was interviewed for a Marketing Manager's position at West-field Corporation. The person who interviewed me was nearly thirty. During the interview she expressed the company likes to hire young people so they can train them to be the future management team. I was floored. I knew at that moment, this interview was a waste of my time. One week later, I was emailed the position had been filled. I could go on and on with interviews of this nature.

It has been an extremely degrading and a humiliating experience, and an ever-growing issue.

Joann Fiorentino Lucas

BIG BOOT ARTICLE

You don't have to be psychic to know something bad is about to happen. It's a feeling that something is just…wrong. Like that science experiment just starting to grow in the vegetable bin, you can smell something is going on; you're just not sure what. The day I learned of my own layoff, I was just one of nearly 7,000 let go that year—downsizing, offshoring, rightsizing. You choose the corporate buzzword: I was canned.

I'm getting ahead of myself; I can't tell you where I am unless you know how I got here. It's a familiar story; many of you out there have probably used the same career path tool I did, which I've coined, "the bouncing ball." Everybody's seen that carnival game where you drop a ball into a narrow glass box, the ball bounces off pins all the way down until it lands in one of several slots at the bottom. You get paid off according to the slot you wind up in, big bucks or crapped out. Not too many people aim for "26 years at the same company, followed by lay-off" when they step up to play the game. As a child of the 60s, I, of course, wanted to be an astronaut. Well the myopia kind of put an end to that; "Space Commander Four Eyes" was a position not readily available when I was picking a high school. I could feel myself falling through the pins, hitting a few on the way down.

Well, I blinked, and all too soon I was picking a college. I figured, "Why not become an aerospace engineer?" That was it, "those who can, fly into space...those who can't..." well, you know the rest. Skip ahead a couple of years, and aerospace engineers are selling calculators at Woolworth's, so I bumped down a few more pins and wound up in data processing (the Elephant's Graveyard, where a lot of failed engineers wind up). I finally landed at the telephone company (years ago that's all you had to say... there was only one phone company), but I was sure it was only temporary. Twenty six years later I was still there, making a nice salary, working with some good people (and some jerks, but that's everywhere), and not having too bad a time overall.

Then the big boot dropped.

The day I found out was bizarre. Companies pay thousands of dollars to learn how to fire people properly. Ostensibly this is to make the experience as easy as possible on those being dismissed; personally I believe it's to keep the incidents of disgruntled employees "going postal" and returning to plug their manager down to an acceptable number (10-15% maybe?). It was almost like a divorce, I was told "It's not you, you're great...it's us, we have to cut costs, or reduce force, or whatever." I was also told that being fired was not a bad thing, but an opportunity. I'd be able to go to school, or really do something I wanted. In fact, all I wanted was to NOT BE FIRED.

OK, back to being fired....I was also told that I was being given the opportunity to find another job within the company, that outside consultants were being made available to help me with resume preparation, interviewing skills, job search, anything I, or my downsized colleagues, would need to be successful. All wonderful opportunities, I thought. With that my boss promised to do what he can, and ran out of the office as fast as possible. This was followed by some condolences from the guys in the office, and Big Boot Day was over. So I went home.

It's a very strange feeling, not having a job to go to, I was lucky that I had never been unemployed, in a career nearly thirty years long. As much as we may complain about work, there is a satisfaction in knowing you do your job well. People depend on you, you get paid for your efforts, and if you're lucky you get to make a difference. Unfortunately many people tie their self-worth to their careers. They wonder how they could just be discarded. What did they do wrong?

The most vivid memory of those first few days was the overall fog I was in. There were a lot of things I needed to do, but I had time. Thirty days to find another position within the company, which I was pretty sure I could do. Cut to the chase, few separated employees find other positions within their company. Everyone is cutting back and there is a stigma with being canned and looking for a desperation job. I would sue; I'm sure I had a case. Well, not much luck there, $300 for a lawyer to tell me it would be basically impossible to prove discrimination. OK, I would "whistle blow", I had plenty of dirt on these bastards, and I could go straight to the top. Well, no one cared. The people I worked for could have killed *Hoffa* and no one would have cared. I am sure, dear reader, that you are now getting the picture. Everything had changed and there was nothing I could do to get it back.

My company was very professional with the whole process. They knew they had completed the tough part, telling me. Their attorneys had done their part, and isolated them from liability. They made the pretense of helping those about to go by providing resume writing classes, and outside placement advice. The calendar was now on their side, the thirty days would pass quickly, and I (along with many, many others) would soon be gone. My last act was signing a litigation waiver (or risk losing my severance money), and getting walked outside like a trespasser. I was gone, nice and clean.

OK, so I would start fresh. I assessed what I had to offer, composed a killer resume and cover letter, and discovered that looking for a job had become an impersonal, computerized, blind date. The corporate employment offices of years ago, where you could go and submit a resume (even talk to a person), were all gone, replaced by internet job boards like Monster and CareerBuilder.com. Well I could see my ball bouncing towards some great opportunities. With hundreds of jobs showing up on line, I'd have a hard time sifting through all the offers I anticipated getting. I picked the best matches in my field, and hit the send button. My big concern was hoping I could take a few weeks off before starting my new career. Rushing back to work, I learned, was not going to be a big problem.

To be continued…

Joe Iudice

I HAVE BECOME A CHEAPSKATE SINCE MY JOB LOSS

I am very upset and worried, so much so that I have become a cheapskate. At the age of 50, I no longer have a steady job. Usually I am very thrifty and so is my other half Joyce, but reality means I have to get back to work. But I really don't think at my age I can get back into a very good paying job. I now don't buy expensive wine, but I do like expensive wine. I am wearing very plain clothes which I now purchase at the thrift shop. I can't believe I have become such a cheapskate. I can also tell you the signs of an unemployed person are to cut coupons, study the flyers that come in the mail and sign up for all the cards for discounts every day and everywhere. This is quite unreal. Most people say that when you get older your expenses will get less, but when you are older other things creep up which evens it out. At this point, I do know that life is short and my parents and grandparents led long good lives. So I guess being a cheapskate is something I have to live with since it's something new to me since my job loss. So freelancer is my new name, and cheapskate is my new game!

In a split second things change, but I am here to say I have made the best of it. When I think of the dollars I used to waste never thinking about a rainy day or that this would happen, I realize that now as a cheapskate I am better off as I get older, but it's kind of funny because I used to rant about cheapskates before, so I guess I joined the ranks of the jobless empire of middle income candidates. Guess it may be time to make the donuts!

Anonymous

THE AGEISM PROBLEM IS PATHETIC

J une 13, 2006

Hon. Tom Suozzi

Nassau County Executive

One West Street

Mineola, New York 11501

Dear County Executive Suozzi,

I am writing to you as a concerned resident of Nassau County and on behalf of the "desperate job seekers" who reside here. We just had our weekly breakfast "pep talk," if you will, and the results are still the same. Resumes and interviews later, we still don't have jobs.

We have grown up here, were educated here and raised our families here. Many of them went to local colleges. My daughter and her family reside in Queens because they cannot afford Nassau County.

I very much want to stay a resident of Nassau County—my family and friends are here. My home is here. We have been unemployed for about three years—all of us college graduates who previous to this, were highly employed individuals, at the top of our game. Now, we are unemployed. Each of us is coping with the skills we have. I have taken a mortgage on my previously paid off home, in a last ditch effort to remain here. I will be selling within a year if things don't change.

We are a group that has fallen between the cracks – 50 and over. The older employee has become a throw away—experience and the loyalty and work ethic that we were trained with have no value today. It's the youngest who get the jobs. When comparing interviews we hear the same phrases repeatedly "they want someone with less experience that they can mold," "how long do you plan to remain in this job?" and the one that blew my mind, was when I was told "I can't believe you would want this job, it seems like such a come down". I'm sure that this a politically correct way of saying they want someone who will work for less. But, ironically, we have realized that we, despite our previous salaries, are willing to work for the same salary. I should point out, these are with reputable companies, names you know well.

Recent articles are focusing on the older employee, but to date, our government has done nothing to indicate they are aware of this problem. My friend in Florida sent me an article touting Nassau County as the best place to live, and I used to think that myself. How sad, that in addition to driving out young people with the high cost of living, an older generation, who have worked to make Nassau County what is today, are now being forced out.

All things considered, we are looking forward to finding employment. We do not give up, we meet weekly to encourage each other and share leads.

I would appreciate it if you would look into this. Perhaps hiring someone of our age to work with the your Department of Labor to research this and come up with a plan. Maybe there is money out there to help us.

An overwhelming amount of people voted for you; you had it all. You were young, energetic and we were hopeful. You had new ideas and a young family and we were counting on the fact that you wanted the best for them. You inspired us and we believed. Sadly, we are disappointed.

I would welcome the opportunity to hear your thoughts and what you believe would be a course of action that would be of assistance. Hiring people with experience should be a plus, not a negative.

Sincerely,

Stephanie Jeffery Carlino

WHAT HAPPENED TO HUMANITY?

W ell, here I am. Sixty-seven years old and wondering what the hell happened! It was not supposed to be like this. I was promised happily ever after and a house with a white picket fence! Where's my knight in shining armor? Why are the kids still here?

Let's start at the beginning. I grew up in 1950's America—*Father Knows Best*, Campbell's Soup, Hula Hoops, and a mother who was waiting for me to come home from school with milk and cookies. Idyllic times. A shame the kids of today will never have that experience of safety, innocence, an intact family, and a belief in something bigger than oneself.

I followed the rules. I gave up pursing a career in law and got married because I was supposed to, had children because I thought I would be sorry if I didn't, and bought a house because it was part of the American Dream. Marriage is over, children never left, house is a money pit. So much for that fairy tale.

Needless to say I was unprepared for divorce, and the prospect of making a living and taking care of my children was terrifying. I had taken up body building while getting back in shape after having my children. I decided to parlay that into my own business, and Barbara's Body Shop was born. I built a very successful business for myself, and managed to support my family nicely. This was in the Opulent Eighties. People had so much money they did not think twice about spending it. The years passed and little by little the gyms and fitness clubs started to spring up on every other block, or so it seemed to me. Slowly but surely my business was eroded, and a few years ago I found myself down to just a few clients. Now I am in my sixties and back in the fitness field trying to get hired as a personal trainer and fitness instructor. I could have tried to find a job in the workplace, but 20 plus years of huge hourly fees made that very unpalatable, to say the least.

It got to the point that I had no choice but to go back out there. Well, what a surprise to me that no one wanted to hire a woman in her sixties. I had 30 plus years experience teaching fitness and yoga classes privately, teaching adult education and a background in diet and nutrition. Every interview I went on I found myself competing with 20-something year olds who knew nothing about motivating people, no experience working with seniors, and no private training or teaching experience. They had no poise, no wisdom and nothing that I could see that would make them a better candidate than me for the job. What they did have was youth, and that was a commodity that I would never have again.

Disgusted and defeated, I used nepotism to get a job at the veterinary hospital where my daughter works. I was hired as a customer service coordinator. It was fine for my needs. I got to stay active, talk to people, use my brain and kiss the animals. We often got visits from Corporate to see how things were in the trenches. Whenever they were there they would pretend to care about how we felt and ask for our input, thoughts, concerns. I noticed that no one ever opened their mouths, even though I knew how dissatisfied they all were as we discussed it regularly. Being at that age where I am not afraid to say what's on my mind, I addressed a concern I was having about the way we were being rated on job performance. The next day I was told I was being taken off the schedule. There was no explanation, and no one had a conversation with me about it. I have not been put back on the schedule since that happened, about six weeks ago, despite numerous conversations with my Practice Manager. She keeps telling me she can't fit me in with my availability. This of course, is an attempt to have me quit.

So what do I take away from this? After I got over my indignation and outrage, I started to think about this in human terms. It saddens me that people are so cold, callus, calculating and insensitive to others. I am a senior citizen with a limited income and half of it was taken away from me. Fortunately for me, I am not in the position of losing my house or starving to death, but did they know that? NO they did not, and judging by their actions, they probably would not give a damn if I were. What happened to integrity, kindness and fairness? I guess it went by the way of the Hula Hoop. Sad. I am grateful though, that I did get to grow up in a world where people had their humanity in tact.

Barbara Kiprik

I LOST MY JOB A FEW MONTHS AGO

Did I just get headless, and careless and thoughtless? There are times that I lost many things and couldn't find them. Is that careless? The other day I lost a set of glasses so I kept looking all over for them—no luck. Now I think about the fact that my job is missing, too. Did a coworker steal it, or maybe a neighbor, or even the mailman? If I look at the statistics for where the jobs are, it is evident in the records that many thousands of jobs have been lost, and the jobless applicants are looking in niches and networking events searching for jobs that were lost but may be re-ignited.

If you think about this, the approach to look for a job has changed. Yes, there's Google. Yes, there's the job clubs. Yes, there's events. Yes, there's the library talks. But as you read and read these days the only way to stay alive and find opportunities is by doing the actual face to face meetings to chit chat and meet great people. And if you do lose a job, what does is mean? Does this matter to the company? No, but it matters to you and me. Have all the jobs gone straight to hell or heaven?

The current job situation for the experienced worker of advanced age, has given me chance to consider other options. I could place my name on a sign and stand on the parkway. I could also put a note in the "lost and found" in the airport but, then again, does anyone ever find an item they lost at the airport?

In my heyday, I knew that my friends lost both their significant and insignificant things on a monthly basis, but it's something else to lose a job which took up your entire life—forty hours a week.

So I continue to be positive, search for new ideas and know someday maybe I will find the key for the loss of the job I truly liked. Till then, I will keep talking the talk, and walking the walk, and always show up. But I will always keep in touch with the member of LIBC, they are the heart and soul of Long Island.

Anonymous

HE HAD MY BACK

My name is Jane Vassil and I grew up in New York City in Astoria, Queens. Throughout my life, starting at a very young age, I was faced with several issues that had skyrocketed over time and finally disabled me when I was in my late 50's. I was always, and still am, a very positive and outgoing individual who believes in a strong value system. Goodness and kindness, as well as respect for all beings in our ever-changing world is most important to me. First and foremost, my hero is God who was and still is my protector, healer as well as my eternal Father in Heaven. My family and my friends are next in line after my Lord and Savior. While I was brought up in a very loving and giving family who taught me values and respect for others, I had experienced many traumatic occurrences outside the home as the years progressed. Even though I struggle on a daily basis, fighting with severe pain throughout my body, I will never give in to the pain and never allow it to control me. I am in charge - not the pain. I just forge forward and do what is needed every day. I never give up and never will! I always feel that there are rainbows after every storm.

I have a strong faith that I will be able turn my life around and be healthy again. I also believe in people to help you get there. We all need people to survive. I am finally learning how to receive from others as I have always been a giver, and still am.

I have worked since the age of eight. I sold the Herald Tribune Newspaper door to door, pumped gas, worked in a hosiery warehouse as a stock girl and then fulfilled outgoing orders for 32 stores until I was asked at the age of 16 to operate a store on my own. I then worked in sales in a jewelry store and then onto the corporate world in Manhattan. I first worked at the JC Penney Company, McGraw-Hill Publishing, Quantum Chemical Corporation, Hansen PLC, Viacom, and finally ended up in Healthcare with Saint Vincent Catholic Medical Centers. I worked in the Human Resources Department in every organization. My last position at the hospital before its closure and my total disability was Corporate Director of Human Resources Benefits/Services. Despite all of the adverse occurrences I have faced in my life, I always kept a positive attitude and was very spiritual, believing that God was always in control of me and my life. He is the driver on my life's road.

Over 45 years ago while babysitting my nieces and nephews, I conjured up a story while I was trying to put them to sleep. They loved it so much that when I became disabled, I decided at some point to finish the story and have it published. From start to finish, it took me a couple of years to research all the dos and don'ts of having the book published since this was a new experience for me. I did the majority of work on this project myself without much help. The book is a children's book called "Martha and Me" (A Handicapped Child with a Purpose in Life). This little girl "Martha" is the main character who you can't help falling in love with. She is sassy and very smart. Martha is physically challenged and yet that does not bother her in the least. She forges on with her life while she is being bullied in school and raised by a single parent. She experienced her father's demise when she was a toddler and yet she keeps him close to her heart. This book reaches out not only to children but also to adults who have faced any kind of adversity in their lives. Martha is a very positive child living in a negative world of prejudice and bullying. She also has a confidant named "Nickel," her one-eyed teddy bear, who is with her in good times and in bad times. The book focuses on values that are missing in today's world. It also has lessons for children to learn that will help them in their day-to-day activities. I have been given positive feedback from many children and adults on how they enjoyed reading this book as well as how it has helped them in some way or another. That warms my heart! In summary, I believe that when you give out positivity in life, the universe will send it back to you in some small or big way. No matter what I am faced with, I always stay positive and know that God has my back and will always be with me in my time of need no matter what. He is the constant in my life. Who is yours?

Jane N. Vassil (author "Martha and Me")

UNEMPLOYED AT A CERTAIN AGE

As someone who has recently been eliminated in a cost-cutting measure by a large organization, it takes a certain amount of personal growth to not take it personally. The phrase "it's just business" is a weak excuse for management to excuse the fact that they have not led an organization to success. I have seen many talented, but not valued employees eliminated just to give the impression that issues are being addressed. It always comes back to the same shell game. Disrupters scare most to try to do a better job or actually do what they were hired to do to drive an organization. It's best to eliminate those who actually scare them into being better employees. It's that old game of those who are liked best are kept, regardless of the true efforts brought forth every day. Is this a generational issue? I am sure it is. Multi-generational workplaces are ripe for lack of effective communication styles. As an example, Baby Boomers will pick up the phone vs. Millennials who would not even consider calling. Currently, we have four different generations all working for a common cause for an organization, but the approaches are very different. It's the diversity topic but in a new way, we don't have ageism we have "experiencism" and the generation not at the helm suffers greatly. In April the unemployment rate for Baby Boomers was in the 8% range and that doesn't include those who stopped looking or are under-employed.

The only way to survive this new era of employment is to have a clear understanding of your career path, self-worth and financial stability. Long gone are the days that one organization is going to help you on these paths. You must get creative; this is not for the weak of heart for sure. You have to find your inner resilience, strength and resources. No one told you this or showed you how to do this. Now you are unemployed and the challenge is on full steam ahead. What are you going to do? How are you going to do it? Who can help you get there or assist in the process? I have found many people are more than willing to help. It's human nature to want to help someone, and many do. They call this paying it forward. Little did I know that I have been doing this all my adult life and have adapted these skills to each and every situation that has been presented to me during my interesting career. I am very grateful to be a world traveler and feel that by having the many wonderful opportunities to travel alone or in groups it has given me the skills to depend on the person I am. Most people have not had these opportunities or desire to stretch for these dreams. The fear is real, painful and debilitating. The challenge to each individual is personal. It's how you approach this new aspect of your life. Now is the time to continue to learn, build up a network that you actually speak with and meet, test yourself on a daily basis for what you really need. As one of my greatest sponsors told me during this latest development in my career "it's just a moment in time on your journey." I'm moving forward with the best possible attitude!

Dolores Kornely

JUMPING THROUGH HULA HOOPS

Well, here I am. 67 and wondering what the hell happened! It was not supposed to be like this. I was promised happily ever after and a house with a white picket fence! Where's my knight in shining armor? Why are the kids still here?

Let's start at the beginning. I grew up in 1950's America. Father Knows Best, Campbell's Soup, Hula Hoops, and a mother who was waiting for me to come home from school with milk and cookies.

Idyllic times. A shame the kids of today will never have that experience of safety, innocence, an intact family, and a belief in something bigger than oneself.

I followed the rules. I gave up pursuing a career in law and got married because I was supposed to, had children because I thought I would be sorry if I didn't, and bought a house because it was part of the American Dream. Marriage is over, children never left, the house is a money pit. So much for that fairy tale.

Needless to say, I was unprepared for divorce, and the prospect of making a living and taking care of my children was terrifying. I had taken up bodybuilding while getting back in shape after having my children. I decided to parlay that into my own business and Barbara's

Body Shop was born. I built a very successful business for myself and managed to support my family nicely. This was in the Opulent Eighties. People had so much money they did not think twice about spending it. The years passed and little by little the gyms and fitness clubs started to spring up on every other block, or so it seemed to me. Slowly but surely my business was eroded and a few years ago I found myself down to just a few clients. Now I am in my sixties and back in the fitness field trying to get hired as a personal trainer and fitness instructor. I could have tried to find a job in the workplace but 20 plus years of huge hourly fees made that very unpalatable, to say the least.

It got to the point that I had no choice but to go back out there. Well, what a surprise to me that no one wanted to hire a woman in her sixties. I had 30 plus years experience teaching fitness and yoga classes privately, teaching adult education, and a background in diet and nutrition. In every interview I went on I found myself competing with 20 something-year-olds who knew nothing about motivating people, and had no experience working with seniors, no private training or teaching experience. They had no poise, no wisdom and nothing that I could see that would make them a better candidate than me for the job. What they did have was youth and that was a commodity that I would never have again.

Disgusted and defeated I used nepotism to get a job at the veterinary hospital my daughter works for. I was hired as a customer service coordinator. It was fine for my needs. I got to stay active, talk to people, use my brain and kiss the animals. We often got visits from Corporate to see how things were in the trenches. Whenever they were there they would pretend to care about how we felt and ask for our input, thoughts, and concerns. I noticed that no one ever opened their mouths even though I knew how dissatisfied they all were, as we discussed it regularly. Being at that age where I am not afraid to say what's on my mind, I addressed a concern I was having about the way we were being rated on job performance. The next day I was told I was being taken off the schedule. There was no explanation and no one had a conversation with me about it. I have not been put back on the schedule since that happened, about six weeks ago, despite numerous conversations with my Practice Manager. She keeps telling me she can't fit me in with my availability. This, of course, is an attempt to have me quit.

So what do I take away from this? After I got over my indignation and outrage, I started to think about this in human terms. It saddens me that people are so cold, callous, calculating and insensitive to others. I am a senior citizen with a limited income and half of it was taken away from me. Fortunately for me, I am not in the position of losing my house or starving to death, but did they know that? NO, they did not, and judging by their actions they probably would not give a damn if I were. What happened to integrity, kindness, fairness? I guess it went by the way of the Hula Hoop. Sad. I am grateful though, that I did get to grow up in a world where people had their humanity intact.

Anonymous

WE'RE GONNA BE IN PICTURES

You are so right about support and laughter, it really gets you through. When I first had ageism experiences and started to talk about it, I did not get any support. People thought I was crazy or making things up; they just couldn't perceive what was going on. After a while I started to find people who shared the experience; right away they knew what I was talking about. On that note, a documentary filmmaker headed for New York who was in the market for smart, savvy New York women to help fight ageism and produce a video of folks who experience age discrimination in the second act. We were asked to be part of a documentary and quickly ran together to a local office to use a conference room; again karma kept happening to us.This phone call resulted in our group being chosen to be the savvy New Yorkers in the video, which is a cross country video for *Ageism Speaks*.

In early 2010, Susan Sipprelle, a documentary filmmaker and founder of Tree of Life Productions, contacted us regarding the online multimedia project *Over 50 and Out of Work*. Our group was asked to be part of this very telling documentary, including 100 Americans over the age of 50 who had lost their jobs in the Great Recessions. We were in the good company of experts including economists, academics and researchers among the fifty-plus demographic in the U.S.

Marc Levin from Blowback Productions followed members of the Long Island Breakfast Club for several weeks in making the *Hard Times Lost on Long Island* HBO Production documentary, spotlighting the challenges facing highly-skilled, well-educated Long Islanders who lost their jobs. After speaking to many members, one of his colleagues stated, "Being unemployed for two years is not just a financial loss. It's an emotional loss. It's a loss of friendships. People disappear; you can't socialize. It changes every facet of your life." Marc entrenched the club after attending many of our spirited events.

Come Fly With Me is how we were featured on local television news with Jim Altamore, now an international jazz singer of popular standards from what is known today as *The Great American Songbook*. Jim Altamore, who is a featured performer, came to our club, worked with the group, and the group again was asked to be on a show with him on a local news channel talk show.

David Gussin, the king of networking on Long Island, started off our story in a big way on CNN News Money & Main Street with *Are You Ready Are You Ready, Let's Get it On!* On this noteworthy day, Christina Yates, CNN Producer, visited with the Long Island Breakfast Club and arranged for CNN News to come to the little town of West Hempstead. Working with Alex Jacobsen from Lakewood Stables on this wonderful day was probably the best compliment and media attention we could have ever received. Hell, if we were employed we would have received a very, very large bonus for this. All this for making our members go ride a horse for the feeling of something different. There were so many interesting discussions on that day viewed on *Money and Main Street* with our members here on Long Island, discussing the ways people can change their life midstream after losing a job.

. . .

If we can't get power through knowledge, maybe we can get power through numbers. If enough of us become vocal, someone will hear. The trio of women and one token male became very excited about being in a documentary which may help to fix the problems that we were experiencing. We made it to the big time we thought.....we had a lot of fun and we also felt like we were making some type of difference for every other experienced woman and man in the world who was downsized.

Valentina

Chapter Four

TIPS FROM THE "FRONT"

Committing to find a job or change your future is not an act, it's an attitude!
~Valentina Janek

VALENTINA'S TIPS

Get a Mentor.

Ask questions, even if you think they are dumb.

Volunteer. Volunteer. Volunteer.

Take a class and learn a new skill (even if it's a social one)

Think about why you do what you do and discuss it.

When you have successful day, share the applause and credit with the people who helped you have that great day.

Be as humble as ever when you get the corner office.

Be open to all networking possibilities, because you never know!

Valentina

DON'T STOP WORKING TOWARDS YOUR FUTURE

Being unemployed is hard. If often carries a feeling of shame from being laid off or even fired.

In reality, a lot of people have been laid off—better known as fired. I have been there. It is not a time that I felt my best self. Don't give up. Don't stop working for what your next move is. Use the time as an opportunity to regroup and get into a fit that that can really provide you a step towards your goals.

And in the meantime, there is no shame in working a side job or even a role you may have never thought you would be in. We all have bills to pay. I respect the people who, even when times are less than ideal, take pride in continuing to work toward their dreams and never let their responsibilities slide.

You've Got it. Never Give Up.

Anonymous

IT'S NOT WHAT YOU SAY, IT'S HOW YOU SAY IT

Your voice is unique. It defines and differentiates you from everyone else. It's one of the many things that makes you who you are, as a speaker—and a writer.

In writing, your voice is the way you choose your words, describe what you see, and view the world. It is the individual perspective that only you have. And writing true-life stories in the first person requires a particular use of voice.

Develop your voice and create compelling and uplifting inspirational stories.

• Recognize the hallmarks of a strong voice.

• Analyze the elements of voice: authenticity, honesty, simplicity, humor, and courage.

• Know the difference between style and voice, and how they are related to one another and can be developed.

• You may be very surprised at how easy a voiceover can be once you realize this is a potential job for an over-fifty candidate.

Valentina

SHOCK AND DENIAL

You're so happy in your work. You've just finished working long hours on that project which was a big hit with the firm's biggest client. After a restful weekend spent basking in the sunlight of a job well done, you go in to work on a seemingly average Monday, make the usual complaints about the fact that it's Monday with your peers but nevertheless proceed to put in your hard day's work. Toward the end of the day, your boss calls you into the conference room, a little out of the ordinary, but not a big deal.

"Maybe she wants to privately congratulate me on my fabulous work and tell me that I'm getting a raise, a promotion, my own office, an assistant...or maybe all of the above!" You're on top of the world with excitement—so proud, so confident, feeling completely rewarded by your work. "I did choose the right career after all."

As she begins to speak, her lips move but you can't quite make out what she's saying. It sounds like, "We have to let you go." But that's impossible.

"I'm a great worker—so dedicated, so loyal to the firm which I am so proud to be a part of. I get along with literally everyone in the firm and I am simply good at what I do—that project speaks for itself."

"Excuse me, could you please repeat that?" you ask, certain that you mind was playing tricks on you just seconds ago. Then you hear it- only this time as clear as a bell, "WE HAVE TO LET YOU GO." Like daggers through your heart.

"Wait. What??? Me??? No, not me. You must be mistaken." But this is not a phone call. Your boss did not make a simple error and buzz the wrong extension. She's standing right there in front of you— wondering why you suddenly have a hearing problem. At that moment you realize why she wanted to see you in the conference room...... and your life is never the same.

The good news is that if you're willing to be open to new opportuni- ties, it can be even better than it was before this horrific experience. For those who find themselves abruptly unemployed, life has changed, but not ended. The thing to keep in mind is that losing a job is just that—A LOSS. Therefore, you must grieve it. Be sad. Get mad. Com- plain. Cry. Do the "Shoulda-Woulda-Coulda" dance for a brief moment. When you've finally worn yourself out, you must boldly ACCEPT what has happened.

For many people, acceptance is the hardest part of this process. The challenge of acceptance is that while it may sound easy, it can actually be quite painful. Denial conveniently shields us from the painful reality that has just slapped us in the face. Denying that X happened keeps the pain at bay. The problem with denial is that you can only stay there for so long—it's not reality. Or as Billy Joel so aptly put it, "It's just a fantasy. It's not the real thing." The truth is you can run but you can't hide.

The best way to get over the pain is to go right through it. Meet it head on and yell, scream, cry, sob into a pillow when you need to, but just GET IT OUT! After you let the feelings flow freely for a while, you may start to feel depleted and empty, like you have nothing left. That's when you'll know that the time has come to rebuild. You must create your own brave new world. After all, your life will never be the same.

… And maybe that's a good thing."

Beth M. Moretti

FINDING THE RIGHT JOB

From Labor Day Jokes and Funny Stories

In honor of Labor Day, here's a first-person report of someone who was not quite as successful as he had hoped to be in the job market:

As a young man:

My first job was in an orange juice factory, but I couldn't concentrate on the same old boring rind, so I got canned.

Then I worked in the woods as a lumberjack, but I just couldn't hack it, so they gave me the axe.

After that, I tried working in a donut shop, but I soon got tired of the hole business.

I manufactured calendars, but my days were numbered.

I tried to be a tailor, but I just wasn't suited for it. Mainly because it was a sew-sew job, de-pleating and de-pressing.

I took a job as an upholsterer, but I never recovered.

In my prime next I tried working in a car muffler factory, but that was exhausting.

I wanted to be a barber, but I just couldn't cut it.

Then I was a pilot, but tended to wing it, and I didn't have the right altitude.

I studied to become a doctor, but I didn't have enough patients for the job.

I became a Velcro salesman, but I couldn't stick with it.

I tried my hand at a professional career in tennis, but it wasn't my racket. I was too high-strung.

I became a baker, but it wasn't a cakewalk, and I couldn't make enough dough.

I was a masseur for a while, but I rubbed people the wrong way.

I managed to get a good job working for a pool maintenance company, but the work was just too draining.

Later in life:

Then I became a personal trainer in a gym, but they said I wasn't fit for the job.

I thought about being a historian, but I couldn't see a future in it.

Next, I was an electrician, but I found the work shocking and revolting, so they discharged me.

I tried being a teacher, but I soon lost my principal, my faculties, and my class.

I turned to farming, but I wasn't outstanding in my field.

I took a job as an elevator operator. The job had its ups and downs, and I got the shaft.

I sold origami, but the business folded.

Finally: I took a job at UPS, but I couldn't express myself.

I tried being a fireman, but I suffered burnout.

I became a banker, but I lacked interest and maturity, and finally withdrew from the job.

I was a professional fisherman, but I couldn't live on my net income.

I next worked in a shoe factory, but I just didn't fit in. They thought I was a loafer, and I got the boot.

I worked at Starbucks, but I had to quit because it was always the same old grind.

So, I've retired, and I find I'm a perfect fit for this job! For those of you who still have life left in you.....

Pat Barrow

JUST AN OPINION

There is little debate that Corporate America continues to favor younger employees over "longer termed" more experienced ones. The reasons are many and varied: alleged updated, advanced technical job skills, financial benefit to the companies in the form of lower wages and employee benefits, and perceived flexibility in managing a more junior person. It seems that age, experience and demonstrated loyalty to the enterprise are just not valued as in the past. Couple this with corporate America's preoccupation with creating additional efficiencies by effecting general workforce reduction and it creates a very challenging environment for the older employee.

Robert Reich, the former Secretary of Labor in his book, *The Common Good,* touches upon this notion. He argues that industry has essentially abandoned a corporate mission model that once stressed **stakeholder value,** defined as a commitment to the community in which the business functioned, commitment to the employees that supported the enterprise and finally commitment to shareholders who invested in the enterprise. That model has now eroded to a mission of simply driving profit for the sake of providing **shareholder value** only. The covenant with company employees—particularly older ones—is largely a thing of the past. He reasons that this evolution has been in vogue for the past three to four decades. The notion of "downsizing," "rightsizing," or "consolidating" has created a legion of workers forced to scramble for alternative job opportunities, or simply forced to leave industry "before their time." The older worker is often confronted with the option of facing an alternative lifestyle prior to his or her intention to do so. For my own part when the corporate consolidation initiatives were in full vigor, I was given the opportunity to remain with the company that employed me. My options were limited, however, to working in a different, less challenging capacity that would require a significant geographic relocation. Weighing my alternatives, I chose the opportunity of taking "early retirement" with all the financial incentives that the corporation at that time afforded me.

Now, I hate the word "retirement". It makes it seem as if someone contemplating the end of a particular business career is about to disappear from the planet. Consider the synonyms that the dictionary uses to describe the word retirement; "withdraw," "go away," "shut oneself away." Is it any wonder that we older folks are often reluctant to terminate a career choice and move in a new direction? Is it any wonder that when a job, career or industry opportunity has reached a logical end, usually decided by the employer, an older employee is loathe to face the reality of the situation?

In actuality, statistics support the idea that workers are attempting, in the face of a hostile environment, to hold onto jobs longer. Statistics show that the percentage of workers 55 and older, which was 12% of the labor force in 1990, is expected to rise to 24% by the year 2020. Part of the reason is changing demographics, lower population growth, people living longer, and of course, the perceived financial benefits of deferring Social Security benefits, IRA distributions, etc. "as long as possible". The so-called experts, financial advisors, psychology types, et al. extol the virtues of staying on the job as long as possible. They seem to not give credence to the fact that, often times, the older employee is working in a hostile, unsatisfying and/or even stressful work environment. The toll that takes on mind and body can exceed the case made for financial and emotional security that can accrue from "staying to the bitter end." No consideration is given to the physical and emotional toll taken by staying in a place where *you know* you do not belong. No consideration is given to the opportunity cost of early retirement years that might be better spent pursuing new interests, or a new career or just plain settling into retirement mode.

I have always been a contrarian thinker, an outlier of sorts, but as an "early retiree" I want to tell you that there is life after exit from the professional world, and it can be safe and secure and generally more satisfying than that which you encountered in your later years in industry. I also want to tell you that there can be exciting life options out there without encountering financial disaster if you open your mind and your heart to new possibilities, new interests and are willing to reshape your own economic structure. Here is how:

Conduct an economic house cleaning or, to put it another way, do the math. Separation from a job, no matter what the circumstances, should necessitate a thorough review of economic requirements. Explore all aspects of your existing lifestyle. Start with your home. Often times, the kids are gone but we remain in a home that is no longer required either for perceived convenience or merely to avoid change. If you can overcome the emotional attachment to remaining in "the place where you brought up the kids", you will find that your place of residence is not "sized properly" for current or future needs. In like kind, review all expenses, spending patterns, etc. While you were in full employ, your spending habits such as dining, clothing, travel, and other general consumer requirements are rarely reviewed. In addition, understand the economic benefits afforded you if you are no longer drawing an active salary. This can come in the form of real estate tax, energy cost, other utility relief. Most folks get themselves in economic trouble simply because they refuse to scale their economic require-ments to their current economic realty. Failure to take some action in this area, creates needless financial pressure and often limits your ability to live your post career life to the fullest. The economic benefit of scaling down your living situation is far bigger than you can imag-ine. In many cases, the economic benefits of a lifestyle "reorder" out-gain the damage cause by separation from your job.

· · ·

Do something for someone else.

In my own case, in building a four-decade business career, I reasoned that I had neglected my obligation to provide service to my community. Upon opting for early retirement, I determined to take the expertise developed over my career and offer those services to the community at large. Since my expertise was and is in the financial field, I have provided free income tax preparation, financial counseling and related services. In addition, I provide other more generic services under a number of community outreach programs. These efforts having been going on for a number of years now and I cannot begin to tell you what a rewarding experience these efforts have provided. Under these programs I have increased and varied my knowledge base, kept my mind and skills sharp and met some very wonderful, dedicated people who I consider my new colleagues. The experiences gained in these not-for-profit endeavors stand in stark contrast to the heavy-handed, most political, non-collegial and somewhat stagnant environment encountered in the latter part of my business career.

Move On–Move Out.

Don't have your confidence shaken by (what Miss Janek defines as) "The Big, Bad Boot." While a job loss, or separation from a job before planned, often takes an emotional toll, resolve to move on as quickly as possible. Do not dwell in the past and do not hold on to old paradigms. Job requirements and job availability needs change over time. Too often, people "who get the boot" run around with resume in hand reflecting job objectives, skills/interests that got them fired in the first place. Do not waste time trying to peddle old skills. Understand that you might need to refresh the resume. This leads to my final recommendation:

This is the part where you get to "think outside the box"

Early retirement, separation from a long-standing job, "getting the boot", or whatever term you want to ascribe affords one the opportunity to start over. It is the clean sheet of paper you need to lay out the roadmap to change. This can take the form of:

• Exploring new relationships or refreshing old ones. The experts will tell you that a very high percentage of career changes takes place from leveraging contacts or rekindling relationships that you have developed over the years. Go to breakfast with a group. Join a new club. Look at networking options. You would be amazed how new opportunities arise if you afford yourself the opportunity to simply "be with people." If nothing else, this gets you, as I like to say, "out of your own head" and generally keeps you engaged.

• Develop a specific plan to upgrade your existing skill set or, alternatively, develop a new one. Free time affords you the opportunity to explore options that will enhance your skill set. Many of the colleges afford folks the opportunity to "audit classes" either for free or for a fraction of the cost. You will not earn a degree or earn credits but at this stage of our life we are looking for a knowledge base, not a certification. The internet offers wonderful classes from renowned colleges and other institutions if one simply avails oneself of this option. Get up in the morning, get on your computer, and a new world of knowledge awaits. The libraries, museums and community centers provide free seminars, book readings and lectures on a host of topics. If you really want to develop a new skill set, the options are available. Your investment generally is not in dollars, but is paid by simply investing your time.

• Leverage the assets you have acquired while working. This option is certainly not for the faint of heart but it a viable alternative for some who want to build a new career or develop other income alternatives. This can be as simple as renting out a part of your existing home as a means of generating income to as complex as refinancing your assets, home, IRA, insurance plan or other personal assets to start that new business venture that you have dreamed about for years. I can tell you that I have a number of friends and acquaintances who have explored this option and have met with financial success. But, greater than their new-found financial benefits, they all extol the benefits of being out of the "old grind" and the joys of "doing their own thing."

I have not said anything profound in this essay. Much of what I have said is common sense or has been espoused by some or most the so-called experts in other times. This is less a primer on the things to do upon job separation and more a call to action and plea to stay optimistic in the wake of facing a job loss or retirement option. Too often older employees ascribe some personal guilt or assign personal failings to their circumstances. More often than not it is a corporate failing, economic happenstance or some other non-controllable event that put them "on the sideline." Look at "the boot" as an opportunity to start anew. Guaranteed, new vistas await. Seize the opportunities that lie ahead. You deserve the chance.

Anonymous

DIFFERENT PERSONAL QUALITIES CAN LEAD TO YOUR OWN INDIVIDUAL SUCCESS

Different personality traits help you in your professional career in a variety of different ways.

For example, if you are the type of person who can drive projects and excel with socializing as well as project work, you are probably always a very giving person and can be a member in charge of a team that ignites yourself and your team to succeed.

If you are a serious planner, and always have your goals logged in daily and check off your planning business days, you probably are a person who gets things done with ease and perfection with much success.

Maybe you are a questioning person who has to do much research before making a decision. It's a good trait because you are a thinker and a planner, which will help you to continue to make things happen because of your ability to think it through towards total completion because of your own high goals.

Then there is the person who I call a rebel. Rebels are sometimes difficult to deal with but need a reason to make something happen and succeed. I know some rebels who will not do something just because someone told them to do it. I call this being rigid, but most rebels can find their way to success as long as they are deciding it's what they want to do, and it was their idea.

Knowing that you are in touch with who you are—and why—is what will drive you to be the best you can be professionally, socially, and independently. Every day and every journey has its starts and stops.

But when you wake up and smell the coffee to realize where you are now and where you were before, that's the good news.

Valentina

MY INTERVIEW WITH MILLENNIALS

Do you remember when you were the youngest person in the office?

I'm sure you do. Everyone was friendly and willing to let you in.

Now, you're one of the oldest, and younger people frequently distance themselves from you. Worse, you may be unemployed and wondering how you get a new job with most of your career behind you.

I did it 10 years ago, and I'm ready to do it again. Here is my story.

The hardest part of getting back in the workforce wasn't the networking, but the interview. After being unemployed for several years (working as a substitute teacher, resume writer, and sporadic jobs consultant); I found myself at a precipice: At 52, I had obtained an interview at TCI College of Technology for a Career Services position I never held, and a meeting with 4 people between the ages of 26 and 40.

The biggest challenge was making myself relatable to the group. In addition to being significantly younger, they were people who never worked in the private sector. How was I going to explain my experience (which was predominantly Fortune 500 experience), to a group who worked in a vocational college?

The following interview checklist is for "Baby Boomers" who find themselves at an interview with "Millennials"

1. Don't talk about the past—focus on your related skills and the value you can provide to the team.

2. Give relatable stories—no dates, no ancient history, no examples about how you did it in the past. No one cares. You may be interviewing with people who were not born when you started your career.

3. Focus on the company and the job at hand.

4. Ask relevant questions about process, implementation, decision-making and goals and objectives.

5. Feed off the interviewer's statements and then frame your experience around that issue or concern.

6. Sell your maturity, responsibility, dependability and trust without saying you are old, mature, or seasoned. That will be obvious when you walk in the door.

7. Make the interviewer(s) feel at ease—become part of their conversation—don't get preachy.

The interview process was grueling for me because I had to jump the giant hurdle of age; not because the questions were difficult or complex.

When I was offered the job, I realized that I had achieved a milestone. Many people are not able to transition in their 50's the way I did.

I was employed at TCI College for nine years. The school declared bankruptcy in July 2018. Now, I am on the job search again. It's even more difficult now at 62. But, I did this before and I will find another full-time position. At least I know that I have the ability to communicate with anyone regardless of age.

Vincent J. Gomory

THE MEASURE OF SUCCESS

All successes must be measured by your own yardstick. Success that looks good to the world but does not feel good in your heart and soul is not success at all. Of all the forces that make for a better world, none is as powerful as hope. With hope, one can think, one can work, one can dream. If you have hope, you have everything.

BE ORIGINAL. THINK BACK TO BASICS.

WHEN WE SPEAK ABOUT ORIGINALITY, WHAT DO WE MEAN?

ORIGINALITY IS A PAIR OF FRESH EYES.

GO BACK TO BASICS

DO COMMON THINGS IN AN UNCOMMON WAY.

CREATION IS THE TRUE ESSENCE OF LIFE.

MOST OF THE TIME, SUCCESS DEPENDS ON AN ORIGINAL IDEA.

BE INQUISITIVE. BE FAIR.

BE RESPECTFUL. BE INSPIRED.

BE ABLE TO LOOK AT YOURSELF IN THE MIRROR AND SAY
"TODAY'S THE DAY."

WHEN YOU ARE NOT FEELING JUST RIGHT ABOUT THE LAST
INTERVIEW YOU HAD, THINK OF A PERSON WHO TRULY
INSPIRES YOU AND SAY, "WHAT WOULD HE SAY?"

Valentina

THE CHALLENGE

As we journey through this experience called life we are all challenged in many ways with hits, trials and tests on every side. It seems that once we muster the faith and the courage to overcome one issue, we get hit with another one! But, the truth is that these are only mere distractions to keep our focus off who we are and what we can truly achieve if we just had a vision and true understanding of who we are and know the gifts and talents that we have all been born with.

When you allow yourself to be distracted, pressed, overwhelmed and afraid, you tend to focus on the problem and not the solution. This is where you get stuck and produce more of the same. We lose sight of what makes us who we are and where we are going and what we would like to accomplish.

As such we begin to focus on doing just enough to survive the storm by pacifying our fears and creating a false sense of security and settling for the "Status Quo."

You know what I mean. You're taking a job only because it pays the bills right now. It is ok for a time while you are setting your goals, and figuring out what YOU would like your life to look like. But letting that job become your master rather than you staying true to what you truly desire to be or do is not good! You were meant to rise above your challenges and use those challenge to become stronger, more determined and focused to achieve your goals so that you can be the master of your own dreams, goals and life.

Or maybe you never tapped into what your gifts and talents are and what makes your heart sing because someone else, like your parents, family or friends, told you who you were or what path you should take, and you did it just to please them. Or you have a family of your own with a lot of responsibilities, so you must do whatever you have to do to maintain and provide... I get it. That is not uncommon. In fact, that is more common and the most accurate scenario of most people.

Statistics show that better than 80% of Americans hate their jobs because they don't feel appreciated. They feel overworked and underpaid and out of control of their future while realizing that they are building the dreams of others and their jobs are not giving them the lives they want to live. The reality is that they are just surviving and truly not living!

Often, for most people, it takes having the rug pulled out from under them and having that false sense of security, getting a consistent paycheck, to disappear before they decide to take control of their own lives and future. Sadly, for most, if that doesn't happen you find yourself allowing years to go by living in a fog, a false reality, not even getting close to tapping into who you can be or were meant to be. You allow someone or something to dictate the quality of your life and shape your experiences while building a legacy for someone else and not your own.

Then there are those who have found a way to use their talent in a profession for a time and some life event comes along that forces them to have to redirect and reinvent themselves and they get stuck there focusing on what they once had. Wishing things remained the same because they got comfortable or even complacent where they were.

If that is your story, then you too have found yourself in a place where you are having to grow through while you go through!

If there is a common experience for everyone, it is that change is inevitable and the only question when change knocks at your front door is, are you going to find a way to control your future or are you going to let that change control you?

What will YOU do? What will your future look like and what legacy will you leave behind for your family?

YOU have The Power to Design the Life You Want regardless of the circumstances!

The Journey:

Like you, I have had to pick up all the pieces and figure out "what's next" or "what am I going to do now?" when life didn't go the way I planned it.

One of my first experiences with that was as a young teen. I had a dream to play professional football and to be an entrepreneur, so I could do what I loved and be able to help other kids and families.

Some people told me that I wouldn't even make my high school team let alone accomplish such a huge goal. But I had a vision of where I wanted to be in life and I refused to let anyone talk me out of it!

Well, I made the team, which was awesome and exciting, of course. I went to Bayside High School in Queens, New York, and in my first season with the team, we went undefeated.

But life started to present challenges for me that seemed impossible to overcome at the time and threatened to pull me off the path and goals I wanted to achieve. After that season my family fell apart. My parents divorced, and my household became so uncomfortable for me I had to leave at 14 years old.

So, I ended up getting two McDonald's jobs at two different locations doing maintenance at one and cooking and cashiering at the other and working them both at the same time. Alternating days and sometimes working at both on the same day. I rented a room all while still going to school and playing football. Can you imagine what that must have been like for me or what my schedule must have been like?

Having a clear vision of what I wanted to accomplish and where I wanted to be was a driving force for me. I didn't want to become just another statistic and I was determined to have the life I wanted and not what someone else said I could be or have!

Subsequently, my team and school went on to win 3 straight NYC Division One Championships in the late '70's and early '80's, which had never happened before by any school and hasn't happened since!

I managed to overcome many challenges and kept good grades. However, two more challenges threatened to derail my dreams.

The first, was that I became seriously injured, playing tight end, while catching a ball over and in between defenders in the middle of my senior year when recruiters were coming in and out to scout us and select us to come to their schools. It almost ended my season, but I managed to make it back on the field by our championship game 6 weeks and 5 games later. That could have ruined all my chances to be recruited to a top school, get a scholarship and stay on track to reach the professional level.

The second, was that I missed so many classes, because I had to work that the school refused to let me graduate even though I officially passed all my classes with high grades. There was a rule that said that if attendance wasn't up to the standard they had set, which I didn't know about, the right to hold me back another year and that's what they decided to do, effectively making me what they called back then, "A Super Senior!" Again, another major hurdle, that threatened my dream.

As it turned out, I learned that a very important principle was affirmed for me while playing football back then. In fact, other famous coaches like Phil Jackson of the Chicago Bulls and Vince Lombardi of the Green Bay Packers, employed this ancient principle to help propel their teams to championship status. Though I wasn't told the source of this powerful principle back then, and who had successfully used it, I later discovered that the use of prior visualization or the human imagination is an amazing tool that will help guide you to and be a strong catalyst to help you achieve the desires of your heart. Today we have many words for it like: *Vision, Purpose, Mission, or Your "WHY!"*

All these coaches employed the technique of visualization, or imagination, of a desired goal by asking us to close our eyes and imagine catching the ball and scoring a touchdown or perfectly executing the plays/game plan they had taught us for a game we were about to play. As it turns out, this tactic happens to go back as far as the oldest book known to man today, called The Bible"! (Basic...Instruction...Before... Leaving...Earth)

Not only did we run and drill the plays we learned physically, we also played back the execution and the desired result in our minds over and over before we even touched the field on game day! As you can see from what I told you about the three straight NYC Division One Championships we won, the results are undeniable! In fact, I stumbled onto this principle even before I made the team because I had the goal of making the team in the first place and imagined myself doing it before I did it and it was further confirmed by all I was taught while playing for the team.

We had an unprecedented number of players from one school who managed to get scholarships to Division One Colleges and many other players that made it to other colleges and universities that year! Three players from my high school team during those years went on to play professional football!

What I learned from those experiences shapes my life even today. Even though I had an injury and then did not officially graduate with my class could have held me back. But I employed the principles. My athletic period kept me focused even while having to leave home at such an early age to fend for myself, and despite those circumstances, I refused to let them deter me from accomplishing my goal of getting into a Division One College Football Program and then getting to the professional level.

That *Vision and my WHY* helped guide me to find a program given at York College in New York to prepare for something called a G.E.D. (General Education Diploma). I never told my coaches or confided in anybody what I was going through at the time, but the determination to never let go of my goal fueled me and even guided me to opportunities and resources I didn't even know existed at the time. I enrolled and passed with one of the highest scores in New York City at that time. Then I called he University of Iowa; they had recruited one of the players from my team and several other players around the city from my senior year. There were several other schools that had done the same, but this school happened to look like my favorite professional team and wore almost the exact same uniform, was also in the "Big Ten," which is a big time college division I wanted to be in because they get to play in the Rose Bowl and get heavily recruited into the NFL. The twist was that I originally wanted Michigan to select me but with the injury in my senior year a lot of schools that were showing interest, prior to the injury, did not continue to show interest after that.

Getting back to what *Vision and a strong WHY did for me and can do for you.*

I called up the University of Iowa and spoke with a counselor and told them my situation. Normally, your coaches would have these kinds of talks with the schools that show interest in you. But, because I never shared what my personal situation was with them; not graduating, and having that injury during the season, the conventional tools they could use to discuss my athletic or college future weren't available to them, so I didn't even ask for their help. Fortunately, the counselor at the University of Iowa told me that there was a way that I might be able to enroll there even though I had a G.E.D and even though I didn't take the college level entry test. But when you have *Vision and a strong enough WHY the HOW to will take care of itself!*

So, they told me that if I could figure out a way to get there, then they would let me enroll as a non-matriculating student in a few summer classes to prove I could handle the work and take another kind of college entrance exam called the A.C.T back then while taking the summer classes, and if I passed it and got good enough grades in those summer classes, they would enroll me as a matriculating student (official student with credits toward a degree) in the upcoming fall semester which would also allow me to officially play football there!

Then came the next step, I called the coaching and recruiting staff on my own, told them who I was and who I played high school football with and they listened. Well, it didn't hurt that they had recruited and given a full scholarship to one of the players from my team and had already scouted us; they knew who we all were. It didn't hurt that they already had film of me playing so they could see what I was capable of. I guess they were impressed with my attitude, determination and the film they saw so, despite my lack of "officially" graduating and my injuries, knee, ankle and turf toe, they invited me to work out with the team as a "Walk On" (a player that tries out and joins the team without a scholarship initially).

Next thing I know I'm on the field running routes with a receiver who ended up going pro and was signed by the New Orleans Saints and catching passes from a quarterback who ended up playing for the San Diego Chargers. The running back that came from my high school team went in the first round of the draft to the Buffalo Bills and just barely missed the Heisman Trophy which went to another running back from Ohio State University that year!

Back to me, as it turned out I was still affected by those three injuries, so they decided to unofficially "Red Shirt" me (hold me off the roster so I could still have four years of eligibility to play for them going forward), my first year/season. Let me heal up and be ready for next season while still working out with them.

So, I went ahead with my classes and ended up with a 3.75, which is an A-average for the summer as a non-matriculating student, and in the fall as a matriculating student! The team went on to appear in the Peach Bowl that year, because of all the recruits they got from New York, 6 in total, including myself. The next year, they recruited a 7th player, my high school quarterback who went on to sign with the Seattle Seahawks as a running back.

Iowa had not appeared in a Bowl game in many years before that and subsequently went to the Gator Bowl and The Rose Bowl after that!

Unfortunately, during that time of my life, while technically still a kid, I had to make some tough choices. It was quite painful. I received a call from my little sister saying that there were major problems back in New York with our parents, so I left college during my spring semester of my first year with intentions of coming back to study and to play football finally for the next semester. But life got in the way. Love compelled me to stay in New York and work there and be there for my sister. I ended up laying my dream down and never went back! All six of the New York City high school players that were at Iowa with me went on to play professional football. I don't regret choosing love over my own dreams, and what I was fighting for, because to me my sister meant more than any of that, and I couldn't imagine not being there for her. Though I must admit that I was affected by it so much that I couldn't watch football for 10 years! I never regretted that decision because I believe it was made for the right reasons.

In spite of having to re-enter the workforce as a 19-year-old kid, with a G.E.D and no college degree and my original goals rerouted, I still came away with some of the greatest lessons and experiences that a college education doesn't teach you, and subsequently prepared me to win at everything I put my hand to later on.

Within two years I was able to go from being one of the top sales people, as an independent rep, for a nationally recognized brand, to being offered the opportunity to run my own business as a distributor for them. Another opportunity was given to me in a different field which made me co-owner of a different type of business by the time I was 21-years old. So, the entrepreneurial side of my goals were in full effect.

I would occasionally run into some of my former elementary, middle school and high school classmates and they would tell me of their exploits having a hard time finding a job with their college degrees, and as such would ask what I was doing, and when I told them, knowing I had to drop out, they were amazed.

The other part of my goal was to be able to help the kids and families in the communities I lived in. I thought football would give me the platform to do that, but without it I didn't know how.

However, *when your Vision and your Why is big enough… the How To will take care of itself!*

. . .

As a result of all the lessons I have learned and am currently using, and am sharing with you, I have worked to improve the communities that I lived in and did non-profit work in for better than 26 years across America teaching, mentoring, and coaching youth and adults in sports and in life. Also availing resources to them and I am currently working to bring medical, educational and housing assistance to villages in India, Kenya and Ghana through the international ministry that I founded.

Currently, I own my own business and provide legal, identity theft and business consulting services to small business owners to help them protect and grow their own businesses and also provide services to families to give them affordable access to the legal system, including services to protect them from the plague of Identity theft. I have run this business for 17 years now.

This also allows me to *"make a living while making a difference"* and provide career opportunities for people who have had an unorthodox start, like me. To give students and recent grads who are just getting started and don't have experience yet, a chance, as well as, people over 50 years old who are finding that they no longer fit in the traditional corporate structure.

I have owned and operated other businesses and have the distinction of being my own boss for at least 26 years overall.

All this goes to show that it was within my power to choose the direction that I took, and I shared this story with you because the bottom line is that we **ALL** have the power to choose and **YOU** *have The Power to Design the Life You Want regardless of the circumstances.*

The Plan:

It's all up to you now. All human beings have the ability to access a force and tool called imagination which gives you creative ability.

If you can see it in your mind and have the audacity to believe it, you will, with discipline, diligence and determination, most certainly achieve it.

Nobody but you will be able to stop you because that is how we were made to function. *"As a man thinketh in his heart so is he."* Whatever you meditate, focus on and give most of your attention to, you will manifest in your life. In most circles they call that studying.

Have you ever noticed that when you buy something you never really noticed it as much before you bought it, then suddenly you start noticing more of them after you bought it? It's because now your mind is tuned in to that thing or frequency.

That is how the mind is wired. It was all around you the whole time. It is the answer you need. It's the provision or opportunity you need, but because you didn't tune into that thing with focus or vision, you were not drawn in to it and it was not apparent to you.

You may find yourself in a position where it's time to change your career or to reinvent yourself, the best course of action is to design your life the way you want it to bet. Take some time and really examine what is important to you and what you want the next chapter of your life to look like.

Don't settle and don't let fear trap you. *Fear is only... False... Evidence... Appearing... Real.* That is an acronym that I learned some time ago that is so true. Most of the time fear is only smoke and mirrors designed to rob you of the thing you want and when you begin to move forward through that fear you will find that there was nothing to fear at all.

In fact, I have said previously that if your **WHY** is big enough the **HOW TO** *will take care of itself.*

When you figure out what you want to achieve and you refuse to live without it or if it would adversely affect someone you love if you don't achieve it, then you now have a *big enough* **WHY** that will propel, motivate and push you to stay focused and achieve what you need to achieve.

Step one: Think of what you want or need to achieve then write it down as your own personal **vision** or **mission statement**.

Preferably, it's something that's really important to you and that lines up with your natural gifts and talents. This way, whatever you do won't be like work and will be something you would want to do whether you get paid for it or not. It will be something noble that makes your heart sing.

Notice that most successful companies and organizations have a vision written down so everyone, especially their employees, can see it to achieve it. Everything they do must line up with that vision or mission statement. It is this kind of focus that makes them successful and helps you too. Because, if you don't have a clear destination in mind, any destination won't do; you could end up far away from where you want to be.

Step Two: Really hone in on **WHY** you *must* accomplish your vision and use that as a driving force.

It could be out of concern over a loss, or a need to do something for a loved one. It could even be the realization that your retirement plan isn't going to be enough for you to live comfortably down the road. Or you really want your life to have meaning and purpose. Or it could be that you want to leave a legacy behind. Whatever it is make sure you write it down. Sometimes your WHY can be a short-term goal like getting a new car or getting a child through college, and once it is achieved you may have to refocus and readdress it. Your WHY could be a life mission, if it is, write that down, too. Whatever it is, keep it before your eyes, speak it, and imagine achieving it every day. This will fan your flame, keep that burning desire in your heart!

Step Three: Continuous Meditation on both your Vision and Why will create **Belief!**

This is necessary because there will always be some sort of obstacle which will threaten your ability to achieve what you desire, and this will be the fuel that will push you through to victory.

• • •

In Conclusion:

Whatever you choose to do, do it with your whole heart because there is nothing worse than regret.

You don't want to look back over your life and be filled with remorse because you may have a slew of "woulda… coulda… shoulda's" that play loudly in your mind, tormenting you.

We all have one life to live and one chance to get it right!

Your time is **NOW** and, as long as, you have breath in your body it is never too late to accomplish what you desire!

YOU have The Power to Design the Life You Want regardless of the circumstances!

Attuquaye Okai

CONFUCIUS SAY DO WHAT YOU LOVE

When you are looking for answers in the second act:

Well we all know Confucius says "Do what you love."

What does this mean? For me, it means wing it, don't think about it too much. Fuhgeddaboutit!!!!!

I say don't think too much. If you'd like to ride a bike, go mountain biking because you never did. If you like dogs, take a very long dog walk in the mountains. If you like to exercise, go to an outrageous gym or spa. Sing in the car when you are driving with a great song you loved when you were younger.

Don't be so hard on yourself. Don't dwell on the past. If you find yourself burning out from the lack of interviews and lack of responses you get, you are not alone. If your friends are fun, brainstorm with them, if they aren't adventurous, then join a new group just for new ideas. Sign up for something you have never done. Ride a horse. Go to an amusement park and ride the roller coaster.

Keep it going, Keep a magic board nearby if you have a possible thought of trying something new, just put it on the board where you work on your computer. DO NOT SIT at the computer day in and day out.

THE MOST IMPORTANT THING YOU CAN DO EVERY DAY IS GET OUT OF YOUR DRIVEWAY, GET DRESSED, AND SHOW UP SOMEWHERE! It can be Starbucks, Dunkin' Donuts, a meeting, an event of an industry you are interested in, a hotel lobby looking very professional. Start a conversation with someone, you never know. Crazier things have happened. Believe in yourself.

Valentina

THE RUSH

My cousin's children Vanessa and Toni Lee were up to New York for the summer; they had just lost their mother and the entire family was very distraught. My other cousins Tom and Flo and their children Nikki and Anthony were living in Boca Raton, Florida. I took the girls and my family to a Mexican restaurant the night before they were to leave for Florida. My son Michael was twelve at the time and his sister Joelle was fifteen. He was being so annoying at the table and I said, "I wish I could send you to Florida, I cannot stand you."

The girls starting screaming, "Yes! Aunt Macky send him down to Florida" There was no room for him at their house, but he could probably stay at Aunt Flo's.

When we got home he was relentless; finally I called Flo and she said, "Send him down. We would love to have him." She was coming back to New York in a couple of weeks and would bring him back. The ticket cost $400—the best money I ever spent.

The next day we were going to my cousin's house in New Jersey for a BBQ, and on the way there we would drop him off at Kennedy Airport. This was the first time he was flying. I was very nervous, so I walked him to the gate. He was fine; he could not wait to get there. My cousin Leroy was going to pick him up. My stomach was bubbling, and I knew that I had to go to the restroom fast. I felt like I was not going to make it.

I starting running to find a restroom, I almost did not make it in time.

The bathroom was dirty, but I had no choice, I put my handbag around my neck and got to the business at hand.

When I finally finished I looked around and there was no toilet paper. I ran to the next stalls bare ass naked. No luck—there was no paper in the entire place. I was mortified, sweating and felt a panic attack coming on. What was I to do? Naturally I had no tissues in my bag. I just stood there in fear hoping that someone would come into the restroom and help me. At the time I did not have a cell phone, so I could not call any of my family members waiting in the car to rescue me. Crazy thoughts were running through my head. I had a dress on, should I use my underwear to clean myself? Fat chance, I had on a string bikini. I was taking so long I was worried that my boyfriend would have me paged. Then what? Should I pull up my drawers and hope for the best? How about using my bra? Fat chance it was so padded that I would not get it into that area. Just five minutes before I was thinking of using it as a toilet. I started praying, hoping for an answer.

What did I have in my bag that was paper? Oh my God—my check book!

I decided to use the deposit slips to clean my butt. It took several but it worked. I thought to myself, how resourceful! It was not an easy task with my handbag hanging around my neck. I was worried that my checking account number was now a logo on my butt, but I was now able to walk out of the bathroom with dignity. I was considering patenting the deposit slips for toilet paper, however, they are a little rough on that delicate area.

The moral of this story is always check for tissues and keep some in your bag and bring your checkbook. You never know how many uses there are for deposit slips!

This was not the first time this kind of incident had happened.

I was going for a sonogram and had to drink gallons of water. When I got there they told me I had to wait about a half hour. I thought to myself I will never make it. Sure enough, ten minutes later I was running to the bathroom that was down the hallway. Oh no! I missed and had urinated on myself. Oh what was I going to do?

I took off my sweat pants and underwear and put them in the garbage. All I was left with was my slouch socks, and a 3/4 leather coat. Another dilemma. I had to think fast, because my test was in about fifteen minutes.

So out of the restroom I went with a coat that barely covered my butt. The office was on Rockaway Avenue in Valley Stream, so I took myself down the street to find a store where I could buy some pants.

I walked into a thrift shop. No luck, so I keep walking. I got to a store and was able to buy a pair of sweatpants. I asked the salesgirl if I could put them on. To hell with the underwear. My dignity was saved again.

The moral to this story is if they are going to make you wait, pee on the floor, and they will think twice about telling someone they have to wait the next time.

Macky DiGilio

JUST DO IT

Well, if we go way back to when the first "Just Do It" version of the song came out, it's very enlightening to think that this song is still going strong, and in today's world, it is one of the most widely used terms when going for excellence in many areas of life, living, sporting, music, education, recreation and religion. I can go on and on.

I say those of us who Just Do It will eventually find our way. Just be sure you are doing what you are doing for the reasons that you want to do it, not someone is telling you to do it. If you want to, JUST DO IT. Get the audio and play it in the car when you are going on an interesting interview, or venturing into a new arena of business, entrepreneurial, or even if you are going on a date after many years. JUST DO IT. When you JUST DO IT, you are actually trying something new and you may be totally surprised.

Valentina

TO WISH PEACE

I have always been hungry for knowledge and embracing a diverse spectrum of people. Life is given to all for a purpose and/or for a great story. I was in college at the age of sixteen—eldest of three raised by a single parent. Incredible accomplishments academically, but very naive with life. I have had many experiences that would help the people of the world feel a bit better about themselves, especially that they are not alone, but this one in particular is for you.

My parents were married less than seven years. I was six years old in 1963 when I saw my father leave us and never return. My sister was only six months. I am an old soul always in search of justice and I grew up very quickly to help my mother. I worked several part-time jobs while attending school and helping at home. My uncle stepped in when he could from his own busy schedule and he was my male mentor. I learned to survive quickly. Attending Catholic school through college balanced everything for me. Until today my faith is my best supporter in good or bad times. I am also a very loyal person and when I do not receive it, in return, I am infuriated on the betrayal. There is a lesson in everything we go through, so I keep going on forgiving but not forgetting.

I was married at twenty-one years old and this was doomed from the beginning, unfortunately. I thank him for my son, who is my biggest accomplishment. I worked at EF Hutton during my marriage until they merged with Lehman Brothers while I was on maternity leave. The company misplaced my position as a manager in the accounting department until I called and straighten it all out. I should have stayed home raising my son, but then there would be no story to tell.

One year later I was traveling to Manhattan from Long Island heading to the Twin Towers for a meeting with American Express where every month we would consolidate and balance accounting ledgers for both companies. Unbeknownst to me the department I managed was being investigated for fraud. I was fired and in shock.

I was happy to be home, but I needed to be independent from my husband. While my son attended school I started a vision board. I immediately started a day care center out of my home on weekends. This grew into a twenty-five year business along with my computer company. I became a New York City Vendor. I did medical billing, data-entry for many different companies and IT/Billing Consultant for Optimum all out of the home. I divorced my husband of twenty-six years and it was annulled for free by the Diocese of Rockville Centre. That is a story in itself. I kept the house and I raised a son who is a great, compassionate and noble person. He is a certified teacher with a double Masters, has his license as a real estate agent, coaches baseball and is studying for his insurance license. I am disabled and retired at the age of fifty-nine with no regrets. I am an inspiration to those who care to know my story and I wish everyone peace.

Aida Brothers

A FEW TIPS FROM ME

You have got the stuff success is made of. Success takes less than it seems. No—dreams don't come true by themselves, as that requires some help from you. It's not nearly as much as you would really think. All it takes to light and ignite yourself is a single spark! WITH PURPOSE, PASSION and a response to both you can achieve anything.

After a job loss, you may find yourself in a bad and dark place, and your thoughts can alter the way you really feel. When you are searching for work and feel like your resume is going in the big black hole, and you're getting into a negative path, think about this. Is your life better without that job and the stress you were experiencing? I suggest right then and there you STOP and you STAND.

Put your focus on getting out of the negative jungle of being unemployed. Only you can do that. How? Only you can make it better. Get involved in a project. Volunteer for a passionate project that can mean something to you, this will not only add to your resume, but it will benefit your self esteem. Hell, you may even like it! Gaining more confidence from stepping outside of your comfort zone will help you to change your thinking, ideas, and absolutely help your career in the long run.

Don't forget what Stephen Covey says: there are three constants in life - change, choice and principles.

Work hard to stay in the period of liking yourself and others forever. Feel good about yourself but feel good about others, too. If you don't love it, forget it. Stay in the liking period. Liking someone forever means they really do like you back. If someone you think you like follows you on a fun experience like open mike night, than that's when you know you like each other for sure!

Don't let being unemployed suck you with the illusion of unhappiness and the illusion of self-worthlessness. Be your own person. Make your own mind, have your own decisions, and above all, don't be afraid of anything! IT TAKES TIME TO GET THERE, BUT YOU WILL!

Remember: Knowledge is Power. Find out everything you can about the passion you have in a certain subject matter; think it, drink it, eat it every day, then take it to the next level. One of the most desirable traits a person can have is intelligence, knowing the whats and the wheres. Too much confidence can have its downside as well as no confidence at all. I believe the simple idea of having other people you are interviewing with think you are brilliant, must start with sincerely believing in yourself. Yes, that's right—YOU. If you believe in you, others will also.

Volunteer, volunteer volunteer. I have found my volunteering efforts to be probably the most rewarding time of my life. WHY? It's actually different for every person. For me, the truth is that when you volunteer you are always around people who want to be there, not people that have to be there. You are always appreciated for what you do. You can be late one day, absent one day, and they are always thanking you where you volunteer with a smile. So many community projects are out there if you take the time to be involved on one that you may be passionate about. Even if it is only twice a month, you will walk out on those days with a big smile. Try it, it works.

IN LIFE YOU HAVE CHOICES—GIVE UP, GIVE IN, OR GIVE IT
YOUR ALL.

BE BOLD. BE BRAVE TAKE RISKS—STOP PLAYING IT SAFE.
YOU MAY JUST LIKE IT!

IF YOU BELIEVE, BELIEVE, BELIEVE.
YOU WILL ACHIEVE, ACHIEVE, ACHIEVE.

Valentina

FEAST OR FAMINE

It has been said: "Be ready to answer for the gifts one receives in life."

I have had a wonderful life.

My career was moving and I was making a lot of money until one day the world changed.

In the blink of an eye your world will be turned upside down.

You lose your job or lose a loved one.

You look around and ask what is going on.

You need to be able to walk the walk and talk the talk.

Be careful what you wish for because it does happen before you know it.

In this world God runs the show and speaks to you while you are not focused.

He will tap you on the shoulder and see if you notice.

If He thinks he has your attention, He will begin to test you.

It's the random things that seem random but then take shape.

Each one of us affects each other.

Every day we see, pass and notice people, and may even say something to one.

Say "hello" to someone. That could make that person smile when arriving at work.

This person now is having the start of a great day and approves a car loan for someone.

Be rude to someone and that same person may decline the car loan because of anger for the previous rudeness.

Every day is an adventure, so take life one day at a time.

What you have today you may not have tomorrow.

The Long Island Breakfast Club was great for me because helping people help other people feels so good to see.

You know who your real friends are, and many times they are strangers and not family or people you know.

"Pick yourself up, dust yourself off and reinvent your self!" has always been my tagline.

I practice it every day.

I say thank you to God for the people I know and for the health I still have.

Money pays the bills but can blind you when others need help.

Giving your time, or money, if you can, goes a long way for those in need.

Feast or famine can come at any time, just be ready for it.

When your parents need help, be there for them, because when they are gone, it's too late.

Do now what you can put off until tomorrow.

Tell family you love them and do not be bitter, but be there for them.

Do not look at what others have because their grass may not be that much greener on the other side.

Be humble in all that you do because you do what is right not because you have to.

Learn about Philotimo, the Gospel, set your spirit free and build a life —don't just live it.

Most of all get to know Him. He is always watching the world with one eye, and with another eye on you.

I am the co-founder of the Long Island Breakfast Club and love the people I have met in my life.

Many others have hidden themselves from helping you and only care about themselves.

Feast and famine knows no place, no color, and no religion.

When it catches up with you, be prepared to answer for all your gifts you have received.

Chris Fidis

Cofounder, Long Island Breakfast Club

LIVE LAUGH LOVE!

To me, there are three things we all should do every day. We should do this every day of our lives. Number one is laugh. You should laugh every day. Number two is think. You should spend some time in thought. And number three is, you should have your emotions moved to tears, could be happiness or joy. But think about it. If you laugh, you think, and you cry, that's a full day. That's a heck of a day. You do that seven days a week, you're going to have something special.

I just got one last thing, I urge all of you, all of you, to enjoy your life, the precious moments you have. To spend each day with some laughter and some thought, to get your emotions going. To be enthusiastic every day and [as] Ralph Waldo Emerson said, "Nothing great could be accomplished without enthusiasm"—to keep your dreams alive in spite of whatever problems you have, the ability to be able to work hard for your dreams to come true, to become a reality.

Valentina

SURVIVAL SKILLS & TECHNIQUES

Surviving multiple job loss for 10+ years (while over 50 years old), depression, injury, and financial challenges at the same time can be daunting and overwhelming. My tips, story, and how I kept going are below.

Job Recovery: Frustration from industry changes and many short-term positions had me exploring new skills.

Solutions:

• Career>Connect through the JCC Sid Jacobsen, (516) 484-1545

◦ LinkedIn, Networking, Interview Techniques, Resume Writing

◦ Practice Interviews with real headhunters and HR people

◦ Support Groups

• Hempstead Works, Department of Labor, (516) 485-5000

◦ Job Search Techniques, Excel, Access, Word, Social Media Job Search

◦ Scholarships to Continue Education (e.g. $5,000 toward a Project Management Certificate)

• Networking

◦ Expo/Trade Show and Sessions (learn new skills)

◦ Industry Networking - find or create networking with people in your industry (e.g. for me, Marketing, Advertising, Ad Sales were the types of people I connected with. I formed a group of unemployed Ad Sales people across magazine and television genres that met monthly and shared leads. One Ad Sales person actually sent me a job listing that became one of my future jobs.)

Depression: I'm lucky I found the help to make it through many losses in my life—the right therapy and medication. Gratefully, I was able to obtain Disability to ease the financial burden, anxiety, and depression, too.

Solutions:

• Mental Therapy (weekly)

• Psychiatry for Medication (monthly)

• Meditation (e.g. Guided Meditation Tapes and How To Meditate Books at the local library)

• Gratitude List—I text a friend a list of what I'm grateful for daily—if I can always find something to be happy about, I'll be less depressed. Some days I'd list just "Grateful for sunny day." Other days a very long list, which included, for example, friends, family, job interview, finding jobs to apply to, new networking buddies, exercising, getting out of the house/apartment, coffee, food in the refrigerator, etc.

• Volunteering took me out of my situation and gave me an opportunity to give back to others (putting me in a happy place). I've listed an excellent place to volunteer under my financial solutions section—free food, too!

Injury Recovery: I had an ankle injury over 10 years ago, which was fixed 3 years later, yet I never was able to do the 2 miles of running every day I used to do. My weight increased with decreased exercise and menopause hitting the same time. The injury led to back and hip problems as I compensated for the injury before having the surgery to fix it. At one point, I was receiving Ladacane Shots in my joints and walking with a cane. I was told I had herniated discs in my lower back, bursitis, and osteoarthritis. Hip Replacement was even suggested, yet I am still successful at delaying it. After completing many intermittent physical therapy and aqua therapy (water physical therapy) sessions, I realized I had to do regular exercise to get back to a more normal life. I found water exercise was less strenuous on the joints and I could bend more in water than on land at first. After only 6-9 months, I was able to dance and do other favorite activities again.

Solutions:

• Pool 2x/week

◦ Water Walking (started with 5 minutes then worked up to 7 minutes each)—walk forward, high marching steps, backward, side to side (overlapping the legs) each way.

◦ Swimming Laps (started with my upper body only, then a few months later added a very slow kick, too)—8 crawl, 8 breast stroke, 8 back stroke.

◦ Echo Park Pool offers the most inexpensive year-long membership in my area. There are discounts for over 60, disability, non-incorporated villages.

◦ Lido Beach Town Park in the summer has free weekday swimming in a pool and beach as well as fun activities and entertainment.

• Yoga 1x/week (Local libraries, recreation centers, and churches I found offer inexpensive sessions without having to commit to any gym memberships.)

Financial Recovery: I became creative in my solutions to find a budget that worked. Overwrought with more expenses than I could cover I found the following answers.

Solutions:

• Roommate—I rented out my second bedroom (2 different times) and am lucky to have found wonderful tenants, who have become friends as well. Craigslist was the source of both.

• Public Assistance, Medicaid, Food Stamps—See if you qualify (usually $2,000 or less in assets not counting your house and car).

• Disability—Do you have a permanent reason you are not able to work full time? There is a program for the Working Disabled, people who can work part time.

• Free or Cheap Clothing—Clothing Swaps (e.g. "Stop 'N' Swap part of GrowNYC.org, (212) 788-7900 for free clothing and things) and Thrift Shops (e.g. MyUnique, Savers, Goodwill, Salvation Army) are excellent sources of finding much needed clothing and items.

• FREE HEALTHY FOOD (most is organic), Clothing, Flowers / Plants, Toys, Household Items, & Things. Available EVERY WEEK including rain, blizzard, holiday (only time we've been closed is a state of emergency when the roads are closed). All food shares are outside, so dress accordingly and bring a way to carry the food (bags, cart, boxes, luggage on wheels, etc). You may keep going on each line as many times as you want for more food. Vegan meals also served at the Hempstead and Bedstuy locations only. Just show up; no proof of need required. Volunteer and donate by just showing up at any location at the day and time mentioned and ask somebody. We're 100% volunteer run and the largest vegetarian food share in the nation! CommunitySolidarity.org (People outside the New York City metro area might find FoodNotBombs.net helpful.)

◦ Sunday 2pm, HEMPSTEAD, W. Columbia Street--Hempstead LIRR parking lot (across from the bus terminal). Next to GPS: Village Pizza, 63 W Columbia Street, Hempstead, NY 11550

◦ Tuesday 7pm HUNTINGTON STATION, E 6th Street and Fairground Avenue (near 110 & Pulaski). At the Fairground side of GPS: All Weather Tire, 100 Depot Rd, Huntington Station, NY 11746

◦ Thursday 7pm FARMINGVILLE, (near Stonybrook) Horseblock Road & Woodycrest Drive or Park Place. Across the street from GPS: Danny's Unisex Barbershop, 21 Park Place, Farmingville, NY 11738

◦ Saturday 12 noon, WYNDANCH, where Garden City Avenue (#1 on Google Maps) almost meets Straight Path (back parking lot of MLK Jr. Health Center, 1556 Straight Path). GPS: 1 Garden City Avenue, Wyndanch, NY 11798

◦ Saturday 3pm, BEDSTUY, NW corner of Herbert Von King Park, which is at Lafayette Avenue and Marcy Avenue GPS: 709 Marcy Ave, Brooklyn, NY 11216.

Anonymous

MORE TIPS

G ET OUT OF YOUR COMFORT ZONE.
GET OUT, GET DRESSED, LOOK YOUR BEST, SPEAK TO
AS MANY PEOPLE AS POSSIBLE. MAKE AN IMPRES-
SION. ALWAYS DROP A SEED—A BUSINESS CARD PORTRAYING
A TAG LINE OF YOUR COMPANY & SKILLS.

VOLUNTEER—VOLUNTEER—VOLUNTEER

DO SOMETHING YOU HAVE NEVER DONE BEFORE.

TAKE ACTION TO GIVE BACK AND IT WILL COME BACK
TO YOU.

WORK WITH A TAG TEAM OF DIVERSE INDIVIDUALS, BOTH
EMPLOYED AND NOT EMPLOYED. THINK ABOUT WHO YOU
KNOW, WHO THEY KNOW AND EMBRACE COMMUNICATION
BETWEEN EACH OTHER

KEEP IN TOUCH WITH FORMER EMPLOYERS, CO-WORKERS

. . .

GEOGRAPHY. GEOGRAPHY. GEOGRAPHY.

WHO DO YOU SURROUND YOURSELF WITH?

BE A DRIVER AND NOT A PASSENGER.

COMMIT TO FINDING NEW OPPORTUNITIES

IT'S NOT AN ACT. IT'S AN ATTITUDE

TAKE A CUE FROM THE VOLKSWAGEN COMMERCIAL IT SAYS "IN LIFE THERE ARE DRIVERS AND PASSENGERS, TO REBUILD IN THIS ECONOMY TODAY DRIVERS ARE NEEDED."

LIFE DOES NOT COME WITH DIRECTIONS. MAYBE SOME DAY IT WILL.

Valentina

Chapter Five

LEANING ON OTHERS

The size of your future you actually experience will largely be determined by one factor: the people you choose to connect with.
~Valentina Janek

MY DOWN-TO-EARTH FRIEND

Most of us have some fairly intelligent friends. Several of mine rank up there with some of the best, but one in particular seems to stand out. He has advanced in his career, achieving some impressive credentials along the way, yet it's easy to feel comfortable in his presence. He doesn't use a two dollar word when a dime one will do. He is humble and—well—ordinary. People often described him as "down to earth."

When my mom lost her job, she was quite angry, scared, and very distant with the family. Her good friend made the difference during the time she spent wallowing in the past and not the present. This down to earth friend made her always feel at ease, and become more optimistic at the time of her job loss. Most people who knew him enjoyed having him present whether it be a family dinner, a night at the bar, or watching sports with a beer. Conversation flowed without difficulty and she was always delighted to see him.

He never acted like he was better than any of us with a superior attitude, which made us always feel terrific. But the truth is he was quite the superior and quite the knowledgeable, but he shared his knowledge with us. Most people tend to avoid these types when meeting them for the first time, the difference being here that no one really knew but my mom exactly how powerful he was.

Thinking about the phrase "down to earth," I realized that this is the characteristic of Jesus Christ that made Him so approachable. We sometimes have difficulty grasping that we can relax in the presence of the God of all creation and converse with Him as we would a friend. I sometimes smiled at my mom who always gave me advice which was always very well stated as poetry with a flair. Sometimes it would be in the kitchen, mostly as she was cooking for a friend or family individual. She continued always to make great recipes for this down-to-earth friend. He loved her so. This friend always gave advice to her and came up with many ways that she could improve herself, her family, and her friends as well.

He was our down-to-earth friend, and from his advice, and kindly ways, he made everything he said seem simple and understandable, even though he was an extremely well-versed, very intelligent man. Some may say he was Our Success for where we are today.

Thank you, my Down to Earth Friend!

Anonymous

TO PAPA: "ALL YOU NEED IS LOVE"

In 1969, the Beatles declared that "all we need is love" and they were right. How right were they; they are still doing well and still preaching the same songs. Love is Life and if we all continue with life and living it one day at a time, time passes when you are hit with a crisis. The cells in our bodies work harmoniously, and as my Papa always said, Power of the Mind can do wonderful things, and I live and dream to believe and know that as a daughter, I did stand through just about anything. There were days in the past when I am sure that we all wanted to be powerful, knowledgeable, creative, wealthy and healthy. In the scheme of today's world and what is going on, the "healthy" is the most important. Many women go through a trauma like I did without a person to help them. Keeping my optimism high and staying close to my Papa made me experience positivity and goodness in my current and future life.

I was in a job loss, and I was not feeling very good about it. When I would speak to Papa about it, he would tell me lots of stories, and I started to relate to some of them. Not only did I get back on track, he pushed me to do some things I never did before. He used to say, "Listen to me, I know what I am saying." I did listen, I did stay open, and I did get back on track. Here is an old saying: "Even if you are on the right track, if you simply stand still, you're going to get hit by that train." When we question everything, we free ourselves to think and when we think we allow ourselves to act.

I am now currently working in a totally different arena as a motivational speaker, personal coach and marketing consultant, including events planning, job placement and business and personal development. I have never been happier in a new and exciting position. Who thought? Ya never know! "All you Need is Love."

Stay optimistic. It will keep you strong, and as Papa would say, "Fight!"

My papa was always a tower of strength to me. A man of many, many words we all knew quite well. His family was his life. His heritage of his country was what kept him going every single day. His love for his family and his native Spadola in Calabria was his legacy. A day did not go by without his preaching about Italy, and all the special inventors of Italian descent who he felt invented everything in the world.

A very strong independent man with a passion for what was right and wrong, he taught us the word "respect," and the act of being kind and giving, to do the right thing for others and be patient and charitable. Being in the Floral Park area for his business for many many years, he must have made everyone in the town a walk-in closet that is still standing in their homes today. He also must have made for every baby in the family, their in-laws and their friends rocking horses, signs, name plates and many other unique items. He tirelessly spent his time woodworking special items for everyone who crossed his path. Maybe this was part of his secret and recipe for his life, knowing he left a legacy to everyone who touched his heart. If you did something for his daughters at any time, you received a piece of wood with a carving specially made for you to remember him.

And then there were his vitamins. I can't tell you how many bottles of vitamins he bought for me, my husband and my daughters and then how many times he disposed of my regular medicines in my home, because he thought medicine was poison to your soul. Sometimes I think Papa really knew what he was talking about!

Papa loved to cook and would get so excited when we called so he could make us his famous Italian Frittata on Saturday and Sunday morning. He spoke to his grandchildren always and told many, many stories of the old times and the wonderful things he did in his country and things he made for his family and friends.

A very difficult man at times, a calm man he was not. I believe he taught me what it is to really "Stand." In the last few weeks of his life, he uttered a thought to me which I will keep with me forever. "When you feel you have done all you can and it's not enough, you just "Stand."

One of the last things he said to me was, "What do you give when you've given your all, and it seems like your can't make it through?" The answer he said in a simple refrain was "YOU JUST STAND." He told me strength comes from our ability to stand up and walk through it. He taught me to not feel doubt, because with the power of the mind you can conquer almost anything. His determination to not succumb to drugs in the very end is the very reason he lived such a long life. Although we would grin and laugh at the things he would say to us about his beliefs, I truly believe that maybe Papa knew what he was preaching to us all the time. We would always listen and smile, and sometimes laugh, and he would get angry if we laughed, and then repeat it again! When I think of his stubborn tone of making me listen, I know I have gained from him the insight to stand by myself and keep his legacy for me and my grandchildren. He made me believe that I could do the impossible and taught me the most important thing; believe in yourself and what you can do. Life accelerated for Papa in the last month to a place where he made me realize for sure that life is not a race; take it slower and hear the music before the song is over. His song to us will play in our minds forever.

He always said to me, "When I die, you will say he was not a stupid man." No Papa, you were a brilliant man with the gift of teaching all of us how to give and not expect anything in return. If we ever said "thank you" to Papa, he said, "What do you mean? Why are you saying 'thank you?' You are my famiglia." I want to continue to celebrate your life, Papa, and continue to teach your message to my grandchildren and continue the legacy forever. The dedication you displayed to our family can only be learned from greatness which I hope to be able to pass on forever.

Thank you, Papa.

Valentina

THE THREE AMIGOS

Child Abuse Unit - SPCC

Janine Picchione and Karen Martin were the two women known to many as the crusaders of the Child Abuse Unit's power to communicate and educate the public on awareness in keeping our innocent children safe. The Three Amigos—Janine, Karen and I—met in the living room of a Williston Park resident to help plan a fundraiser for the Child Abuse Unit—SPCC. Every few weeks, on a regular basis, there would be a small meeting to discuss the current fundraising and advocacy issues of the unit. The "three amigos" were three spirited and passionate women working together on a mission. Since forming this bond of strength, we had defined the meaning of "feeling like we really did have wings," and putting life into the message of cyberspace safety.

I remember repeating the message…"Never doubt what a loyal group of concerned people can do in a community when challenged to do the right thing." I remember the words: "The success of safety depends on you." As a motivator of this volunteer group, I quickly became very entrenched in this vision. The loyalty of the volunteers had also kept our cause open and enhanced our friendships in the community and business world.

Our goal was to band together and set the standard for awareness concerning Internet safety. Keeping the public and children informed was our primary focus, while securing interest from technology companies, businesses, media organizations and the general public was also paramount. This presented challenges which we overcame together as a group. This charge for which we were committed continued to be very much a part of our personal and business lives. Janine and Karen, two media savvy spirited women who worked on Long Island by day, still found ample amounts of time to volunteer for a multitude of functions. Their passion, vision, and participation to make things happen for many years was building business relationships and community friendships.

Our hope is for this growth to take place safely. But this won't happen unless the Internet industry and the law enforcement community can demonstrate to the public that their children can venture into cyberspace safely. The three amigos challenged the Technology Companies of the Internet to "Step Up and Be the Difference." Too often we tend to be so wrapped up in the everyday minutiae of life that we sometimes forget to be aware of the organizations that are working hard at protecting our children, grandchildren and significant family and friends. We have positioned our board to include some interesting executives in the communications, technology, legal and creative industries.

Anonymous

MAKING LEMONADE OUT OF LEMONS

I was out of work for three years and getting pretty desperate. Almost applying for anything. Just about when I was ready to give up, I went on an interview and was annoyed that they had me waiting in the room with someone else. A stranger. Is there anything more annoying when you are not yourself! And for the same job, no less. Well, she looked nice enough and we started to talk—we were both there for the same job. But, we were older and realized that we brought different things to the table and agreed to phone each other afterwards. We would share job leads and almost immediately adopted the motto of "one for all and all for one." If someone was going to get the job, why shouldn't it at least be one of us. We compared notes, laughed a little and decided to stay in touch - especially once we realized were on the same "circuit". We decided to meet and include a mutual friend, and met at a diner for breakfast, possibly the least expensive meal you can have out. We met a few times, each time sharing news, job offers, etc. Well, one day something happened —we were asked to leave the diner. Can you imagine how it feels to be thrown out of a diner? We walked out, we laughed, we cried and we got angry. It was at that moment we decided to take action and formed the Long Island Breakfast Club. We are an organization that provides support, advocacy and inspiration to the mature individuals who find themselves unemployed. We are growing by leaps and bounds. This is probably the only time in history that growth has a negative connotation. We provide job coaching, resume writing and wit and wisdom, in equal parts.

But the best part of the story are the friendships we formed that most people only dream of. Sadly, our mutual friend Joann has passed away, and while she is no longer with us at the "diner," she is always with us in spirit, encouraging us at every step.

If this isn't making lemonade out of lemons, I don't know what is.

Stephanie Jeffery Carlino

ABOUT MOM

Well, I can say that after having four daughters pretty close in age that my mom's life was never boring. My mom raised me in a local town and was very involved with my school and my dad's hardware and carpenter business in the Floral Park area. Not only did she help her own daughters, family and friends; she was very involved with helping some of the foreigners who lived in the area, getting settled in the town and helping to assist their children getting adjusted to their new surroundings.

The most important lesson I have learned from mom is she always respected others and never had a bad word to say about anyone, no matter what the circumstances. She taught me to look for the good in everyone and respect the people for the individualism that they possess. Mom was a loving, caring individual who never turned her back on anyone, and was always there for her own family, but was never too busy to help someone else whether it be a business cause or a social cause, or just making a plain old meal for someone who needed it.

Owning a business in a local township in the 1940's through the 1980's was not easy in those early years. Although she struggled, I never knew it as a child growing up. I always had the best of everything and attended almost every event there was to offer through the local schools. She always made sure I had nice clothes, and, of course our family dinners were of utmost importance to her. My family values are based on my mom's ability to teach me, guide me, suggest to me, nurture me, love me and most of all, let me become who I wanted to be. She let me stumble and fall, but she was always around to listen and console me and make light of a situation that maybe I think is not the best.

One of the most important things my mom has taught me is to respect the person that your child grows into which might mean doing things like not saying what you really mean, not having the last word on the small stuff and only taking issue with the very important situations that come up. She taught me to respect my daughter as she grew to be the smart, independent woman that became.

I am so proud to have a mom that cared for me and showed me the way to make my daughter's life as wonderful as she made mine.

Valentina

HOW TO BE A COLORFORM AND HOW TO GET TO THE A LIST

I met Jane at a pharmaceutical industry job fair. I was told that they were looking for motivated sales people who could represent products to the medical industry. While waiting in line, I met Jane, who had also been downsized after working for a company for many years. As we stood in line on a cattle call, as I called it, she gave me some tips on how to get to the A list at the pharmaceutical line. If you have never experienced one of these, you get labeled with red, blue or white dots which mean you are fair, good or outstanding. I call it a cattle call. She suggested a cookie cutter dress code: navy classical suit, pump shoe, Dutch Boy haircut and minimum jewelry. This is corporate America. Your abilities were predetermined by dots and it's as if you were a Colorform. Without all the colors in the right places, you were doomed for employment consideration. She had been in the pharmaceutical industry in sales for several years. She explained to me what to say and how to say it to get on the "A" list. There were ridiculous demands to get beyond the red, blue or white dots. Grown women striving for the red dot. Really motivating! We chatted and got to know each other, and decided to visit a local restaurant for a drink afterwards. Since that day, she has been on of the women in the circle who has contributed to this book.

Valentina

WE ARE FAMILY!

I am a 28 year old entrepreneur. I was born in East Meadow, New York, and raised in El Salvador. In the year of 2006, two days after my graduation, I traveled on a plane from El Salvador to the USA to live with my mothers sister, my wonderful aunt. As a graduate of Uniondale High School with honors, I quickly attended Nassau Community College for business administration. Shortly thereafter, to be exact, one year later, like many entrepreneurs in history, I decided not to pursue a formal education, and look for ways to create the true purpose in my life. I believed if I could change the world one family at a time, I would be very happy. I worked diligently in the restaurant business for nine years while simultaneously keeping two to three part time jobs searching for ways to create wealth. One of my first goals was to bring my family together and establish their residency here in the US, which I achieved in 2014. My next goal is in arranging for my brother to live here in the USA ad truly develop a family business.

Thanks to the tough times and crisis after crisis I experienced during my lifetime, I have been able to find my mission and purpose. I believe I was born to act as a bridge and connect people who otherwise would not benefit from one another. My mission is to change the world one family at a time. Soon afterwards during the years from 2015 to 2018, I worked at Chase Bank on Long Island in a secure position. An opportunity to go develop myself into a business owner was placed in my future. After long discussions with my father, we both had to make a decision together which could affect all of us. Should I stay in a comfortable job, living a comfortable life and enjoying comfortable benefits? Should I take a leap of faith and jump off the cliff of entrepreneurship and take the risk of failing or succeeding in business for myself and my family?

All my life, I knew that my mission was to help people. That is why my motto for my business at "Olinda's Cafe" is "We are in the people business serving food!" I do truly believe that's why the opportunity to drive this vehicle of my future helping blend the love of food and love of family was placed right in front of me. I decided to take the opportunity and take over the restaurant. Was it easy? Not at all. I took over a decaying business. I guess I can say that the previous owner was struggling with issues due to serous circumstances in her life. Very happily, I decided to take over the business with a problematic history, but the circumstances never defined my vision. When the dream is big enough, the facts do not count. Well, that is how I see it. As a visionary I could see that my dream potential with Olinda's Cafe was because of my vision to be a leader in helping people as much as I could. The first few weeks were very tough, but we have worked smarter not harder in the business. We developed a great culture and changed the whole business from the inside out. We are still not where we want to be, but we keep making progress every day. Every day in every way, my family business is getting bigger and better!

It was a very proud day for myself, Mr. Roberto C. Ramirez, and my father, Hector A. Ramirez, when there was a very special ribbon-cutting ceremony at Olindas Cafe and Restaurant in West Hempstead, NY. When Senator Kaminsky came with several legislators from the town and county, arrived with such grace and inspiration, I knew that this decision was one that I was meant to make. All of our family members and friends of Olinda's cheered us on that day. This beginning has given our restaurant a new culture and new life for many who visit our location in West Hempstead, NY as we change the world one family at a time. As the song states "We are Family!"

Roberto Ramirez, owner of Olinda's Cafe

THE DESPERATE JOBSEEKERS

I never thought I would meet such kind people while cruising around for employment.

There was a string of women who were downsized on Long Island who came together by pure need and became friends. It is slow to find like-minded friends after a major job change and ones that really understand the bouts of panic and problems women in their forties and fifties face when interviewing for positions. Dealing with the fear of this experience and breaking through it was like a teaching lesson for the future. We all feel we've had an unusual friendship and bonding experience. At times there were even bouts of loneliness which I guess are universal but not incurable. The friendships we made were a renewable resource for the future that has given us the wings to keep positive and spirited and try to laugh as much as possible, and not sweat the small stuff. The abrupt changes from working a full work week to not working at all can be very difficult on your psyche, your pocketbook, your health and your personal life. Some researchers say that involuntary job loss in mid-life leads to stress. I am here to tell you it leads to stress, anxiety, health issues, loss of identity and devastating circumstances emotionally and physical, not to mention the expenses that triple as a result of being unemployed.

One day we actually were asked to leave a Long Island diner in Huntington where we met once a month. We had not even been there for more than two hours—on the way out, we laughed our heads off. Not only were we unemployed, no office to sit in, we were thrown out of the diner! We became a club of Desperate Job Seekers and had weekly sessions where we spoke about every interview and personal problem, and it became fun. It just got us through the days we were at our limit of experiencing the interviews from hell or heaven that were both frustrating and inspiring. We certainly laughed on many days, but other days were full of angst on others and the conversation always proved to be therapeutic for all of us.

We called it our camaraderie. We needed others who understood; we had to share and blow off steam. On this special day, the Long Island Breakfast Club became its own entity. Who would have thought getting thrown out of the diner would make us famous?

It did. It was quite the moment when a reporter quoted us as "They Meet, They Eat and They See—the New Yorkers Long Island Breakfast Club!"

Valentina

THE GOOD, THE BAD AND THE UGLY

With the charity work I was doing, I was always in need of door prizes and gift certificates, and perused many contacts, old and new. One day when I was keeping busy, I called a contact in the wine business, and asked if he would donate some fine wine. He suggested that I drop by the factory where he worked and bring the appropriate papers for approval. As I hardly know my way around driving, I set out early to find the location. After losing my way and driving for an hour, I arrived at the plant, if that's what you want to call it. Finally, stressed as could be, I pulled up to this very large warehouse and was very hesitant to walk in. After pulling into the driveway, many trucks were pulling in and out, dropping off many different items. I thought, "Well, this could be good for the donations." I walked into the office and met a very stern man with a weird raspy voice who I quickly convinced to donate many bottles of fine wine for our upcoming charity event. He was obnoxious as all hell. We will call him "Mr. S". I wondered what kind of operation this was, but did not ask questions. After his ranting and raving at his delivery men and his secretary, and after understanding the kind of work I did for charity, he had one of his trucks back up to my car and load it with fine wines for the event. I was wondering what kind of operation this was, but accepted his kindness, thanked him and drove quickly away with many, many bottles of wine, olive oil and other goodies to use in my prize baskets. Again, I don't know why this happened this way, but I remember thanking God for getting me out of there very quickly.

It made a huge difference for a charity event on Long Island and gave me inspiration that people are nice—the good, the bad and the ugly.

Valentina

JANE'S LUST! SURPRISE SURPRISE SURPRISE!!!!!

Drink! An Affair! An Interview! Not Me!

Jane had been interviewed by many individuals, but one story stuck out in her mind.

After an interview with a management recruiter we will call Joey, it seemed that Joey and Jane had some similar interests and decided to go for a cocktail after the interview.

Obviously she believed the cocktail would be the second part of the first interview. Wrong! What happened? They became very enthusiastic with each other, and one thing led to another, and he proved to be quite seductive! Because she was very disenchanted with interviewing, she thought a drink would be harmless. The drink turned into a personal midlife affair! He came into her life at a time when she needed some attention, some excitement and some love. She thinks it happened because she was really feeling very lonely and not supported by her mate. Support at a time when a woman is going through change is very important. It happened so quickly, but every week she was drawn to meet Joey at a special time in the same place. It seemed he was so much so drawn to her, like no other man had been. It felt very good for her. Although she knew it was wrong, she was drawn to go back every week. Her affair became part of the weekly conversations with our core group, who met every two weeks and discussed potential career moves and job interviews. We became a wonderful support system as we met and shared stories. It was very much a part of the discussion when we talked about each week's experiences—who landed and who did not.

Fortunately it gave our talks more life, but unfortunately, it also gave the other women some food for thought in their own lives that they were missing something. We believe that it was easy for Jane to share the story with us as we were all very similar in age, and going through the loss of being unemployed and looking for experiences to keep our minds busy. It made for juicy conversation, as well as thoughts and dreams of it happening to one of us in the group.

Anonymous

LET EVERYONE KNOW!

I thought I was one of the lucky ones! A major bank on Long Island, where I was employed as Director of Training and Development, was "merging" with another large bank. As the other bank had no Training Department, we were assured that our department would survive the merger. We were fortunate not to have to go through the dismal period that most of the staff did in expectation of losing their jobs. At the very last minute however, everything changed and our department was disbanded!

Since I suddenly had "free time" on my hands, I decided to attend a stockholders meeting of the bank that was now in control. While there, I met a Senior Officer from our former bank who had already transitioned to another bank. Our paths had previously crossed only a few times as he worked in a different division from me. We chatted and I told him I was seeking employment. That evening, he called me about 9 PM and said, "I have just the position for you!" Would I be able to come in the next day for a "formal" interview with the Executive Vice President of the division in which he was working?

We were leaving for Paris the next day! There is some advantage to having "free time". Fortunately, the interview was scheduled upon my return. And, as they say, "the rest is history". I spent many happy years in the new organization in an entirely different aspect of banking.

It is so important to let everyone know you are seeking employment. The call can come when you least expect it!

Anonymous

CAREER PATHS: THE SHORT ROAD LESS TRAVELED

At 52 years old and after 29 years into my full time working career I look back and wonder how l ended up where I am today.

My goal when I first began my career was to work about 30 years or so with the same company until I was able to retire. My Dad's work history in Sylvania inspired me to think that this would be a possibility for me, too. Now I look at that goal and see the humor, especially because my initial path was within the music business which, of course, we now know has had its decimation in recent decades. I lasted about 9 years in that industry. I began in retail management, moved to a small music company behind the scenes—a reception-ist/exec assistant and ended in a larger independent music distributor as executive assistant.

By 2000 I gave up on the idea of staying in the music business for what I thought would be a more solid career, and took a job with Doubleday Direct. This was a direct mail company that housed various book clubs that the public could join and, as you probably, remember members buy several books for a small amount of money with an obligation over the next two years to buy a certain amount more. Then the goal was to retain the customers after they met their obligation. I started out as a Media Buying Coordinator but soon moved over to Traffic Coordinator or, as they first called it, Promotion Administration which was a team who ran schedules for the production of mailings going to both current and new members of book clubs. It was multitasking, meeting deadlines, solving problems and working with many people. The first 7 years were great. We bought our competitor, the Book of the Month Club, and merged with it to be known as Bookspan. The company seemed profitable and there were lots of company camaraderie and perks! Any former Bookspan people today will remember their days working there fondly and wish they could find a company as comparable. I loved working with all the various departments, working in a team setting to help each other out and meeting deadlines even when there were some stressful times.

By 2007 it seems the company wasn't doing as well as we thought. We fell behind in the industry when the company decided not to get involved in the new "electronic" book market. Our corporate company Bertelsmann merged us with other direct mail companies, BMG and Columbia House. Since they had merged a few years prior and turned a profit, they were hoping combining with Bookspan might work, too. Unfortunately it didn't. In December of 2012 my department was eliminated and we were laid off with a maximum package of 8 weeks.

The massive unemployment rate resulting from the banking fiasco of 2008 was still pretty prominent. The government agreed to give unemployment extensions past the typical 26 weeks. I was advised to go to my local career center and take advantage of any free courses they gave to benefit my future employment. Needless to say, as a result of the mass unemployment, they were very busy. When you met with intake counselors they automatically asked you if you are willing to take any job right away. My answer was no, I was going to hold out for another job in my field. They set me up with a career counselor named Gloria who reviewed my resume, gave me suggestions to tweak it and set me up with a local job seekers marketing group that met in Farmingdale once a month. Even though my position wasn't marketing it was still extremely helpful to have this group to network with and it did warrant a couple of interviews. Although they didn't lead to an offer it was still good practice.

During this time I took classes in Photoshop, Indesign and PowerPoint to keep me familiar with programs that I'd be either working with or programs any creative team would work with. I networked and uploaded to job sites learning the challenging craft of updating my resume to match keywords that a job listing might have and keeping an ongoing list so if the Department of Labor wanted proof that I was looking, I could show them.

After 5 months I was offered a job with Estee Lauder as Traffic Coordinator for their flagship brand website. I sought and accepted the job because it was a Traffic Coordinator position which was similar to what I've done, and Estee was a big solid company that's been around for awhile. This was a newly created position for their team and I now surmise that they weren't sure who I should work under, since my first boss was Director of UX design. I really didn't have connection to her but I did work with the Project Manager of ecommerce and the International ecommerce Manager who also worked under her. In addition, I also worked with both retail and email marketers as well. All projects were domestic and international campaigns that had to be created, reviewed and launched onto the Estee Lauder sites. The creative team that worked on these campaigns were located on 59th Street. I worked in the 23rd Street office. My daily routine became going uptown every morning for a half hour meeting with the creative team to discuss active projects and prioritize their work. Between multiple layers of approval and decision makers in endless meetings this proved to be a challenge. One year into the job the Director of UX was laid off due to the completion of the new site and I was now working under the Creative Director. After 20 months in the job the Creative Director and his boss VP of sites explained that they were changing the role. My skill set no longer matched. I was given a package and, once again, by February of 2016 I was out of a job. I now can see where they were hoping that I would have enough initiative to work with all teams to keep projects on schedule. I also had to learn the subtle art of working for a large corporate company and the nuances of who to connect with and who not to. I didn't show my true potential of what I knew I could do. They probably needed a different type of personality for that role and, yes, different skill sets.

My first instinct proved successful. I reached out to my network right away, letting people know that I was once again looking for a job. One of my former co-workers from Bookspan reached back and said there was a similar position to what I did at Bookspan. This was a small ad agency that was about 21 years old and their major client was a well-known life insurance company. They produced monthly mailings that were sent out to both current and new clients. The job was temporary with a possibility of becoming permanent. I came in for an interview and was offered the job that next day. I was back working in less than a month since losing my previous job. I picked up the process very quickly and established good working relationships with all departments as well as the external client and printer. I was respected right away for my adaption to the company processes. By the fall of that year I was offered a permanent job but, unfortunately, due to the company having a very small budget, I could not afford to live on the salary they were able to pay so I had to decline. By February I was back looking for another job.

I once again reached out to my network to let them know. I also kept in touch with the career counselor I worked with at my local career center. She had since retired from that job but was offering night classes in job searching as well as free advice via email. She told me to reach back out to the job seekers marketing group I was previously working with and advised me to connect with another network group via LinkedIn called LI Seng, a job search networking group. I also took a refresher course at the local career center.

About two months into the search I found a job on LinkedIn for a Traffic Coordinator at J.P. Morgan. Again, I thought, a good solid company that's been around for awhile and a similar position I've done. Some of the job description fit me and some I would have to learn on the job. One was metrics, the other was SharePoint. I mentioned this at the interview. The team interviewing me, I guess, didn't seem to mind because I was offered the job and by May of 2016 I was working full time once again.

Although J.P. Morgan offers an array of various online classes to help improve your skill set, these two new tasks for me were not that easy. The metrics, as I was shown by one of the designers covering it, was simply refreshing the document for new data to populate through. I did not have to actually run pivot tables each time as the pivot tables, charts and graphs never changed. When the system changed, it was a struggle which led to lots of mistakes and learning curves to understand the relation of the charts and numbers. This did not go over well with my manager, who by August was commenting point blank, "My expectation of you is very low." As I tried to take various online courses to improve my skills and continued to make mistakes, my manager continued to make negative comments including, "I don't trust you."

In addition to the reporting challenges, I did get the hang of the Share-Point content management system. However, communication was not so clear with my manager about next steps for the yearly update. When I met with her in December to discuss next steps she berated me for being late with next steps. The updated site launched in February, which by the way, is when it launched the previous year as well.

At this point my feeling was I could find a cure for cancer and my manager would find something wrong with it. I'm pretty sure she was done with me. After two improvement write ups, and many phone calls with Employee Relations, I was terminated in September 2017.

So back to pounding the keys on my laptop, networking and trying to get into the career center again to once again brush up on some programs. My lesson to take away would be I'm not necessarily good at my own initiative. I do need some guidance in the beginning and some initial helpful feedback to know I'm on the right track. As much as my intention was good to "learn on the job" I really shouldn't commit to that if I don't know I can. The two previous jobs for Estee and J.P. were essentially solo Traffic roles. The successes I've had were working with teams and processes in place. So with interviews and phone calls I now know what questions to ask.

My sister suggested I reach out to a temp agency. It would get me some gigs and money and you never know if that can lead to something. I signed up with Long Island Temps. They got me on one temp job as a marketing surveyor. It was interesting temp work and I kept in touch if they ever had anything else.

It's February 2018 and I'm at the career center waiting to take a class, and my phone rings. It's my rep from Long Island Temps. One of the versions of my resume I submitted to them was for Customer Service Rep since I had done that for 13 years with a part-time weekend job I recently had. Sure enough they were calling about a Customer Service Rep gig at a food manufacturer 10 minutes away from my house. It was a temp to perm job and the pay was decent for Long Island. The role is similar to Traffic as it's a lot of meeting deadlines quickly, multi-tasking, problem-solving and working with many people. I am part of a team and they train you on the job. I've been a month into it, and as I tell people "so far, so good." I've picked the process up very quickly, the people are nice and appreciate my work. Ironically it's a combination of two major food manufacturers that service distributors to restaurants and retail who have both been around for many decades. Due to the merger we are outgrowing our warehouse, so they are moving into an additional warehouse and they are hiring more people, including recently an HR director.

OK, so things seemed to be working out. "So far, so good" is my attitude. With a growing company, however, comes growing pains. The girl who is my counterpart and I can cover each other's work when needed. She was over-tasked and ready to quit until they hired me to help take some work off her plate. She liked how quickly I picked up the job and decided to stay. However with new people and training on the fly, the set processes that worked in the past didn't run so smooth. This was frustrating to her and stressful when mistakes on customer orders were being made and process was not followed. In addition I was learning that I have to be more careful with numbers so some of the billing I was doing was taken away from me to concentrate and getting pricing correct when processing orders. By August she gave notice and will probably be gone by the end of October. To make matters worse, with the end of summer comes the season of bees, specifically yellow jackets! We manufacture sweet syrups which were improperly disposed of outside and which attracted these insects, who made their way into the building and specifically my office! The first day I left early. The second day a few of us confined ourselves to a room that wasn't affected. By the next week the other girls braved it in the affected room by killing as needed (every day) and I stayed confined. I provided a doctor's note that I was allergic to bee sting when requested and I've been confined to a back room since. This year has been especially warm. Now into October, they are still there and the daily killing continues. Two people were stung, but luckily had no bad reaction. My overall view of this company has soured tremendously so, needless to say, I will keep my resume active and keep looking. Even after the bees are gone there will always be next summer and next bee season.

What are my next steps? Do I work back in New York City or does the Island provide a decent paying job in a medium size company that won't fold?

Elizabeth L.

THE REAL BENEFITS OF NETWORKING

A few years ago, I was feeling the urge to pivot at work. I did have an "aha" moment when planning my wedding where I realized that I was buying very differently that I was selling and I wanted to bridge that gap by moving into marketing. I started taking digital marketing courses and set up networking meetings. One of the most pivotal was with Marnie K. Wells. Marnie is one of those people who is impressive right out of the gate, and we sat there chatting about work and life. She was one step ahead of me. As we talked, Marnie pulled out a sheet of paper and started listing the smart, talented women she knew and gave the list to me as a resource.

I recently had a meeting with one of those women. It was serendipitous, to say the least aside, from getting sage advice and learning a shared love of tea. She recommended I get involved with Team Women and apply to their mentor program which I did. It felt like a great full circle moment fueled by a conversation that I was initially hesitant to schedule. So do reach out, connect, build relationships You will never know where they can take you.

Networking can seem so ambiguous, until you realize often times the entire purpose is that you don't quite know what it will lead you to.

Kathy Frankson

EVERYTHING GOOD, INCLUDING THE BAGEL

My road to current 'freedom' (I call it current cause I always know it can disappear) must always be worked on; I never take it for granted. If nothing else makes sense, remember this: follow your passion, give it your all!

My turn around starts with this: instead of killing myself and letting my family collect a $250,000 life insurance policy, thinking they may be better off with the money than struggling with me, I decided, I might as well go for it now, and going for it now meant being the best at advertising, marketing and helping businesses and nonprofits get their message out—bringing value in multiple ways.

I always wanted to get into advertising, but no one was going to hire me. They wouldn't believe I created the Everything Bagel (I did) and even if they did, I couldn't survive on the low pay. While the Everything Bagel is nice, my branding and marketing passion came from LEARN—"Let's End All Racism Now". This is a message that has been in every New York City school and around the world, but certainly needs to be spread louder - with loving hearts and greater understanding. At its simplest; I'm not telling you to LEARN; I'm asking you to say Let's End All Racism Now, too. The more people say, Let's End All Racism Now, the more children will learn. We all know about racism, we can't keep away from it if we wanted to...I'm convinced that it's a great idea to educate and inspire the future to oppose racism.

The Everything Bagel; and especially LEARN led to 516Ads.com & 631Ads.com—Long Island's Business/Community Network. On one hand we ignite business to create smart business activity, provide resources and help businesses turn themselves into a resource. We call it a mixture of web and warmth—using multiple on-line tools (website, email, blogging, social media) but still going 'old-school'—to bring people together; face to face - in breakfast, lunch and evening formats - to make introductions, build relationships, and hope to bring value to all who attend.

All of that is nice, but it's all business. The kicker is we attempt to use our platforms to spread positive instead of negative. That might sound eye-rollingly nauseating, but in a world and media where "if it bleeds, it leads"' and hate and controversy make headlines—it's certainly needed. You can't make a "good newspaper"; it sounds nice but doesn't work. But if you can help businesses; then you can use your platforms to spread positive instead of negative.

That's our passion; what's yours? Whatever it is; I'm confident Valentina's book will be helpful in moving you in the right direction.

David Gussin

LETTING GO AND FINDING MYSELF

My story began in 2012 when I unexpectedly lost my job after eight years as an Executive Assistant to the President of a small insurance brokerage. The company lost a big account due to the client being bought over and was no longer able to be our client.

I was unemployed for about eight months and was hired as an Administrative Assistant/Customer Service Rep but was let go a little over a year later due to downsizing. Last in, first out—nevertheless, I was let go again.

My daughter was getting ready for college. My husband had lost his job of 22 years when his entire department was let go in 2007. Our income decreased tremendously when he could not find another job in his field and was now making pizza for a living. We also lost our medical benefits for the family.

I started sending out my résumé, applying for jobs while our bills were piling up. After months and years had passed, I was frantic because I wasn't getting calls for interviews, and if I did get called, I did not get hired. I would search through the job boards, newspapers, magazines, and go to workshops and networking groups as a volunteer to keep my skills current. Nothing.

I was finally hired as a Customer Service Rep at a small company where there was no communication between the employees. It was a toxic environment because everyone working there was unhappy. I became unhappy even though I was working, which was not like me. A few months later I was let go, but not given a reason why.

It was January 17, 2016, as I was reading through the newspaper, I came across an article written by a retired Career Counselor, Gloria Schramm. From the article, she seemed to really care about people. I just thought to take a chance and connect with her on LinkedIn. Although I had seen a Career Counselor before, I did not get any answers or help with finding a job. Gloria willingly accepted my invitation to connect and had me send her my resume to see if I had something missing. She gave me a few tips but thought my résumé was surprisingly good!

Gloria would give me the boost I needed to apply to the next job or go to the next interview. We would talk every day about what I was going through and gave me the encouragement I needed to keep going. Gloria was my sounding board, my "go-to person" for advice about the jobs I would apply to, the interviews I went on and whenever I was let go, she was there to help me through it.

I began my search again but now I was frantic, and anxious! After searching awhile, I was hired as a Customer Service Rep. I needed a job and would take anything at this point. I was surprised that I was hired during the interview and was able to start on Monday! Little did I realize that once hired, I was placed in a Call Center, calling people and asking them to sign on with this radio station, which I felt was not what I was hired to do. Needless to say, I was let go again because I did not meet my quota of people signing on.

I was beside myself! I was frantic, anxious and now depressed—what was wrong with me? I was losing it! After months of searching I was hired as an Administrative Assistant but I was placed in an Order Department with no phone, just processing orders via email and fax, all day. This made me more depressed and after two months, I was let go again.

As I mentioned I volunteered to keep my skills current. I was volunteering for a non-profit company and crossed paths with Mark Hubbard who is a Wellness Practitioner at MKH Healing Arts. I started to speak with him about my situation—searching for a job, having no income as my unemployment ran out, bills were piling up, and I was trying to stay out of foreclosure, not knowing what to do next. Needless to say, I was very depressed.

Mark helped me to see that I was not only depressed about my job situation, but I was dealing with depression from 2006 when my Mom passed on and I stopped "living in the now." If I had not crossed paths with Mark Hubbard at MKH Healing Arts, I would not be where I am today.

I am now working full-time as an Executive Secretary for a President of a small finance company and am there ten months. I am very happy at my current job and am able to feel good about myself, pay my bills, and be aware of my surroundings—see colors of birds, butterflies and rainbows, actually hear words to songs while listening to music, things that I did not realize were happening around me. I had blocked out everything in my life when my mom passed.

So, after all these years of being let go and searching for a job, I can honestly say I am not depressed anymore, I am happier now than I ever was when I was first let go in 2012 and I now have a friend named Gloria Schramm.

Rita Barone

REALLY AND TRULY I'M TOO OLD AT 50???

I am now 50 years old, and look like I am 40. It's very difficult to realize that according to our life plans and journeys, many unforeseen things happen to us. I always worked in corporate America, and have to say I was pretty darn good at what I did. I received many accolades, promotions, and awards during my career as a operations media voice of the company. I have to say that after learning about some unsettling happenings at the company, and sharing them with management, at fifty, I was told '"You are not fitting into the culture anymore," and I was laid off. I took that as a knock on my age. I also took it as a betrayal for helping to change a situation that was not built on integrity. I guess you can say I was a whistle blower on the inside but not the outside of the company.

Two weeks later, I was transferred to another department and told I would have to take a cut in pay as the department was downsizing. All I could say was, "Really and truly, am I too old?" That's how I felt. I was smarter than most and found a little bit of a discrepancy in numbers to bottom line financials. I had never been betrayed like that at a job, was it the discrepancy or was it the financial loss I uncovered? I guess I know the answer. It was both. I guess this was really a God moment. I think of some moments when St. Joseph had betrayal in his life. I was shattered. I tried to stay in the new role, but felt very discriminated against. It was a department of very young new hires, and one that was very difficult to work with. The company offered me a package to leave, which I took. When I left the offices, with the package in hand, I felt a stream of relief to my body and soul, and had a long conversation with the man upstairs. "Really and truly, God" are the words I uttered for a few months when I came in touch with a priest who started to mentor me.

Needless to say, this priest was a guardian angel for me. He wrapped me with his kindness and his positivity, and gave me something different to focus on. I was really never that attached to the church, but this job change brought me back into the church. This priest guided me back to a better place in my life, and believe it or not, I ended up with a position in the rectory running the administrative and bulletins for the church members. It was the easiest change I ever made that has not only made me into a more cultured woman, but has opened up doors to a social life working on some of the programs for the members of the parish, and some of the students. I even now teach religious instruction to teens.

Really and truly, God, I never would have thought I would do this. There was a time when I did not see a light at the end of the tunnel as I looked through the window; when that happened I gave into a religious effort for support. Really and truly, God. Thank You. I now know that when stuff happens in life, it's all part of the plan that God has in store for us. I guess my plan was always there, but I never knew it. In a church organization, age does not matter! Why is it that it matters in corporate? It really and truly does. I know, as I experienced it for sure.

Anonymous

GET OUT OF YOUR COMFORT ZONE

In 2003, I was in my early forties and unemployed for the first time in 23 years. The resources I had previously used to find work were no longer available. The New York Times employment section had shrunk to a shadow of its former self and there was no longer a plethora of employment agencies able to schedule several job interviews for me in one week. I now had to be my own job coach and recruiter. I attended job search workshops, I received, as part of my severance package, advice on how to learn how to market myself and network with anyone who would give me five minutes to talk about my job search goals.

I am an introvert. In the beginning, I was uncomfortable with networking, but over time it became easier and ultimately lead me to my current employer. Eight months into my job search I contacted a former colleague who gave me an important contact: the name of an executive in the company I wanted to work in. I knew that if I called this person during the day her secretary would screen the call and the message would go in the circular file, so I called the executive in the middle of the week at 6:30 p.m. The executive answered the telephone. I gave her my 30-second elevator speech and she wanted more. We spoke for 20 minutes and she requested that I send her my résumé.

After a series of difficult interviews and a two-month waiting period, I was hired by the company. I am still employed by this company. Job search is hard. Get out of your comfort zone and you will succeed.

Anonymous

WHAT MATTERS MOST

Ten years ago, several supernatural phenomena and dreams inspired me to write a collection of vignettes. But it was mother's death in 2016 which unconsciously drove me to write about her, my enduring impressions from childhood and the players in this collection of memories. Before I wrote this I thought I could never "access" my mother again. After writing *What Matters Most, a Memoir*, memory and the present are not as estranged; after writing this memoir I have given my mother back "life" within the context of those memories and dreams which remain and define my life.

On the surface, *What Matters Most* is a rumination on author Ann Zalkind's relationship with her mother—but within these indelible personal reflections are universal themes with which almost anyone can identify. Both poignant and at times, chilling, Zalkind has created a memoir unlike any other in this impressionistic portrait.

With each moving, often profound vignette drawn from early recollections, Zalkind uses masterful descriptions of the supernatural and poetry and demonstrates a remarkable use of imagery, narrative, and language.

"Memorable. Terrific moods and settings with poetic language," reads one extraordinary review on Goodreads. "The supernatural descriptions were chilling. Also moving recollections of family and lasting impressions from childhood."

A remembrance of her mother, and also the various characters from her mother's world, Zalkind has created a collection that draws from oftentimes difficult memories and addresses the timeless connection between life, death, and memory—and in doing so, utterly stirs the soul.

Ann Zalkind

MORE THAN MENTORS TO ME

T o the reporters I was lucky enough to work with for many years in the publishing world:

I wanted to say that during the time I worked in a weekly tech news environment for most of my career, I learned everything by sitting in a bullpen surrounded by smart, intelligent, tough, witty reporters while watching stories unfold. Being an integral part of news meetings, sharing ideas and respected like an important part of the process of publishing amazing stories weekly is a time of my career that I have never forgotten. Having worked with editors and reporters, and watching the day-to-day news cycles come to light, has given me the best education in my career. I have the utmost respect for reporters because of the integrity, passion, and storytelling I witnessed for many years working with top editors. When I first started in the editorial scene, I was totally unaware of the impact it would have on me and I quickly realized that the days spent during those years gave me exactly what I needed to know after receiving the big bad boot of downsizing. Back in those days, working side by side with these very intelligent individuals gave me my own passion for making things happen after my downsizing.

Having witnessed so many serious, yet funny, scenes in the bullpen area and management offices afforded me an education I could never have received in a university. Those years I treasured, and I thank reporters everywhere for their hard efforts in printing the news with integrity and passion! Many of them are my heroes who taught me so much moving forward in my current life and gave me the chutzpah to make things happen socially, professionally, and sincerely with enthusiasm after I moved on.

A special shout out to Bob and Camille DeMarzo, who have been in publishing for decades. What an education I received under your publications.

Valentina

Chapter Six

RANDOM MUSINGS

Experience impacts the world beyond imagination!
~Valentina Janek

REASON FOR LEAVING MY JOB

According to a survey by Glassdoor, a job site for recruiting, fifty percent of adults say they would consider looking for a new job this year, which is the highest number ever, according to a survey. How about that—does this mean nobody is happy these days?

I worked for a company that felt like family to me because of the fact that no one got along. How sad is that?

After three years, four months, two weeks and five days six hours, 7 minutes and 44 seconds, this is my last day here at my job. I worked very well with clients, did some great business and also achieved awards and increased profit. Even had a few picnic frisbee contests and once had an accident which broke my nose at the job. Got raises, bonuses, and promotions all the way up to senior assistant vice president in a blink. Rose from lower management to middle management. After some time, I even received a new chair to catch my breath on. I wrote a note to my colleagues today. I have to say that in the time I worked here I wore out my welcome, so many will easily accept my departure because many rarely gave me the right time of day and knew that I existed here. Although we had our differences as in right and wrong, I know I was right and you were wrong. Little did I know that my latest review showed I was a leader and exceeded goals.

Still it's always a privilege to team up with colleagues who are smart, professional and dedicated, but I could not ever say that about anyone here. Although this organization felt like family to me, it was just because no one ever really got along with anyone else within the operations. If I called any of you my friends, the reason is that outside the office I have no friends. So let me take this chance to come clean. Many times I often caused paper jams in the printer, and never said it was me. More than once while flying on company time, I put dramamine on my expense statement. And let's not forget I could have worked harder, too. Very often I shut the door of my office and napped for six hours. I do have my regrets and owe all of you an apology. Truth be told, I'm leaving so I can finally steal the stapler! As I start a new job in two weeks, I am inspired. Sorry if this sounds like gloating, but right from the get go they are going to give me a chair!

Ecstatic I am leaving! Ta Ta! I guess you can say I am happy to move on.

Anonymous

THE BULLY AVENGER!!

My 17 years as a senior support person at a health system was going well until I needed to assist my family members, due to old-age and illness. Then the trouble began. I worked for a place that promoted wellness, ethical culture and was totally against bully bosses. I found out it could not be further from the truth.

There was no understanding that I needed to receive phone calls from family to get them an ambulance for my ailing family member, or the trips to the hospital to meet the ambulance. I always returned to work and went to the hospital again after work. The boss turned into a bully. I wound up in the hospital myself due to stress and the boss didn't care, just wanted to know when I would be returning.

It continued to go downhill to the point where I asked to be transferred because I couldn't take the stress of that situation; it was making me sick. At first they said they would help me find another position, but then I could see that they were not going to help me. I was out ill for two days and the bully boss demanded that I come back, or he would have to get someone to take my place. He suggested I could work in another area of the department, where there was another bully that the bully boss protected time and time again. Of course I refused.

I always gave more than 100% to that company and couldn't believe the way I was being treated. The bully chose not to understand what I was going through with my family, even though I had helped the bully's family and employees throughout the years with their issues. There was no way I was choosing the job over family.

I went in when I was better and packed up my stuff, left and got in touch with a lawyer, which was the best thing I ever did. I received the severance and medical benefits that I wanted and never had to see those people again.

At first I was very depressed. It took a few months to settle down and realize how much better I began to feel. Today I'm having the time of my life.

"The Bully Avenger"

SEPTEMBER 11–AFTER MORE THAN SEVENTEEN YEARS

For several years, I would, each month, go to the 25th floor of One World Trade Center, the North Tower, to attend the Board of Directors meeting for Empire Blue Cross Blue Shield which became WellChoice, Inc. Normally, I would drive to New York City and arrive early for each meeting. That meant I would walk into the building around 9 a.m. Back on 9/11 the North Tower was the first one hit – 8:46 a.m. That would have been close to the time that I normally arrived at the building. For that reason, I will never forget that awful attack on the lives of innocent Americans and so many others from around the world.

It has been estimated that almost 3,000 people lost their lives in that attack. The person directly responsible, Osama bin Mohammed Laden, hid for almost ten years. But, on May 2, 2011 bin Laden was killed by Navy Seals who raided his compound in Abbottabad, Pakistan.

9/11 was a terrible day and included two other serious incidents. One plane flew into the Pentagon and killed hundreds of people. Another plane, because of the resistance from passengers, ended up crashing in a rural Pennsylvania field. In total, counting passengers and people in the two buildings, there were over 3,000 killed by the terrorist attacks.

At the time of the attacks, my wife and I had just purchased a weekend condo out in Greenport, New York. When I heard about efforts to build a memorial for 9/11, I decided to help out. The memorial stands on a pier visible from the dock near Claudio's Restaurant. Designed by Roberto Julio Bessin, it consists of an Osprey, sculptured with wire, sitting on metal salvaged from the World Trade Center. The theme of the sixty feet high 9/11 memorial was—that like the almost extinct Osprey which has come back—so shall the United States.

Then an interesting opportunity arose. One of the members of the Memorial Committee owned a company that had been responsible for salvaging the metal from the World Trade Center and moving it to waste facilities. My law firm did some environmental work for his company on Long Island. You may recall that some of the salvaged metal went to create the bow of a new U.S. Navy destroyer. The rest was discarded. I was asked if there was any interest in a small Osprey sculpture on World Trade Center metal for my home?

"Yes," was my immediate answer. Now, I have a wire sculptured Osprey perched on World Trade Center metal. It stands about three feet high and sits next to the fireplace in our living room. It is a constant memory of the 9/11 experience. Like the Osprey, the United States and buildings at the World Trade Center shall rise again.

Robert R. McMillan

WHERE I'M FROM, I AM

I am from the Age of Disco and Gucci bags.

From bell bottom pants and platform shoes.

I am from antipasto and manicotti on Sundays to home cooked meals every night.

I am from a family of cooking, cleaning and setting tables.

To a beautifully decorated home and educated artistic parents.

From Japanese gardens, antiques, pottery and tapestries.

I am from a close knit family and many distant relatives.

I am from love, devotion and compassion.

From Daddy's little girl to Mommy's eldest.

I am from public schooling with high standards.

From a grand high school prom and a small graduating class.

I am from piano lessons, dance recitals, and homemade Halloween costumes.

I am from a family who celebrated every occasion.

From a hard working Dad who gave us everything.

To a mom who was always there.

I am from parents who worked for all they had.

From vacations in the Bahamas and Cape Cod.

To weekends spent with relatives and friends.

I am from beach parties and sunsets.

From a childhood of wonderful memories.

I am from friends, old and new.

Childhood friends from forty five years ago.

I am from a strong Italian family.

From having a sickly brother growing up.

To having a much younger baby sister.

I am from nieces and nephews who I love like my own.

I am from sleepovers, manicures and pedicures and shopping sprees.

I am from a story book romance thirty five years ago.

From St. John's University to living on Long Island.

From having two beautiful daughters, different in so many ways.

From learning disabilities to Dean's List.

To making us the happiest parents in the world.

I am from molding my children into the women they have become today.

I am so proud of them both.

I am from traditional parents.

Now I cook, clean and sweep tables.

To take care of them.

I am from christenings, communions and sweet sixteens.

They are for my children.

I am from Sunday meals and vacations.

Now they are different

I am from having a carefree childhood.

To being a responsible adult.

Life has changed

I am still from laughter and excitement.

I am from fun loving memories that will never fade.

From a family who has taught me how to live, love, and give.

I am truly Blessed.

Brenda Picone

DEFENDING BILLY JOEL AND THE BAY MEN

B ack in the summer of 1992, an interesting event took place at an East End beach on Long Island, New York. Billy Joel and his wife, Christie Brinkley, the actress and model, gathered on an Amagansett Beach while several bay men demonstrated the outlawed haul seining for striped bass.

Haul seining is a form of fishing with a net taken out into the water and then hauled back to the beach with a catch of fish. Haul seining had been outlawed by the State of New York to prevent the taking of too many striped bass from the waters surrounding Long Island.

As the net was pulled in, Billy Joel and his wife went to the water's edge and carried striped bass out of the water. They and the bay men were then charged with violating New York law. Next, there would have to be a trial.

How did I get involved in this case? It started when I received a call from Tony Bullock, the East Hampton Town Supervisor. Tony said to me that Billy Joel and the East End bay men needed legal help in a court trial. "Could I please help?" I agreed to take on the case.

Next, I went out East to meet with Billy Joel and the bay men to get all the facts and prepare the defense. One of my partners, an expert in environmental issues, and I went to Amagansett for the meeting. We spent around two hours going over the facts and examining the tickets issued for the haul seining and taking of striped bass.

On returning to the office, our employees asked as the first question, "Did we get to meet Christie Brinkley?" Billy Joel was second on the list. Unfortunately, we had to answer that Christie Brinkley was not at the meeting.

The next step was the trial before a judge of the East Hampton Justice Court. Based on the review of the tickets, our best defense was an error, which was made in the filling out of the tickets. As I summed up our defense, my closing words were, "The bay men of the East End of Long Island are as endangered a species as the spotted owl in Oregon." Interestingly, the television coverage of the trial ended with that quote from my summation.

The judge decided in favor of Billy Joel and the bay men, based on the technical defect we had found in the tickets. The case was over, but the bay men were still not permitted to continue haul seining in Long Island waters.

Robert R. McMillan

HOW THE DREAM JOB BECAME THE NIGHTMARE

If you have been following along, you know that I am considered an older employee in the workforce. Older yes, stupid, NO!

The problem with job seeking today is that there are too many applicants for every job. This gives the potential employers the feeling that they are in control, and to a certain degree, they are. But just because the applications keep coming in, doesn't mean the applicants themselves are qualified for the job. I think the young people today just send resumes in hopes of landing any job. I'll use an analogy I got from a teacher friend—when asked how she read all those boring essays, she said she didn't—she threw them up the stairs and graded them in the order of which they landed. Not exactly what I expected for an answer, but it was an answer and it did solve the problem. I think that's how the job market is run today. Well, that's not true. You never know when meeting someone can lead to a different job.

As an older person in the job market, I am respectful of my time—the networking it takes to reach the right person, develop a rapport, send a resume, get and ace the interview and eventually land that dream job. I also consider the time of the interviewer—I don't apply for jobs that I know I am not qualified for.

. . .

But here is where we get to the point—I did all of the above and landed the dream job. It was a job I could do in my sleep—in publishing, my home court. It was putting on events, which I have done all my life, securing sponsorships, checking, and overseeing the arrangements up to and including day of, check, check and check. Having done this for years, I know how it should work—there is a timeline, there are parameters, sometimes you are furnished what I like to call "hit lists" and other times, you are to do your own research and create your own. I have done both, successfully.

As the newbie in this position, I was excited and anxious to get going. And yes, my co-workers were younger than me so to some extent I was wanting to prove myself and my worth—to myself and them—and to other seniors out there wondering if they had what it takes to do it. My answer to them, is YES, YES, YES.

But this is the serious part—and I mean this to help employers as well as employees—when you have a job that you want to get done, assign the right person to do the job. In this case it would be me as I was hired for a specific purpose. My marching orders were clear, or so I thought, but apparently only to me.

The first time out of the box, I was reprimanded for calling on another person's client. If that was a rule, I should have been given a list of people not to contact, but that was far too organized for this place. I put it behind me and marched on. As I started to put my plan of action together, I realized that I didn't have any information about the event —not concrete information—every time I asked a question or for more information, I was treated like the enemy—little did I know it was on a need to know basis and apparently they felt I didn't need to know anything. Are you following along? Does this in any way sound like a recipe for success? Not by a long shot.

To make a long story short (and put us all out of our misery) I will get to the end of the story—the job was a bust. I left because I couldn't function with chaos. Moral of the story—help your employees help you by providing them the information needed to succeed. THE

BLIND LEADING THE BLIND WAS HOW THIS ENTERPRISE OPER-
ATED IN THIS VERY SUPPOSEDLY ASTUTE QUEENS AND LONG
ISLAND EMPIRE.

Valentina

THE LAST SUPPER

You never know the last time you might speak to someone. Growing up, my mother always told me "Don't ever end a conversation with fighting!" "Yeah, yeah, whatever mom," I'd say sarcastically. "What did she know? She acts like she knows everything." I was a very stubborn child. Looking back now I wish I had listened to her more carefully. Because that sentence will now haunt me forever.

A few months back in my home, at 5 o'clock in the afternoon, I decided to make myself dinner. Hungry, stressed, and exhausted from a full day of work, I didn't want to be bothered. "I'll make some pasta" I said to myself. I opened the kitchen cabinet and grabbed a box of pasta and one container of sauce, I put it on the counter, and grabbed a pot to put on the stove. As I was filling the pot with water, my father snuck up behind me, trying to lighten my mood. I clenched the pot in anger. "What the hell are you doing?" I yelled. My father smiled and said "I saw you're making some pasta and was wondering if you could make extra for me before I go off to work." I looked at him with disgust. "Can't he see that I'm exhausted? I'm obviously not in a good mood. Why can't he make his own God damn food." I thought to myself.

The two of us stood in the kitchen, not uttering a single word, just staring. I wondered what he was thinking as he stared at the pot I had been holding. "I'm hungry" I said. "Is there a reason you can't make your own food?" My father's smile faded as he sighed and walked out of the kitchen without saying a word. I didn't care. I just continued on with my cooking. About ten minutes later, he came back into the kitchen while I was stirring the sauce and asked again, more politely than before, "I'm not trying to annoy you, but I don't have time to cook after you're done. Can you please save a bowl for me?" Angrily, I shouted "FINE, you can have some if there's extra, BUT ONLY IF THERE'S EXTRA!" "Thank you", he said. A few minutes later when I was finished cooking, I deliberately poured all the pasta into my bowl. "Maybe next time he'll learn to make his own pasta," I said sullenly.

A half hour later I heard my front door open, then close, indicating my father had left for work. He didn't ask me why I did what I did, he didn't even bother to say goodbye to me before he left for work. I didn't care though. "I'm tired. Now he'll understand to leave me alone when I'm in a bad mood," I said.

The next morning I heard a screech from my kitchen. I ran downstairs as fast as I could to see my sister hysterically crying. I nervously asked, "What's wrong with you? You're scaring me." She tried to control her breathing, "Dad is face down in the basement and he's not responding to me. Why is he not responding to me?" "Call the police right now!" I yelled. A few hours later we were told my father had died from a major heart attack.

Even now, as summer has ended and autumn leaves begin to fall from the trees, that last conversation with my father still and will always haunt me. Sometimes when I close my eyes, I see my old kitchen, my father's smile fade, and the two of us staring at each other. I hear his "Thank you" and the quiet footsteps leaving our home that will never return. Knowing what I know now, I will continue to value moments I share with my loved ones because I may never know when those moments with them will be my last. As my life moves forward I will always remember, how sorry I will always be, for my father's last supper.

Dana McDermott

PASSAGE

An enclosure of time
A sail to guide me on
an ivy pass not emerged
until one treads the ridge
and builds the past
Where the path is obscured
on the screen of muzzled
communications
Impacting a common era
observing a margin of history
lured by my reflection
As I lay inert
when I travel an edge
between my shadow

a frontier on either side

and love a threshold

where construction is viable

Perceptions yield to a passage

toward a dream

The zenith of my sight.

Ruth Poniarski

ruthponiarski.com

EVERY TIME YOU GET KICKED... IT'S A BOOST UP!

I t was October 2008. My boss called me into the office and told me that my department was being downsized and that I was, unfortunately, being let go. He was very sad and felt so terrible that I ended up comforting him! I was then called into an office down the hall where my HR representative explained what my package would be, and asked me to sign off on it. Also in the room was the head of our division who thanked me for my contribution. Now let me explain that I am a professional stand-up comedian and had performed and was an MC for several events for the bank, gratis of course. I had been at the bank for 13 years and I knew I'd get a nice package when I did leave. Not life changing, but enough to help me get by. I had just gotten remarried so I had, as the kids would say, a "friend with benefits." And by benefits I mean medicare part A and part B! So I didn't have to worry about getting a new job right away because I had a husband who had a pension, and benefits. So now what?

Well I saw a unique opportunity. Though I had taken classes at Nassau Community College, and I was a licensed Stock Broker and Insurance Broker, I never got any formal education. So I decided to go back to school. On my train rides into and out of Manhattan I would fantasize that if I ever had time I would take long walks in the mornings, and go back to school. So I enrolled myself at NYU and got my professional certification in Life Coaching. It inspired me and invigorated me. I was learning something new and it was exhilarating. I was an 18-month course and I loved every minute of it. That led me to having clients, most of them women over 50. I heard a recurring theme when coaching women. They were having trouble coping with life changes that come with a life over 50. The women I talked to felt marginalized, and though many were hard-working, intelligent, kind women they saw themselves as much less. So that inspired me to write a book called *Who's Better Than Me? A Guide to Living Happily Ever After.* It was my way of saying "give yourself credit for all you've done and for all you do." It's never over until you say it is. If someone locks the door climb out a window. If there's no window, build a tunnel!

As I mentioned I am a professional comedian so I combined my life coaching expertise with my comedic talent and I am now a funny motivational speaker, and I speak primarily to women's groups around the country. I'm writing my second book called *It's Not Gray, It's Platinum … Finding The Joy In Adding Another Candle To The Cake!* I was inspired to write that book because I also talk to seniors. They love having a reason to laugh and finding positive side to coping with the challenges that age brings. Nothing is all good, and nothing is all bad. It's what you do in the wake of major life changing events like losing your nice stable job. The bad new is that you lost your nice stable job. The good news is it freed you up and offered you the opportunity to do something different, that you may never have done without being forced. In my case the opportunity to go back to school, and to start a different career—one that gives me great joy and personal satisfaction. Granted, my life circumstance at the time was such that I could take advantage of it, but, without losing my job I never would have quit to pursue the path that was granted to me on that October day in 2008.

"Kites rise highest against the wind, not with it", said Winston Churchill, along with this gem, "Success isn't final, and failure is not fatal: It is the courage to continue that counts." And I did.

Nancy Witter

YOUR HEADLIGHTS ARE ON!

I've been business networking for about 11 and a half years. About 10 years ago, I was at an event and we were all going around the room giving our 60 second speech.

I was wearing a light pink t-shirt. I was so nervous—sweating and chilly at the same time.

After I stood up to give my 60-second speech, I went into the ladies room.

As I stood in front of the mirror, this woman who I never met before started laughing and said to me, "Your headlights are on."

I was mortified. Not only were my underarms coated with sweat, my nipples were hard.

That's what a hot and cold feeling can do to one's body.

I was so embarrassed.

I never knew that there was such a thing as slightly padded bras.

I'm so glad that I learned about them that I went out and bought slightly padded bras.

Anonymous

THE "LOVE BOAT"?

A t the ripe age of 65, I landed a part-time job at a very high level, established assisted living on Long Island. It was a position for a community activities liaison at a classy facility, which was extremely beautiful, very spacious, and was occupied by 125 residents, and 60 plus employees.

You received free lunch every day which was quite delicious, and I was responsible to be there for the residents in this highly quaint but exclusive operation. Not having ever done an activity liaison job, I thought it would be pretty easy to work with staff, play games, and talk to residents. The dress code was very business professional. I was thrilled to have landed a job in such a beautiful location.

Needless to say, after a few days I realized this was really a job exactly similar to the gal on the TV show "The Love Boat". I believe her name was Julie. So here I was (we can call me Julie), extending good wishes to everyone, and training with a very young trainee. Roller skates were needed to get through every hallway, elevator, the garage, the employee kitchen, the three dining rooms, the libraries, the huge movie theater, the massive gym, the mailroom, the crafting room, the card room, and the lobby. This did not include all 125 resident sleeping rooms which were on several floors, and the parking lot which was is the basement. It was strictly run by a schedule so that each resident could possibly attend 3-4 activities a day, have three meals a day, see a movie, and enjoy a concert in the evening. The residents were a mix of many nationalities as well as all religions.

I found the facility to be quite beautiful but hard to keep up the pace. At 65, I thought this would be a breeze. Was I wrong! Not only did I have to learn so much, I had to be a movie theater guru and learn how to put on the movie twice a day, make sure the walkers were out of the way for each resident, listen to many people who wanted the sound lower, higher, or needed special attention during the movie! What was I thinking? I never knew how to run a movie, a big screen operation! Then there was the gym. I had to learn how to lead a class in exercises. Having my own issues with moving around, and being on the larger size than most gymnasts, there I was doing "one, two, buckle my shoe" in front of many senior residents. I did enjoy that part, and it was healthy for me, but it was exhausting. There were always several performances a week which were enjoyable, but again, each resident had to be comfortable, and there was always parade of walkers to be put aside in the room where the performances took place. Some adorable seniors would sing to the music, and then there were those who did not like the music. Talk about a mix of different opinions, it was quite challenging, but cute to be watching. I continually got lost in my travels running from event to event and room to room, to make sure each activity was taking place on time and everyone had what they needed. As I continued my training, I was in total shock of how busy this job was, but I really did like most of the people and the atmosphere. Here I was with the rich and the famous enjoying the lifestyles of retired people who could afford very expensive living. Most of the residents asked me every day if I was a new resident. No matter how I tried to tell them I was the new activity employee, they thought I was a resident. I was always dressed very professionally, so I guess they got me confused with their friends and neighbors. Be that as it may, as I am a very strict Catholic, when Friday came I was told that I had to do the Shalom Shalom Ceremony on Friday evenings every week. I was puzzled and quite amused, but I mastered the SHALOM SHALOM! It included the cutting and covering of the bread, then the pouring and serving of the wine in small glasses. This was followed by the the candle ceremony and then the coup de grace, The SHALOM SHALOM TRANS. I had to learn the words and how to intone them. There I was, a strict Catholic woman singing tunes to SHALOM SHALOM. I found it very amusing, as my background was never exposed to this ceremonial religious moment. A rabbi would come every Friday evening, and I was commissioned to do the tasks so the Rabbi could just do the talking and praying. Then each glass of wine and the pieces of leftover bread needed to be taken back to the kitchen, which was miles away. So off I went pushing a cart with all of these items back to the kitchen and thinking "what am I doing here?" I realized very quickly that this reminded me of the "Love Boat" TV show and I remember Julie was the cruise director who always smiled and never looked tired. By the time I left every day, I really wasn't smiling, but was committed to staying at the job.

At 65, if you land a job, consider yourself lucky, and being the young one around the seniors was motivating and kind of comical.

I had a difficult time keeping up with the activities, although I enjoyed the location, more than the job. The best part of the job was seeing how the rich and the famous lived while I was training for a few weeks. By the beginning of the fourth week, I was unable to keep up, but I will never forget how I learned how to do SHALOM SHALOM while actually sounding like I was part of the culture and learning the ins and outs of what is actually correct for the ceremonies!

It was a nice experience, with a bad ending. On the last day of the fourth week, I could not walk, and became unable to continue doing the job. At 65, I was the youngest person there with the residents, so I felt pretty good to be a part of this culture. Seniors are such interesting people, and it made me so aware of what it's like when you retire with a nice chunk of change to live so proudly and elegantly as these seniors did. It made me think about my future even more, and whether or not I am prepared for the third and fourth act of my life to be able to live so eloquently in later years.

Many residents, although they had the "life of Riley" as I put it. were very lonely. Money does not buy happiness that's for sure! They did live it up but they really didn't live somedays because of their moments of loneliness. There were many residents who missed their families tremendously, and just needed someone to talk to.

Lesson learned by me for sure! On the last day of my job at the center, I could not walk and decided to resign because of the pure physical labor involved. Working in a facility of this type had professional advantages, but was just too difficult for me to physically handle. Sadly, I left the position after four weeks like a bird flies away, but I was not flying, I was practically carried out!

Valentina

"CONFESSIONS OF A SERIAL AUDITIONER"

Dateline: Late '80s - early '90s
The heart of The Great White Way, BROADWAY!
Scene: Equity Headquarters (AKA the Theatrical Actors Union)

It's a bone-chilling morning that begs the predawn sunrise to get off its sorry BLEEP! and aid the approximately fifty aspiring, anxious, fidgety, slightly delirious from lack of sleep actor-hopefuls that already line the city street, waiting (and waiting and waiting…) for their three minutes to audition for their chance to be in a Broadway show. And I, the "Serial Auditioner", am one of them.

Me…with my frozen gluteus maximus permanently adhered to the hallowed concrete sidewalk.

Me…with said tush that won't budge, lest I forfeit my coveted spot in the queue for my audition later that day, or earlier, depending on how my appointment time fits into the schedule of said day. Now, this typical day is comprised of my full time, "survival" corporate job, organizing an entire tax department (now, what genius thought *that* was a good idea), and the other two auditions that occur within an half hour of each other, on opposite ends of town, that I will squeeze in, if it kills me, damn it!

Me…with my head crowned with my best "Melanie Griffith/Working Girl" coif and my brain abuzz with chatter between its two lobes, obsessing on how the hell I would pull the whole thing off. And, bless my 20-something heart, 90% of the time I would succeed!

Now, do not be alarmed, but the following comparison to the Google definition of a "Serial Killer" will prove my former life status of "Serial Auditioner":

"Serial Killer: One who commits a series of murders, often with no apparent motive and typically following a characteristic, predictable behavioral pattern."

Just substitute "murder" for "throwing myself onto the stage, any stage, to get the coveted lead in a musical production, somewhere in some theater in some part of New York City, and there you are, or rather, there I was.

Ask my now husband, who works for the Treasury Department (the out-of-work, broke actress and the watchdog of US Banking, a match made in heaven!), who at the time was my bewildered boyfriend. I was obsessed with my quest!

Oh, I remember that February day in 1993, when I excitedly got in line at the Winter Garden Theater to be among the over 500 hopefuls to be cast in the chorus of "Cats." Now, I had no desire to be in "Cats", but I definitely was obsessed with joining the cast of "Les Miserables." I was so driven by that dream that I got intel where the music director of said show lived and I set up shop in front of his apartment building, waiting to introduce myself, his next great Eponine, the waif in Les Mis! Upon being confronted by this rabid actor, he calmly referred me, with a shaken voice, to the "Les Mis" casting director and then hurried into the building, and probably called his real estate agent looking for a new address. Anyway, back to the Winter Garden Theater! I knew the casting director of "Cats" was casting "Les Mis" as well, so I showed up for the cattle call, where 500 hopefuls who look painfully similar to each other stand in a line, while strangers behind a folding table literally check them out, head to toe, deciding which ones are the "type" they're looking for. (Think police lineup and you're a perp, but I digress…) Now you really can't blame them for instituting this procedure of torture; after all, do you know how many hours it would take to listen to 500 individual auditions? Excruciating!

And there I was, dressed as The Waif, from head to toe. I'm still not sure why they kept me. I don't have extensive dance skills. Maybe, maybe, they were thinking "She might be right for "Les Mis!" So I was asked to stay. Lucky Number 150, scheduled to sing at the end of the day, considering my previously mentioned daily juggling schedule. An audition would go for 1.5 minutes on average, so that meant at least a 3.5 hour wait for my moment in the sun. Now, a hungry, nervous New York City actor with stars in her eyes can be a ticking time bomb, in this case, not a danger to anyone, but herself. As the minutes crawled along, my self-talk grew more and more toxic, and my energy less and less, to the point when I finally entered the theater area to sing my exhausted heart out…

THE COVETED THEATER AREA OF
THE WINTER GARDEN THEATER!

I was totally ungrounded! Disconnected from my precious life force that got me to that theater and had me stand on that demeaning cattle call line in the first place!

Well, suffice it to say, it wasn't pretty. I don't even remember what I sang (selective amnesia) But, bless my broken heart, I'll never forget the high note at the end. And neither will those beleaguered auditors. For when I reached for that high note, well, uh…

IT GOT SUCKED INTO THE STRATOSPHERE BY "THE GRINCH
WHO STOLE 'LES MIS' FROM ME"!
(In other words…
it cracked.)

The return trip to my apartment in Hoboken was but a blur. Upon entry, I threw myself on the floor, wailing, wishing I were dead! Too bad the "Les Mis" folks didn't get to witness that performance. Then, they would have surely hired me!

But the worst part was the real story that happened that day. The day was February 26, 1993, the date of the first bombing of The World Trade Center. The day I was so obsessed with stardom and my epic fail that I was oblivious to the tragedy that had befallen my fellow man.

Looking back over that wonderful, crazy era of my career, my serial auditioning days, I see it was all very necessary. I had to learn that my obsession with being a star, simply for the sake of being seen, was my undervaluing the gift I had been given by God to use for the sake of humanity. Now, twenty-six years later, I have cultivated that gift, and so many more gifts than I ever imagined I had, and I am offering them to the world, with an open, exuberant heart, as the playwright and composer of my own shows, that I perform in and produce for aspiring hopefuls! And, thankfully, I have officially retired from my life of "Career Crime!"

Doreen Firestone

NEVER THOUGHT YOU WOULD GET THERE...THE AHA MOMENT

After you have lived many years striving for the perfect job, life, marriage, home, relationship, car, or vacation, one day you will realize that the most important thing for you is spending every day happier than the last—and not to sweat the small stuff anymore. It will happen to you. Things in your career that may have happened quite some time ago, will make you chuckle or reflect "did I really react that way back then?" Also, your tolerance for certain scenarios will lighten. I believe this for sure. My mom always said, "Life is not a dress rehearsal," so just be ready, don't wait for a bomb to hit you, and don't let the door kick you in the butt on the way out! And remember always, "What you give is what you get!" Mom was right!

Valentina

AN UNEXPECTED TURNING POINT

S hortly after graduating from the University of Massachusetts at Amherst, I received a call from my favorite journalism professor. He presented me with an opportunity—I could interview with *Computer Reseller News*, originally launched in 1982 and published by CMP Media of Manhasset, New York.

Growing up in Cherry Hill, NJ, I had never even set foot "on" Long Island, but next thing I knew I was joining this band of seasoned journalists. I decided to move to Long Beach, a barrier island off Long Island's South Shore. My logic seemed sound to the 23-year old version of me—it's nicknamed *The City by the Sea* and there seemed to be a whole lot of beaches, bars, and bagel shops—what else did I need!

Over the course of the next four years, a band of grizzled journalists, misfits, geniuses, and characters became my family as we covered the dawn of the Digital Age. I wrote hundreds of stories, once got tossed out of a press conference by computer mogul Michael Dell, and was tricked by many of those same friends into thinking that I was going to get the paper sued by the Commissioner of Major League Baseball.

Life was good, until CRN was purchased by London-based United News & Media's Miller Freeman in 1999 for $920 million. But the dotcom era was booming, and I received an offer from rival publisher

Ziff-Davis Media to join a spin-off of the venerable *PC Magazine* called *The IT Insider Series*. The position was based in New York City and presented an opportunity to shape a newsletter, conference series, and website from scratch.

Creating a publication from its humble beginning was thrilling, and our small crew was rolling along beautifully about to launch when the dotcom bubble popped. The dotcom era was a period of excessive speculation in the U.S. that occurred roughly from 1995 to 2000, a period of extreme growth in the usage and adaptation of the Internet. It was also a time when it was believed that "old" profit-motivated business models were becoming extinct.

As we now know, the death of balance sheet fundamentals was greatly exaggerated. Once booming businesses like Pets.com, Webvan, World-com, Boo.com and USWeb came crumbling down, and seemingly just as soon as it started, the *IT Insider Series* experiment was terminated at the end of 2000, and my cushy, exciting new job in the city was axed.

I commiserated with my co-worker David (a fellow CMP Media alum) after we were called one by one into the office of our Editor-in-Chief and decided the best course of action was to drink. We visited our favorite watering hole *The Back Porch* on the corner of 33rd and 3rd. We downed our sorrows in an enormous margarita, which the bar proclaimed as "the largest margaritas in New York City."

The description was accurate. We stumbled back to the office, and our shaken boss said, "How are you guys doing?" We muttered something like, "Feeling a lot better now!"

I spent a few weeks in my apartment attempting to train my new pug puppy Rufus, but quickly found that to be a futile endeavor. I began flooding the Internet with resumes and writing samples. I was getting nowhere quickly and growing desperate. I was about to get married and my meager savings as a reporter/editor was quickly evaporating.

I thought back to my days at *CRN*. We were taught to stop at nothing to get a story, even if it meant poking the most powerful people in the technology industry. I realized I was going about this job search in the wrong way.

I discovered a position that sounded perfect with a firm called Simba Information that provided market intelligence, forecasts, and advisory services in the information and media industries. But rather than sending out my resume on a wing and a prayer, I showed up to the offices and asked to speak with the person John who was in charge. Needless to say, he was surprised to have someone personally knocking on his office door handing him a resume. We went to lunch, had an engaging conversation, and I was hired.

Little did I know, this would turn out to be a turning point in my career. After spending four years writing research reports and providing advisory services to large health information and tech firms, I was offered a position by one of my clients. I have since leveraged this opportunity to transition into corporate strategy positions for large Fortune 1000 firms (I apply my writing and reporting experiences every day) recently earned an MBA from Rutgers University, and what once seemed like a door closing has opened up a vast world of new opportunities.

David Jastrow

PHILOTIMO

W illiam James: The community stagnates without the impulse of the individual. The impulse dies away without the sympathy of the community.

Saying from an Aborigine woman on my mother's and Jean Kelly's wall: If you have come here to help me you are wasting your time. But if you have come because you are swept up in my cause, then let's work together.

Superstorm Sandy: We all felt the kind of sympathy that means, "I suffer with you."

The dream that will not die because you were born to love it into full being. Gratitude Journal

This was never so needed than during the aftermath of Superstorm Sandy when vast numbers of Long Island communities suffered overwhelming devastation, loss and despair, from damaged homes and businesses to broken hearts and wounded souls. I've heard that sometimes it takes a natural disaster to reveal a social disaster. To reflect back on this unprecedented moment in time, I have to draw on a great quote from Ben Silliman that speaks to the undeniable American can-do spirit: "American families have always shown remarkable resiliency, or flexible adjustment to natural, economic, and social challenges. Their strengths resemble the elasticity of a spider web, a gull's skillful flow with the wind, the regenerating power of perennial grasses, the cooperation of an ant colony, and the persistence of a stream carving canyon rocks. These are not the strengths of fixed monuments but living organisms. This resilience is not measured by wealth, muscle or efficiency but by creativity, unity, and hope. Cultivating these family strengths is critical to a thriving human community." If I had to pick my one word for this region's response to Superstorm Sandy, it would be "community", how we unselfishly came together to help those in deep distress by pooling our strength and sharing the work and the responsibility. I have never witnessed or experienced anything like it—manifestations of true camaraderie and genuine human-kindness. It was the greatest privilege of my life to have a front row seat at the Volunteer Recovery Center seeing all the myriad organizations easing human suffering together on such a grand scale. We all felt the kind of sympathy that means, "I suffer with you." Whether feeding, clothing, and sheltering displaced families, removing debris from homes or repairing damage, advocating for public policy and victim rights, providing case management and other needed family supports and resources, supplying legal and financial advice, and ensuring a safe and healthy environment not just to live in but to thrive. At the essence of this work are volunteers. I am here to report to you that the humanitarian effort has led the way in disaster relief and recovery. Based on 93 disaster and other organizations reporting, 51,976 volunteers have served 496,744 hours. Superstorm Sandy brought out the best in all of us. The knowledge that being a volunteer doesn't depend on what we do, what matters is that the exchange has been one of reaching out to be a partner in the human condition, in making that connection where you know something profound has happened. It's not an ideal or intangible objective, its real life and certainly embodies the adage, "Volunteerism is not what you give, it's not even what you get, it's what you become." This storm brought us to our collective knees. But we as a community continue to say to the world, "we are still here" and "we will rebuild."

"In all of our communities, I still believe there's more of what Greeks call philotimo—love, and respect, and kindness for family and community and country, and a sense that we're all in this together, with oblig-ations to each other. Philotimo—I see it every day and that gives me hope. Because in the end, it is up to us. It's not somebody else's job, it's not somebody else's responsibility, but it's the citizens of our countries and the citizens of the world to bend that arc of history toward justice. And that's what democracy allows us to do. It's why the most impor-tant office in any country is not president or prime minister. The most important title is "citizen"—and in all our nations it will always be our citizens who decide the kind of countries we will be, the ideals that we will reach for, the values that will define us. In this great, imperfect, but necessary system of self-government, power and progress will always come from...'We, the people.'"

—President Obama speaking in Athens—the birthplace of democracy —during his final foreign trip: go.wh.gov/POTUSabroad

Anonymous

Chapter Seven

THERE IS LIGHT IN THE DARKNESS

The surprising power of believing leads to success.
~Valentina Janek

NEVER THOUGHT IT WOULD HAPPEN TO ME....

After almost 30 years in the business process outsourcing business, I was told just days before my 15 year anniversary that my position was being eliminated. There were other times in my career that I thought it could be the case but not then... However, unbeknownst to me, the company was up for sale and overhead was being cut. I didn't find this out until 6 - 9 months later.

At the time, the range of emotions I felt ran the gamut—devastation, pissed, worthless, the scarlet "RIF," sad, lost, shock...you name it. These feelings lasted a long time in varying degrees. That being said, my former employer did treat me right—gave me 3 months notice, then 6 months severance, paid for COBRA and for me to work with an executive placement firm.

I began looking for a job right away and hoped to land something while still employed. After several promising meetings and interviews, everything dried up as we were going into the Christmas season. On my first day of being unemployed, I was lost, sad and depressed. After diligently looking for a job in January, I knew I needed to keep all options open and think out of the box. I told myself that I hoped this would be the only time in my career that this would happen so take advantage of it.

In addition to the traditional job search, I attend various webinars on different topics including starting a consulting company and franchise ownership. I quickly ruled out consulting but stayed on the path of a job search and evaluating franchise ownership. Not to bore you with the details but the job search wasn't going anywhere in the cold and dreary months of January and February. So franchise ownership really started to become attractive and I found that you could use retirement savings to invest in your business without penalty so I kept exploring.

I worked with a franchise consultant who presented 4 options. Two were ruled out within a few weeks and the other 2 were evaluated for almost 2 months. In the end, my husband and I decided to become a franchise owner with Art Recovery Technologies. In the past 15 months, it has been rewarding, fun, challenging and scary but I have no regrets. I love what I'm doing and the multiple hats I wear.

Sure, I wish there were some things I didn't have to do but at least I'm doing it for me and my family. The biggest challenge is sales—isn't it for anyone? But I feel that we're on the right path to success—we made it past the 1 year mark—an important milestone!

I encourage everyone to remember, "Things happen for a reason." I really believe this!

Deana Caraballo

YOU ARE THE LIGHT

When the world looks cloudy and dark
Remember, you are the light.
With your smile, love, and kindness
Go to your heart, bring out the light.

When the world looks bright
Take in the light for when it is dark.
Remember, you are the light.

It is the flow in which we grow,
Breath in, breath out as you go.
Be the flow and remember:
When it is dark you are the light.

Tildet

IN THE EMPTINESS OF DARKNESS WE ARE NEVER TRULY ALONE; MY STORY OF SURVIVAL, 17 HOURS ADRIFT AT SEA AND A WORLD FULL OF GOOD SAMARITANS

It was midnight. The clouds were moving in covering the moonlight that reflected off the ebony water. In the distance I could see the tiny rows of lights outlining the office buildings of Stamford, which were getting smaller and smaller reminding me I was drifting further east of the shoreline that seemed so close a little while back.

I couldn't imagine feeling any smaller and alone, like a tiny cork floating in an ocean of darkness. It was now Sunday October 6th. I started out the previous morning, Saturday, a pristine unusual summer-like day with temps in the 80's and water at 67°. A great day to launch my kayak into Cold Spring Harbor and chase the bounty of fall fish before the season closed and cold weather moved in.

I loaded up my kayak with fishing and safety gear, put on my life vest and began paddling to Oyster Bay and the Long Island Sound, like I have done over the past 12 years. The day was delicious. In between landing monster porgies, I would pause to watch the colorful spin-nakers balloon full of air then collapse in a blink as the sailboats made their next leg in the regattas against the backdrop of navy-blue water and gold coast mansions.

It was too perfect a day to call short, so as the afternoon passed I headed to the Sound to meet up with the stripers who were looking for late day snacks. I spent the rest of the afternoon drifting on the current off a sandbar near Caumsett Park. As the day came to a close, I packed up my gear and spoke with my roommate by phone letting him know I was on my way back to my launch spot, Lloyd Harbor Beach, but since the tide was running out and the wind picking up from the South, it would likely take about two hours to reach the beach and I would check in by phone when I landed ashore. It was about 5pm at this point.

And then things went terribly wrong. With the tide and wind against me, the waves came over my Tarpon 140 kayak rapidly. Not a big deal for a kayak as excess water simply drains out the scupper holes in the bottom of the cockpit area. Only my kayak had a flaw, the center hull hatch has a Tupperware type lid. Newer kayaks have more reliable gasket lined water tight screw on hatch lids, and my 12 year-old Tupperware type lid was no longer water tight. No big deal, I keep a large sponge on hand to remove water that collects in the hull. Only the waves were so large and quick that I couldn't bail out the kayak faster than the water was entering.

Again, no big deal, I have dealt with this before, I will just paddle to shore, drain the kayak, paddle along the shoreline and repeat as needed.

Fate would not make it so easy.

As I sit on top and the kayak hull fills with water, it becomes less stable. I could feel this as I paddled the 200 yards to the beach at Caumsett. As the sun was starting to set, the laws of physics caught up with me and about 100 yards from the beach, the kayak capsized, throwing me into the water and the kayak upside down. Using the experience from my 12 years of practicing the maneuver, I righted the kayak, grabbed the far side handle and pulled myself aboard, and readied to continue the short paddle to shore. However, this was not to pass as the kayak immediately flipped, and once again I was in the water. The kayak had taken on too much water to be seaworthy.

I leashed the kayak to my life vest and began to swim us to the beach. It was the last light of sunset, but the beach was a stone's throw. At least under ideal conditions. The tide and wind had other plans for me as they endured to push me further from shore and mock my spirited efforts at swimming.

It was now dark, and understanding the effects of tide and wind, I conceded that I now required help to get out of this predicament. I grabbed my dry box to get my phone and make a humbling call to the Coast Guard. The kayak had batteries in a waterproof box to shine my anchor deck lights, so I would be visible to any would be rescuers. Only, I hadn't properly closed the phone dry box and it was full of sea water. I was now alone drifting in the box with my kayak next to me. At least it had lights.

Over the next 4 hours, a few boats raced home, but in the dark with their engines full speed, they could not hear the sirens of my emergency whistle nor see me in between swales. I was drifting nearer to Connecticut and away from Long Island.

By 10 pm, the water had knocked out the lights and so the kayak was of no use to me. I let go saying goodbye to my friend for the past 12 years as we slowly drifted to our own separate fates. It was just me, my life vest and darkness. And my wits. Stay calm and keep my wits.

As a parent of an Eagle Scout, I learned a lot about scouting. For example, the first survival lesson is STOP. Stop, Think, Observe, Plan. Several times that night, I experienced a peaceful calm. In the dark of the night, if you can clear your head, stop swimming and let yourself float, the warm water can be a very tranquil place. The waves are quiet and have a harmonic rhythm that gently rocks you in a subtle and surreal way, as if to cup you in their hands saying "You are safe…for the time being". Okay, we stopped. Next plan.

Stamford was close. Much closer than the bluffs of Lloyd Neck. Reachable close. I began to swim to her shores, using the buildings as if they were a lighthouse marking shore. It would take time. I was a distance runner, so I was experienced in the notion of one step at a time, and in this case, stroke.

Over the next 2 hours I got close to shore. Real close. Close enough to start thinking about walking over to the Stamford train station, which I knew was near the water, and using the cash on hand to hire a cab to take me home, anonymously. But, that was not to be. That tide was running east and for the same reason it pulled me away from Caumsett, it would not let me close the final gap to the Connecticut shore, and for several hours, even though I kept swimming to shore, I was pulled parallel, eventually passing Norwalk.

Through the nights as the tide shifted, I was pulled back to Smithtown Bay, equally teased by anchored boats that were just out of reach. Through the night I alternated between drifting and swimming.

By dawn, the waters had returned me to Norwalk, with a hard easterly (outgoing) tide. After coming within 50 yards of some islands off Norwalk, I changed tactics, conserving energy by trading water and looking to signal passing boats.

The predicted storm that had made the tides stronger than usual had arrived bring drenching rain and over my head waves. It also meant that passing boats would be few and far between and the few that did venture out would be running full engines with the wheelhouses closed. The high waves on top of limited visibility compounded the dire circumstances of a visual rescue. One cabin cruise making the trip from Norwalk to Port Jefferson passed within 100 feet of me as did a police rescue boat who was out actively searching for me, underscoring my urgent need for another plan.

That is exactly the moment it appeared. The Green Ledge Lighthouse, I would later learn, is about a mile south of the mouth of the Rowayton River and marks the underwater reef that is part of the islands I had so closely passed earlier in the morning. All I knew was in the distance I could see a lighthouse that appeared to be off shore, and if it was off shore, perhaps it wasn't in that current that kept pulling me back to the middle of the Sound. Absent of any better plan, I put my head down and began the final 90 minutes of my order.

For the next hour and a half, I would swim, swallow water as waves crashed over me, and look up to realign to that mark. Little by little I was inching closer, and the bigger it got, the closer it would seem. It was slow going. I grabbed my Army baseball cap that was miraculously still with me and used the bill as a flipper in my right hand to help move through the water.

As I neared the lighthouse, I would become more aware of the tide, wondering if it would play another cruel trick and sweep me by my target. I adjusted my angle of attack East to account for the tide.

The more I thought I was going to make it, the more I was aware this might be my one and only chance. No looking back or making alternative plans. This has to work.

I was so close, I angle the tide correctly and now I had to figure out how to get the lighthouse's ladder without getting knocked out by the surf crashing onto the boulders on which the lighthouse stood.

11:34 am. The time reading on my watch as my left hand emerged from the water to grab the first rung of the ladder. It was over.

I climbed up the ladder onto a catwalk, jelly legs and all, and proceeded to blow my emergency whistle, waving my bright yellow left vest which now could be seen by two men fishing the nearby reefs. A few hand signals and they picked up their radio and five minutes later the rescue boats that had passed me by a little earlier arrived to take me ashore.

In the weeks that followed, I learned about the hundreds of strangers in addition to the first responders, family and friends that made up the search party. Scuba divers, jet skiers, fishermen, boaters, the staff at Caumsett, etc. It was a lousy day, surely not one to go out on the water. All they needed to know was that a kayaker was missing, and they stopped the comfort of what they were doing to risk their own safety to look for me. A stranger.

No matter how dark and lonely it may seem, no matter how dire things may appear, you are never alone. The world is full of good Samaritans who drop what they are doing to help total strangers in need.

Michael Diaz

SURVIVAL TO TRIUMPH AND LOVE

I t was 2008 and I had been with The Bank of New York for 8 years. The bank was in the process of being acquired by Mellon Bank of Pittsburgh. For me, the transition of my position to Pittsburgh was almost over and I would then take my 6-month package and leave the bank. The timing of this takeover could not have been worse, as Wall Street was in crisis and firms such as Bear Stearns and Lehman Brothers would no longer be part of the financial world. Millions of people were out of work and unemployment was at a long time high.

At this point in time I knew I needed to do something different until the economy got back on track, which for me was 3 years later. I managed to use my operations, business and HR skills to volunteer with the hopes of landing a position once I had demonstrated my experience and work ethic. I was successful in doing so; however, I needed to get back in the financial service industry and continued to network and seek other opportunities. This was not easy, as my husband at the time was terminally ill. I managed to land a position with a major financial institution in 2011.

In April of 2012 my husband passed away and I had to deal with getting over the financial burden of his care, my loss of someone I loved deeply and dealing with a new job and its responsibilities. Needless to say all of these life events took their toll on me. I am forever thankful for the love and support of my family and friends.

I continued to commute to New York City on the LIRR and a year and a half after my husband passed, one morning on the platform a conversation was started by a commuter with someone else and somehow I became part of that conversation. That conversation provided an insight into someone's life when I had only seen and said "good morning" to as a fellow commuter. That someone turned out to be my soulmate, best friend and husband of three years as of July 2018.

It is important to always have faith and keep yourself open to all possibilities. Life events will always challenge us but, as demonstrated in my story staying on track, never giving up hope and seeking support of family and friends will get you through these times.

Lori Heiman

OFF TO SCHOOL I WENT

I had been out of work for 3½ years due to a disability. I was a 7-year, burnt-out high-end property manager. It was a useless thankless job but I did love it. At the end of a long grueling day I would wipe the brown off my nose, wash my mouth out with alcohol and come home to my children, tired and stressed. I was suffering from property management burn out.

My bills were mounting and I knew I would eventually lose my house. It was now time for me to return to work. I knew if I would return to work I needed to brush up on my skills. I was very concerned about the gap in my resume. When I asked a friend for advice and what to say I was doing for the past two years, he replied "working as a high end call girl," this certainly would not look favorable on my resume (especially I did not look the part who would believe me—only a blind man).

So off to school I went trading in my $400 brief case for a book bag, packing my lunch, bringing an apple for the teacher, but there was no one there to tell me to be good in school. That was where I meet VJ, she was my job coach and we became fast friends.

I was in a financial bind and needed a part-time job after school. I felt like a 16-year-old where I could work CVS, McDonald's (Do you want French fries with that hamburger?)

VJ assisted in getting me a part-time job as a reservation agent for a Limo Company 3 nights a week; we had both known the owner so the job was mine. So on Mondays, Wednesdays and Fridays I booked clients limo services that were flying to exotic places, and yes, I was a little jealous.

School was ending in February so I decided to look for a job at the end of December. I went to the graduation ceremony taking my 26-year-old daughter and Aunt. I was actually full of pride in myself. It was not easy going back to school, especially with kids who were young enough to be my children.

Every Sunday I would read the paper; my favorite section was the wedding announcements, longevity anniversaries and who was turning 100, and especially the love stories. It made me feel hopeful that someday I would be able to send in my story.

However, I did read the want ads. That day there was an ad for a property manager in Lynbrook, managing buildings in Manhattan and Brooklyn, not on site visits. Sitting in one spot sounded good to me; I was older and didn't need to fly from one property to another. No property site visits in high heels, (always needed to look professional you never knew who you were going to meet). After a site visit my feet would hurt so badly I would drive back to the office barefoot; I felt like Annie Goolahee from Dogpatch.

The next day I received a call on the school bus asking me if I wanted to interview; I had to yell to the kids to keep it down so that I could hear what was being said. I was to interview the next day. The bus ride always made me feel like the bus matron. The bus was packed with children in their late teens and early twenties; I was everyone's mother. Scolding the kids for having the radio too loud or asking them to stop throwing spit balls.

During the 3 ½ years at home I had gained over 30 pounds, some of it due to menopause. I was now the proud owner of size 34C "girl-friends, no more wonder bras for me". I always weighed in at about

124 to 128 pounds; I am a little Italian lady. I had lost 25 pounds; I needed to loose 10 more, so I put on the tightest girdle I could find and squeezed myself into my black interviewing suit—took out my three-inch heels (no longer four inch for me) as I could barely walk in my flip flops. It worked. I looked professional.

I map-quested the directions; I am certainly not a descendant of Columbus. The job was on Atlantic Avenue in Lynbrook. I drove up and down at least 4 times before I found the building. It was a warm December day and I was glad I put on my deodorant twice, forgetting that I had already put it on. Happens a lot these days standing in the bathroom and trying to figure out why I am there.

I walked into the office and met the receptionist, Jeanette. Jeanette was an older woman who had started working for the company right out of high school and had been there for 45 years.

I interviewed with Ms. M, who I would be replacing, and Mr. J—one of the principals of the company. The interview went well and I was asked back for a second interview to meet the owner, Mr. E Sr., and Mr. E Jr., who I would directly work for. They were lovely gentlemen and I just knew it was a fit.

At the second interview, in walked Mr. E 30 minutes late (in his early eighties), making no apologies and barking orders as he walked through the office. This man intimated me; he was a force not to be reckoned with. He got right to the point—I had not worked in 3½ years and he was not going to offer me the salary I was making. He needed to take ten phone calls during the interview, so Mr. E Jr. gave me a tour of the office. It was like bingo day at the senior center. There sat the 90-year-old bookkeeper, Mr. E's elderly administrative assistant, and the accountant that probably used a ledger made of stone for accounting.

Mr. E Jr. informed me that the average employee had worked for them over 30 years. At this company they did not disregard their employees because of their age, but valued the years of experience and knowledge that they brought to the firm. I felt like a kid. This was the place for me.

I took the job, and at 51 sat at my desk thinking in 30 years I would be gumming the words to my tenants to "Pay the rent or I will dispose of you!" And so my career began again, and now I am a proud employee of the E Senior Center.

A year and a half later I am still there; I was evaluated for a raise and received a substantial one. The moral of this story is that there are firms out there who value their older employees and don't throw them away like old shoes. They appreciate the knowledge and experience that older employees deliver, and these are the people who have help make E/Burman the success it is today.

That little old man who intimated me has taught me so much, I now know how to renovate a building from the ground up, read blue prints and work with city agencies (if you are gruff, lazy and useless, there is good place to work!)

I am proud to say that I am part of the E/B group and they are what it is all about. The developers of 8 assisted living facilities and many 55-and-older residences.

And yes, back to school I will go, possibly to learn to be more experienced in reading blueprints or obtain my real estate license (failed the first, maybe the second time is the charm).

There is hope for the 55 plus workers, I am living proof that it can happen.

Macky DiGilio

FAILURE ISN'T ALWAYS FAILURE

September 27, 1988 was my last flight in the T-37 jet trainer. The flight represented an inglorious end to my long-time aspiration to become a fighter pilot in the U.S. Air Force. The road began with dreams of flying, as a child. Then came many years of hard work during high school to get the grades I needed to apply to the U.S. Air Force Academy. My initial Academy Physical was a heartbreaker. I was informed that I would not qualify to fly due to my allergies and an eye condition detected during the battery of tests. I fought. After multiple visits to various doctors and optometrists, I was able to reverse the decisions and I entered the Academy as a pilot-qualified cadet, after being accepted in the spring of '84. The road ahead was long--it took everything I had to make it through the Academy. Along the road, I was again informed, after my Academy Graduation Flight Physical, that I did not meet the standards necessary to fly due to an eye-condition. I fought. Hours of staring at pencil tips, trying to get my eyes to work together, and I finally was able to pass the test that had given me so much trouble. I regained my "PQ" status. When the long battle was through, I finally got my pilot slot. I wanted to get going right away so I signed on for the first class available, giving up half of my graduation leave so that I could start pilot training at Laughlin AFB in Del Rio, Texas, in July. That turned out to be a very bad decision. I had underestimated the burnout factor and how big a toll the Academy had truly taken on me. I had little left to give to an incredibly challenging endeavor like Air Force Pilot Training. Added to this, I was mystified, after showing up, when over half my class already had the volumes of "Warnings, Cautions, and Notes" memorized along with all the Emergency Procedure Boldface. I guess I never got the memo that I was supposed to find a former Instructor Pilot and convince him to Xerox off the Dash-1 for me to study at the Academy and over the summer. My bad. I was never a good memorizer so I reverted to my Academy ways--stay up as late as it takes to get the required information loaded into my brain. I stayed up until midnight each night studying. One problem--at pilot training, our show times were between 3:00am and 3:30am. I showed up in a veritable comatose state. Added to this, my First Assignment Instructor Pilot (FAIP), had signed on for so many additional duties that we never got to see him until it was actually time to fly. I was jealous of the other students who received engaged instruction throughout the 12-hour work days. So, each day, I headed out to fly under the hot Texas sun. 120 Degrees on the ramp and 140 degrees under the closed canopy in the T-37. It is no surprise that I got airsick and had trouble concentrating—exhausted, cooked alive, and air sick. Part of me just wanted it to end. Yet each day I showed up, threw up, but tried to learn a thing or two during the limited time my brain was focusing. My instructor gave up on me. Just as I was starting to overcome my air sickness, it became apparent he was trying a little too hard to give me the "option out"—six air sickness events and it's an automatic disqualification from flight training. I would not give him the satisfaction. On my 5th flight, he wrote me up for being "passively airsick." That means that I didn't throw up but he was convinced that I was "not in the game" due to airsickness. I objected. Knowing that it would be a tough sell to disenroll me for a "passive airsickness event" on my 6th flight, he was courteous enough to ask me, at 10 minute intervals throughout that flight, how I was feeling. He knew that if I, just once, said "a little queasy," I would be effectively eliminating myself. I politely responded "I'm fine," at each query. Unfortunately, blood and guts aside, I had fallen too far behind and was eventually eliminated from pilot training for not being able to progress at the required rate. My final mission was on the 27th of

September and, with a strange shift in winds, I was seeing the local flying pattern from a direction I had never seen it before. My fate was sealed. It was the worst day of my life. It was the end of my dream of being a fighter pilot. Sitting alone, in the dark, in my flight commander's office, and waiting for him to arrive so that I might sign my final disenrollment paperwork was a sad and lonely time. But it was also a meaningful and reflective silence. I recalled the real reasons why I joined the Air Force and I knew it was about much more than flying. The reasons were big and transcended any airframe or mission. When my flight commander arrived, he took instant pity upon me, sitting there in the dark, and he urged me to remain seated. I wanted to end this thing right. I popped to attention and fired off my best salute, reporting in as a sharp officer should. A good officer doesn't stop being a good officer when faced with adversity. No, that's the time he, or she, becomes an even better officer. Of the many positive and glowing performance reports I have received over the years, I still love to look back upon a report which many would have burned or buried deeply within some folder of useless paperwork. It's my training report from pilot training. The report is simple and to the point but the final block has meaning for me: "Lt Lange displayed excellent military bearing throughout his training. He always maintained a positive attitude in spite of the difficulties he encountered. Lt Lange is an excellent junior officer and will be an asset to the Air Force." Over the years, I've seen too many people pitch out of the fight when things didn't go their way. That was never my style. The report, perhaps unintentionally, captured a fundamental quality that continues to drive me. I never enter a fight because I think I can win; I engage because the cause is just and the battle needs to be fought--my ability to "win" is irrelevant.

As I walked out of my flight commander's office, the next part of my Air Force career began. I knew that if I could overcome this shock, and still keep my motivation to serve our country, that a whole new world of possibilities would span out before me. While my flying didn't make the cut, my academic average at pilot training, nearly 97% on test scores, more than qualified me for a Navigator School slot. I got lucky. I was actually working in "casual status" at the Outbound Assignments Office at Laughlin AFB when the official message traffic came in that I had been awarded a slot at Nav School. I was overjoyed. Since I was working in Outbound, I actually got to type my own set of orders and had it processed through all the wickets in no time flat. In the dark of an early December morning, with "Ramble On" blasting on my car radio, I left Del Rio for the last time and made my way out to Sacramento, California where I would attend Specialized Undergraduate Navigator Training. It was like getting a second chance and I wasn't about to blow this one. Nav School and the follow-on Tanker Combat Crew Training School both went very well and I've never looked back. With over 3,600 hours of flying time, in all kinds of weather, I never got airsick again.

So, what about failure? Had I completed pilot training, the path I would have been set upon would have taken me away from so many life events that I truly consider to be the most wonderful and significant moments of my life. Everything from completing life goals to finding and marrying my wife and having four wonderful kids. So many things might not have come to pass; things that I wouldn't trade for anything in the world. "Failure" is funny like that. Pilot training wasn't my first bomb. It won't be my last. But time and maturity have taught me that life works in funny ways. Sometimes, our greatest disasters lead to our greatest victories. I often get a doubtful look when I try to emphasize this point to younger folks or, sometimes, peers. But, it's true. I think we end up where we are meant to be. A little humility goes a long way. Also, some of the most terrific people I've met in this world are those who have faced adversity and come out on the other side—survivors. I used to warn people never to trust the knight in shining armor—the armor retains its luster because it has never seen the scourge of battle. The one to keep your eye on; the one to put your faith in, is the warrior riding tall in the saddle, armor dented and badly worn. I will always believe this. Keep faith and never give up the fight. Failure isn't always failure.

David Lange

TRAVEL TWISTS AND TURNS

Way back in 1995 I submitted a resume for a job in the travel department of an investment banking firm in New York City. It was my first job in New York and I knew I didn't have the educational credentials required for a position in a white glove firm like this. So I fudged a little on the college education portion of my resume. I got the job! It was 6 months by the time that part of my application was verified. I was able to get through the Human Resources hearing because back in the early 1970's there were NO computers to document anything and now in 1995 there was no microfiche to view either. Microfiche was not used anymore. They let me stay with the firm. Because of my Long Island Retail Travel Agency experience, I was not unfamiliar with Guerilla Marketing. One day I realized that there were 3000 employees with the company and they all received the company newspaper. *I saw an opportunity* and requested management if I could write a travel column for the paper. They said yes, and the rest was history. I created a 5 million dollar "travel agency" inside a corporate travel department and I was given the title Leisure Travel Manager. It was a great job and truly the highlight of my career in travel.

. . .

I was first forced to *reinvent myself* the July of my 50th year, just after September 11th, 2001. At the time I was working in the travel department of an investment banking firm in Manhattan. Of course, since travel was not their core business my department was the first to go. Finding another job, especially in travel, was impossible during that time. To make matters worse my husband of 25 years decided he "outgrew" me. I now had to hire attorneys and fight for my house. Not easy to do while surviving on unemployment and my severance from the company. Emotionally and physically I was at rock bottom. After the shock and depression wore off I was determined to stay in my home and resume my life. I accepted a position as a *"floater"* in a nationwide travel management company in Rockefeller Center. A floater is the lowest job you can take in my business. I was surprised they hired me at 50. I went from $90,000 plus benefits and bonuses to $32,000 with a three-month probation period. I just wanted my life back, it was a foot in the door. I knew it was important to get up, get dressed and go to an office—back in New York City where I was working since 1995. I just knew I had to start somewhere.

In two years' time I was promoted to East Coast Operations Manager with 13 offices under my supervision. The company continued to grow and joined forces with American Express Travel and then later acquired The Travel Authority. My company was changing, and I began to sense the New York office was not going to be the main hub. The owner stepped aside and became chairman of the board. There were new managers, SVP's EVP's and all the V VP's. The old guard was gone, and I knew at some point I would be too. I was with the company for 10 years by that time. My life was also changing again. This time for the good. My son got married and I now had a grandson, my mother was elderly and needed more attention during the week. Plus, I got married again. I wanted to leave on my own terms. I quit my job the week after we got back from our honeymoon. A few months before I left I started my own travel company, JDK Travel, Inc. and became an independent contractor. For the past five years I've been very busy growing JDK Travel, Inc. and taking care of my family.

• • •

All in all, it's very important to stay positive, be creative, look for opportunities, and keep moving forward.

Joanne DeSalvo Kreusher, CTC

President , JDK Travel, Inc.

MY REINVENTION

Securing a new teaching position made me feel anonymous and invigorated, although it was a struggle to let go of a life of stifling certainty and to embrace a newly emergent life with boundless possibilities. The most compelling part of my transformation involved facing and interacting with the truth. The truth of it is job loss enabled me to realize that I was doing too much, working too hard, trying too hard, relaxing too little and not sleeping enough.

So where am I now in the sunny place at 55 years of age? I am physically healthier, and living a good life in Florida since leaving my friends at LIBC a year ago. I say "yes" to what I want to do and a resounding "no" to what I do not want to do. I have shed some acquaintances, and deeply appreciate the few that are part of my reinvention and job change. I have learned to eat more healthfully, am blessed to have a job that always now interests me in a sane way.

When I joined the club, I was so despairing of my job, my social alliances and my life. At 55, I have a nourishing interior life as well as a phenomenally fulfilling career going on the past six months. Going back to teaching after several years of being in a corporate role has been the best thing for me.

Nothing is perfect, and there is so much more for me I am sure. My evolution was gradual and reflects my commitments to my ideals, my community, my family and myself. My reinvention has been slow and steady and is the part of me that I am most proud of because I lifted the clouds that were covering me and I found the sunshine within and all around me.

I miss all the fun I had with the LIBC, and will be back to visit and follow your press on the website. I will never forget how much I learned by getting involved with the organization, the people and, let's not forget, the fun.

I wanted to let you know I am doing very well. Not rich, miss New York, miss the members, miss the excitement of New York, but rich in self and heart gainfully re-invented!

Charrie Seeler

MOVING ON AND FORWARD

So my husband suddenly dies in March 2018 from a massive heart attack, and my life is now all about moving on and moving forward. At least that's what everyone told me I had to do. Well what if I didn't want to move forward? What if I wanted to stay in my home of 25 years, where we raised our two beautiful daughters and it's the only home they've ever known? What if I contemplate staying in this home because my husband had two insurance policies that I knew would cover the funeral, house expenses, and my kid's college education. So what if I just stay where I am? And then what if I find out my husband did not cover his last insurance premium and two weeks after his death, I find out the insurance company will not honor payment of his plan that he paid into for over 20 years because he missed the grace period by a few days (perhaps because he died within the grace period?) And then I realize I cannot stay in my home and have to sell it within a couple of months because we are months behind on the mortgage payment as well as other bills, which I find out about after my husband's death. So what happens? I move on and I move forward.

Six months later, I am now moved on and forward, but I'm not quite sure, as of yet, where I have landed. All I know is that I did bury my husband, did sell my home, moved to a smaller apartment, stored 90%

of my life in a 10' by 12' storage unit, secretly smuggled my three cats into my new apartment, pushed my daughters into a 'shared space' (God help me!) and found myself in a bedroom where I had to cut off the headboard in order for my bed to fit. I also have a dog (landlord was ok with the dog) who still can't figure out where he is, and waits by the door to go "home".

On the good side, however, and yes there is a good side, my daughters are adjusting. They recently told me that they didn't think it could happen, but they feel "comfortable" in the new place and now allow their friends to visit. Still not happy with sharing a room, one of them moved down to the basement. So there is another good thing—the apartment has a basement.

A few other "good" things: Our apartment is located near the LIRR, which is good for me, since I'll be working for the next umpteenth years. It's also near the beach and boardwalk which is helping the healing process, but don't worry about my therapist, she feels in the blanks when it's raining. And let's not forget my kids—they are happy that our location is also just minutes away from the "happening" bar and restaurant scene. Another healing process!

So six months ago, my life fell apart, and six months later, my kids and I are piecing back together, slowly but surely. Of course, there is much more to this story, as there always is, but you get the picture. Life does go on no matter what befalls us. It is the nature of the human spirit— yes to move on and move forward. And hopefully, sometime soon, even my dog will do the same and come to call our new place "home."

Diane McDermott

IT'S PRETTY STELLAR

I opened a little boutique in a trendy area near my house in 2004 and kept it going for four years. but closed it in 2008. That's when the economy turned and things got a bit tough for a small business. Then I found the job I have now after looking and trying to figure out what the next steps would be. I was temping at some companies to try and figure out what I wanted, and found the company I'm with now. It's only eight minutes from my house, which is pretty stellar. No morning commute. I support the VP-CIO who is also the Executive Director of the Foundation, and have been with him for the past 6 years. I love my job and am so fortunate to have found it. The IT department is about 75 people and I do everything—big and small events, meetings, and whatever is needed. I run to my boss and tell him where and what needs to be done. He's a very nice man and we enjoy working together. I've had some opportunities to move to other departments but won't, because we have such a good relationship. Those are really hard to fine.

The company is about 4000 people and we are the world's largest producer of mozzarella cheese. We are the sole supplier of cheese for Papa John's, Little Caesar's, Pizza Hut and Domino's. We also are into nutrition and make lactose, baby formula, etc. We use the by-product of the cheese, which is whey, and turn that into additives for other food products. It's a $4 billion company and is still privately owned. I count my blessings every day that I found this job and it will probably be the last one until I can't work any longer. I love getting up and going to work every day and enjoy the people I work with and the whole thing. No stress, no issues! That's a hard thing to find now.

Francine Plavnick

AGAINST ALL ODDS, I TURNED IT AROUND!!!

After a life of crime, I beat my demons finally, and graduated from high school when I turned 49 years old. I began taking drugs at a very young age, which led me to the perils of prison life. Along with my trials I had seven children and I lost custody of all of them but one. I have been clean for seven whole years, been out of prison for ten whole years and now as I write this I have all my children back in my life today, because of the positive people who helped me along the way through my traumatic times. How lucky I feel to have made it so far. The best positive news is that I finally received my diploma and I am feeling exhilarated, and overflowing with joy. Family, School, Freedom: that's all I need. I never thought it could happen, but again anything can happen! Sometimes it just takes someone coming into your life that really makes the difference. I have made a future for my family now and am so very, very happy that against all odds, I turned my life around. God Bless America!

Anonymous

EVERYONE HAS A STORY...

A starting point of a journey that led them to where they are today.

Mine began around the time when my father got sick. I'll never forget it. It was Memorial Day weekend 2001. Six weeks later he passed away, on July 4th of all days. That was a hard one...the world was celebrating and I was devastated and crushed.

Not long after that my stepmother passed away too. At this point I now felt broken. I quit my job, avoided everyone and everything, just needing to be alone and heal.

A month later, with the little bit of money my dad left me, I bought a business and went on to successfully run it for the next fourteen years, but I wasn't happy. That business and the industry I was in had changed me, and not for the better. I became miserable and resentful and jaded, something I had never been before. I knew if I didn't make a change soon I'd regret it for the rest of my life. I did just that and got out of that business and the industry that had altered me as a person. I vowed to become my old self again and make it a point to be positive, spread kindness and find happiness.

After a long sabbatical, a lot of soul-searching and going through another disappointing career attempt—thankfully, by the grace of God —I was able to find something that I could be passionate about. Something that gave me the ability to help people and do some good.

I found and partnered up with a company that has a global mission to help people and our planet. A company that I can be proud to be a part of. I have finally found my home.

I am on a different journey now. A path to make positive differences in people's lives and I thank God everyday that I am able to do so!

Jodi Somerstein

MANIFESTATION WORKS!

After a debilitating accident in 2008 I was left unemployed and walked with a cane. Years of physical therapy and surgeries left me deeply depressed and I ballooned up to 219 pounds. To cap it off, my Personal Injury attorney took a bribe from the opposing insurance company (which I didn't learn until after the statute of limitations ran out) and I lost the case with no recourse.

I was destitute, obese, jobless and handicapped with a paltry income of $820 a month Social Security. My big, beautiful house in Huntington Bay was sold at a foreclosure auction, and I had to find a place to live —FAST!

My family came to the rescue with an offer of rent up to $1,800 a month so the search began. They took me to see places that were horrific. One brand new, 400-square-foot apartment, behind a bus depot in an industrial area with a view of the LIRR was $2,200, but they said they could stretch the cost a bit. I hated it. The arrogant realtor who was employed by the complex sneered at me. "What did you expect?" he said, "Rents are high, and this is the best we can do." The complex buildings were new, but there were zero amenities, the constant clatter and moan of the railroad and of course the bus fumes. I said "No thank you," and continued my search.

My daughter took me to a similar complex in Hauppauge, just as pricey and surrounded by highways. The roar from the LIE penetrated the paper-thin walls and there was no room for my kitchen table. There was zero storage, so I would have had to get rid of everything! I thanked her for taking me out, but declined.

My younger daughter called from Pennsylvania and said "Ma, what do you have against Bayshore?" I told her first of all, it wasn't Huntington, which has been my home for 50 years. I have no family, friends or network there. The area she was referring to looked lovely in the ads, but was in a dicey neighborhood on the verge of gentrification. They said I was being "difficult." Of course. I have been "difficult" since I was born.

My son, the youngest, said, "Ma, come live with me in Brooklyn!" I laughed, but was very pleased.

I got a text from the eldest saying she was going to look at a cottage in her town, I could go with her if I l liked, which I did. The cottage was okay. A converted trailer in someone's back yard, about 600 square feet. There were restrictions. There was no outdoor space, but I was told I could put a chair behind the woodpile. I could not have overnight company, or loud parties, OR any flame anywhere on the property. Ugh. The trailer/cottage was situated less than a dozen square feet from their front door. I was frantic and desperate so I took it and gave them the down payment. We were all set to go when they told me I should come and meet the dogs. Dogs? **DOGS!** I have lived with dogs much of my life and am a great fan. "No problem," I said and went to see the dogs. The two dogs were huge German Shepherds bred to be sentinels, watch dogs. They were massive, bigger than the owner. And they only responded to commands in German. He explained to me that they were breeders, and his two dogs would be mated with a male prize-winner so all of them would have run of the property all Summer. Also they did not like me, which he noticed. I did not like them, either since I have "history" with another two German Shepherds. The owner was very kind and gently said "I'm afraid this isn't going to work..." but I was frantic and said "I plan to make this my home..." His response was "On Sunday they bit my mother-in-law..." I left then and told my daughter who exploded in anger. "They think you are too high maintenance! Nobody wants a high maintenance tenant! You have to lower your expectations, this is the very best you can do in Huntington!" I was deeply hurt and at that point almost willing to take anything.

Meekly, I conceded to my family's wishes. I would live almost anywhere. To my daughter's credit she did try to get me something in Huntington township. They were all basements in somebody's house, and one was an attic up three flights of stairs. I am 73. I went as far as King's Park but didn't want to be so far from my daughter and grand-children.

I took things into my own hands but there were zero options. I prayed. I prayed to my mom who always responded. I prayed to the universe. Then I went online to Craigslist and posted "Delightful little old lady seeks light-filled 1,000 square feet of interesting living space that is not an attic or a basement. On the water. For next to nothing." I received a lot of responses from horny men who made inappropriate suggestions. None of them was acceptable. I posted it on Facebook. My kids laughed at me. My son-in-law David chastised me over the phone using a tone of voice that was beyond condescending. Then he said "You're out of your mind. What you're looking for does not exist on Long Island…" He forgot about my mom.

I posted on Facebook, too. EVERYONE in the world knew I was looking when one day I received an instant message from one of my buddies "SA: hey did you find a place yet? ME: No, I am crazed! SA: Call this number, 631-------, but go over now because it won't last and they want to meet you." I called the number got the address and when I arrived it looked from the street like an apartment over a garage. I climbed the stairs and the property opened up to a 180-degree view of the water! The owner was waiting for me. The house is 1,000 square feet, with huge windows, two patios, a garage and a basement. In a garden. On the water. Considerably LESS than the $1,800 budget I was given. I took it.

The moral of this story is Manifestation works. I hope that you have a miracle too! I know I have…

Anonymous

A SILVER LINING

They say that every person will get fired at least once in their lifetime. Yet, at my tender age of 23 I was sure that statistic did not apply to me.

I had been recruited by a middle-aged business woman who I met on the Long Island Railroad. We shared long conversations for months on the way to and from another job in Manhattan. She worked for a prominent business publishing firm and informed me that I was just who they needed at that time. Being offered more money and benefits, I was eager to try something new and happy to boost my resume. She was the Assistant to the Publisher and I was to be the Junior Assistant to the Publisher.

Things were working out well, she taught me a lot. The owner and publisher of the sizable company was smart, successful, well-connected and demanding. They definitely raised my game. Nearly one year later at the company holiday party, where we were all laughing and mingling, she asked me to come into the office we shared so that we could exchange Christmas presents. She gave me a beautiful collectible piano that she knew I would love. No sooner did I open it she also informed me that due to company cutbacks, six people were being let go and I was one of them. I was shocked and devastated.

In hindsight, I remembered a day that stuck in mind as the mark of a changing tide. She had been on vacation for two weeks leaving me to support the Publisher on my own. When she returned to a warm welcome and a fairly snag-free report she asked him how I did. His reply, in a playful tone, was "we did great, we didn't even need you." I saw the look on her face and probably could pinpoint the exact moment that my fate was put in jeopardy. I know that he did not mean it literally and in no way was I looking to or ready to take her job, but I think she thought otherwise.

Long story short, I was given two month's severance, decided that I had had enough of working in New York City, and was about to start a job search on Long Island. A friend suggested that we take a great trip first so off to Morocco and Spain's Canary Islands we went and had a blast. When I returned, tan and mended, I answered an ad for a company called CMP in Manhasset. I had never heard of it, but little did I know that my life was about to change.

I joined CMP, a growing and successful trade publisher, as an editorial assistant in a vibrant, smart, and fun department and began an 11-year fulfilling career. I learned immeasurable skills, worked hard, traveled, received numerous promotions, collaborated with smart and wonderful people, and cultivated a group of precious friends - my favorite being the author of this book. Oh and yes, I met the love of my life, with whom I just celebrated my 30th wedding anniversary. How lucky was I?

Who knew that on that cold December day in 1983, when I cried the whole train ride home, that I had been granted the best favor of my life.

Camille De Marzo

NEW BEGINNINGS

I was educated to be a Speech and Hearing Pathologist. My first position was in the New York City School System. This was prior to Individualized Education Plans (IEPs). And, many days were thwarted by the first New York City Teachers strike! We were told that if we crossed the picket lines the teachers would not let their students out to Speech and Hearing classes! The strike was not over until November!

I was in six schools each week. Two were on Fridays! I had no materials, no mentor, and basically only two normal classrooms. One class was held in "The Matron's Closet" under a flight of stairs in the basement. Not very conducive to students' therapy as other classes are pounding down the stairs to use the bathroom!

Another group was held in the athletic supply closet on the far side of a huge third floor gym. Better yet, most of the windows had no panes so I had to cover them with cardboard! Made for quite a chilly winter. Between being in the damp basement and the freezing gym room, I was sick often that winter.

At the end of April, our very kind supervisor advised us that we would not have positions in the Fall as New York City was having budget cuts! The day after school was finished in June, I went to the beach to think of what I was going to do next. And, quite honestly, I love the beach! I arrived home and my husband said, "I found a job for you in Human Resources at Con Edison!" The following morning I had an interview with the Manager of "Union Hiring" and was employed on the spot! Literally! The Manager asked me to start working that day!

I spent about two years there and I was then promoted to Professional Placement where I spent many wonderful years.

An interesting side note: At the end of August of that first year of teaching, I received all my information in the mail to begin my second year. No one had every bothered to notify us that we had our jobs back! As I was enjoying what I was doing, I chose to stay at Con Edison.

Regrets? I had a few. I enjoyed the children and assisting in improving their disabilities. But the conditions were not proper for what needed to be done. Also, had I stayed and survived, I would be enjoying a very nice pension!

I think the gods knew what they were doing! My husband now has fairly severe hearing loss—even with hearing aids! It drives me crazy!

Anonymous

EVERYONE ASKED ME WHAT ARE YOU DOING?

Back in 2013 I was overweight, unhappy in my job and felt overwhelmed everyday with being stuck! A coworker of mine introduced me to a product line called Isagenix. I didn't know at the time there was any kind of business opportunity attached to it, but I started the program off hoping it would help me look and feel better.

Low and behold, in 3 months time, I felt like a new person. I had amazing energy, had lost my unwanted weight, was sleeping through the night and looked better than I had in 15 years!

It was at that point people started asking me what I was doing. I started sharing the program with others, helping them look and feel their best and starting to earn enough money to get my products paid for.

I then realized what was sitting in my lap—this amazing company that I was a part of now gave me the opportunity to build a business. A real business, with real income and unlimited potential. I jumped in and started to build my residual income. The company offered the best compensation plan in the industry, gave me the tools I needed to be successful and the resources to grow my business.

Since then, I have helped hundreds of people in both their health and their financial well being. I no longer have a job I hate, I am earning a fantastic income, get to fuel my body with the best nutrition on the planet and truly live a life of both financial and time freedom simultaneously!

Karen Vito

FIRED TO FABULOUS

My crazy story started over 29 years ago. I was a young professional who started working at Eastman Kodak only 5 weeks after graduation from UMASS Amherst. I relocated from my hometown in Pittsford, New York to pursue my dream of Living and Working in New York City. I left my college sweetheart to finish his senior year in college and my family to live alone on Long Island. The first year was brutal trying to find my way, literally navigating my sales territory in Queens with a map long before GPS was invented. It was a lonely time and I struggled to make it on my own. In time I learned how to live on a small budget in an expensive city. My second year was harder because my college sweetheart moved in with me, but was not able to contribute to our household expenses. He was studying to be a stock broker and cold calling for a large investment firm. We tried to make it work as a couple, but his lifestyle changed when he started living large trying to maintain the Wall Street image. The "Wolf of Wall Street" was a true depiction of the life a stockbroker led at that time.

One night I met a man at a birthday party for a college friend. He was quite charming and completely different than my college sweetheart. He pursued me until I finally left behind my stockbroker for a certified arborist. My new man had just started a tree care company and was eager to make a living saving trees from disease. I was anxious to use my degree in Marketing to help him with business advice. We were good together when we first met. I made a good living and he relied on me to help him implement business practices and organize the new company. He proposed only 8 months after we met because he feared I would leave him for my previous boyfriend who was now a wealthy stockbroker. We were married only 18 months after we first met.

Looking back at my life I never saw the warning signs; jealousy, insecurity and narcissistic behavior. I was in love with my husband and we were building a company and new life together. I was doing extremely well at my job, so good that the competition offered me an amazing opportunity. I decided to leave Kodak to join Xerox Corporation. I was excited because in my new career I was making 10 times what my husband earned each month. It never bothered me because we were partners in life. I helped with bookkeeping and daily management of our little tree company. I got pregnant but, unfortunately, lost that baby; we were both devastated. After genetic counseling and many doctor visits, we knew the stress of my demanding job in Manhattan may have caused my miscarriage. I decided to transfer to the Long Island office and take a different sales position to reduce my stress. I took a job with less responsibility, an easy commute and got pregnant again immediately. My baby girl was born healthy and entered our world in November 1998. As a sales person, the 4th quarter was the busiest time of year at my company. I needed to return back to work to support my family when my baby was only a few weeks old. My husband was not enthusiastic to be our child care provider because had a tree company to run. We found a family member who was hired to babysit our newborn girl. A few months later I was pregnant with twins. I lost one of the twins early in the pregnancy and had major complications for the next five months. I was on disability and we struggled to make ends meet. I was forced to return back to Manhattan only 6 weeks after my baby boy entered our world. My days were crazy, commuting 3 hours each day to Manhattan, coming home to take care of my babies, my home and my husband's company. My son was always sick and I was having a hard time managing everything. My son was 10 months old when he was hospitalized with a fever of undiagnosed origin. My husband and I took shifts to stay with our toddler while our baby boy was in the hospital. One night while at the hospital, I couldn't sleep. I was responding to work messages at 3am. I sat there staring at my little miracle boy hooked up to IVs with a 105 fever. It was then that I had my epiphany. I had to leave my job and take care of children. My husband encouraged me to take a leave of absence to help him run his company. I thought life would be perfect. I woke up every morning taking care of my kids, my home and my husband. The bonus was using my business degree to actually help run his business full-time. Our company went from a one man show to over 13 employees in our first 10 years together. Business was thriving and we were finally working together every day.

Unfortunately, my husband took on a partner to help runs things while I was taking care of my sick baby. His partner was not a good man. He was a liar and a thief. The partner hired his mistress as an office manager. She set her sights on my husband. When I started questioning the missing money, trips to Florida and large expenses that we did not have money for, I was fired by my husband. He decided that it was best for our relationship that I was not involved in his business. Ironically, I was never a paid employee. I was the owner's wife who invested 10 years of my salary, blood, sweat and tears to build my husband's company. I thought we were partners for life. Sadly, I learned the hard way that nothing lasts forever. The craziest part of this story is that I stayed married to my husband for another 10 years before I finally had enough.

After leaving his company, I started working as a beauty consultant for Mary Kay. I won many awards; Queen of Sales and Queen of Recruiting. I won diamonds and jewelry at our monthly sales contests. I contributed to our household income, but this new job was not the six-figure salary that I earned in my corporate career. My husband grew bitter because he hated my Mary Kay business. He wanted me to return to a full-time corporate job to assist with our household finances. He never appreciated the job I did as a homemaker and mother. He started cheating with women that I knew. Finally, he was caught in a web of lies. I decided it was time for me to fire him as my husband. After 7 years of legal battles and owing my lawyer a fortune, I am finally free. I have no regrets. My children grew up with me by their side. My Mary Kay career gave me the flexibility to volunteer as class mom and to work with other parents in PTA to build friendships. I was a Girl Scout Leader, Cub Scout Leader and used my business skills to help our PTA board by organizing programs for our school district like "Parents as Reading Partners" and our semi-annual blood drives. I am involved in my church, teaching religion for the past 15 years in addition to being a Vestry member for 7 years to help our little church thrive. I was there for my children every day of their life until they were respectively 11 and 12.

After my husband and I separated, I had no choice but to return to work full-time to support myself. I have been a Mary Kay Independent Beauty Consultant for over 15 years with customers who have walked with me through this journey. I managed to maintain two jobs for the past 7 years to make ends meet. My children learned to be self-sufficient and are now amazing young adults, doing fantastic in college. We have incredible memories that I would not trade for any amount of money. My children are my life and my legacy. Recently, I received recognition from an amazing organization on Long Island. I was nominated for Angel Awards of Long Island and won a special award with beautiful gifts. My daughter was by my side as I was recognized for my volunteer efforts in my community. My son cheered me on from college in South Carolina. Everything happens for a reason. I live my life by the Golden Rule: "Do unto others as you would have done unto you." I am grateful for all that has happened to me because it made me into the independent woman that I am today. Looking forward to a brighter future for my children and me. Life is good and is getting better every day!

Heidi B. Gallmeyer-Felix

THE POWER OF PRAYER

About 10 years ago, I found myself in a life-changing situation. I had always worked in an office. I was, at that point, an office manager for a title insurance company. If you recall, around 2007-2008, the real estate market started to plummet. Sadly, the company I had worked for for many years ended up closing.

At the same time, I was dealing with the decline in my mom's health. I had her (begrudgingly on her part) staying with me. I loved her to pieces, but we all know that 24/7 togetherness can get to anyone.

Knowing I needed much flexibility in my schedule and food always being a passion of mine, I ended up taking a part time job in a a local deli. It was hard work, but I really enjoyed it; both patrons and staff.

My mom lived for about 10 months. My plan was to get back into an office. What happened instead was they implored me to work full time at the deli...which I apprehensively did.

Well that turned into 7 days a week, 8 to 10 hours a day. This went on for eight years. At 57, I realize I could no longer do this work. It was both physically and financially draining.

So I decided it was time to get back into an office, rewrote my resume and began the painstaking task of job hunting. I sent out resumes, but also told everyone I knew of my search.

Little did I realize that 57 was not a very marketable age. I dealt with disappointments and many mixed feelings, but kept trudging along and praying. I really believed that if I continued doing this type of work for that many hours per week, I would no longer be able to walk by the time I hit 70.

Well after much persistence and prayer, I was offered and accepted a job in a wonderful company. Now not only am I off my feet, I have health benefits, paid time off and a 401k.

All I can say is the power of prayer and much effort can change your life...no matter what your age!

Eileen Story

REFLECTIONS OF AN ENTREPRENEUR

I recently turned 60, and realized it has been 20 years since I took up a hobby that would change my life forever. In 1998, we redid our bathroom, and I somehow convinced my husband to let me create a faux finish on the new walls. I had zero experience, and no clue of what to do. However, I figured it out and managed to create something beautiful. In fact, the contractors who were still working in my home told me I should quit my day job, because they could not believe it was the first thing I had ever done; they said I was better than any professionals they had seen! I couldn't contain my elation that I was good at something besides typing! I was always creative but never had the opportunity to paint; I even cried when I missed finger painting in kindergarten one day.

I was a legal secretary straight out of high school, and in my last job, was working for the same attorney for 23 years, running his nine-attorney law firm. I spent every weekday living for the weekend. I felt like a robot, barely alive from Monday to Friday, often working late every night. My boss had a toxic personality, and was sucking the life out of me. But it was all I knew how to do, and I was great at it. So I stuck it out to help provide for my family. I had no choice.

My newfound passion of decorative painting remained a hobby for a few years, except for the occasional room I would do for family or their friends. But September 11, 2001 changed everything for me. What a moment of clarity I had, working in New York City, and witnessing the Towers come crashing down from my Midtown office windows. My boss was screaming because he thought his friend was in one of the buildings at a meeting (he wasn't). Yet when I was walking to the elevators to begin my two-mile walk to be with my daughter at her Barnard College dorm, he followed me with work, telling me to do it at the dorm since I was leaving early! That just sums up what I put up with all those years. I realized in that moment that life was both precious and fragile, and I could not work in that toxic environment any longer. I am so thankful I found the courage to change my life. Trust me, it wasn't easy, and felt like financial suicide. But I could no longer let money be the driving force in my life. I had to put my sanity first.

All these years later, I still pinch myself. I get to do what I love and make my clients happy. And I've been voted Best Artist of Long Island for six years in a row! All I had was an insatiable passion for my new hobby, and an urgent desire to exit from the rat race that was my life. Let there be no mistake, I didn't choose an easy path, and it's still difficult, not knowing when and where my next paycheck is coming from. But the rewards are immeasurable. I am in charge of my own destiny, my own schedule, my own happiness.

When I left my job, I promised myself I would never work for anyone but myself ever again, and I'm so grateful that has remained true. I show my gratitude by sharing my talent in ways where it can bring joy and hope to others, such as donating murals and art in foster agencies, schools, children's hospitals, or wherever there might be a need. I have also donated tens of thousands of dollars of paintings to important causes I believe in.

These days, I try to live a tranquil life and be in the "now," which is the total opposite of the life I lived in my corporate job. Just give me some soft jazz and paint, and I'm golden. I am passionate about all the beauty life has to offer, and the heavenly landscapes of Long Island, New York provide never-ending inspiration.

As an entrepreneur I have been forced to do things that are often way outside of my comfort zone, such as figuring out ways to market my art business, finding new opportunities, or being in a room of strangers at a networking event or business seminar. But one thing I've learned all these years is that anything worthwhile is worth fighting for and never easy. It's all up to me to either carry on and continue to put myself out there, or crawl into a corner and give up. But that is not an option for me. I've been told more than once that I am tenacious, and I'm so proud of that. Make no mistake about it, turning nothing more than a passionate hobby into a business, without having any game plan, let alone a business plan, in place, is quite an accomplishment. The fact that I am STILL in business nearly two decades later, is pretty darn awesome.

Debbie Viola

LIVING WITH MS

When I was 13 years old our neighborhood paper boy "Jay" was attracted to me and started to gain my parent's trust. After a few months, they hired him to renovate our bathroom in the den. He would hang around after work and visit me on Friday and Saturday night when my parents went out. My sisters would be upstairs in our split level house, watching TV or sleeping, and I would be in the den waiting for Jay to come around back. A few months after we had unprotected sex, I realized I was not getting my period. I ignored the pregnancy symptoms until my mother questioned if I had recently gotten my period. She took me to the doctor and he determined I was six months pregnant. To avoid embarrassment, my parents made up a story that I was visiting my Grandmother in Florida, but in truth they sent me to a facility on Long Island for underage mothers. I was forced to give the baby up for adoption and a month after her birth I transitioned into high school as if nothing had happened.

Fresh out of high school in 1984, I attended secretarial school and within six months of graduating I landed an interview with Mr. B, a prominent lawyer on Long Island. He was well-known for handling high profile divorce and criminal cases and I worked for him as a legal assistant for 20 years. This job gave me the experience I needed to become the virtual assistant I am today. Working in the field of litigation was challenging and throughout the years I was forced to meet with the attorney's constant deadlines. These long hours at work were an interruption into my family life. On top of the high demand and stress of this job, in 1994 I developed symptoms of Multiple Sclerosis (MS) at the early age of 29. I was diagnosed within a year and I pushed through the MS symptoms of slurred speech, double vision, facial paralysis, fatigue, etc. for as long as I could. The symptoms continued to worsen, and once walking became difficult I had no choice but to retire and take care of my illness.

Without a job to help support my family I filled my time volunteering, attending physical therapy to keep my body strong, and taking care of my family. I met people through my involvement with local associations, chambers, and clubs. Networking opened up a whole new world for me to further gain independence. I have received awards such as "Hometown Hero," "Business Person of the Year," and "Woman of Distinction," because of my dedication and community service.

Recently I have become involved in freelance work at home and it has proven that anything is possible despite having and living with MS. Just like anyone else I have bad days, but since I started using Young Living Essential Oils daily, I am empowered to make a difference in my life and to assist and help guide others to live their best lives by using and sharing Essential Oils with every home in the world!

Patricia Locurcio

THE GOOD IN GOODBYE

"The greatest glory in living lies not in never falling, but in rising every time we fall." Nelson Mandela

On December 12, 2017, I retired as Executive Director of the Long Island Volunteer Center (LIVC) after 20 years. It was a symbolic date for me--the feast day of Our Lady of Guadalupe. Joan Imhof (the LIVC founder and my dearest friend) passed away on that day 6 years ago and we opened "Hope Floats" in her memory on that day 5 years ago to ramp up for Superstorm Sandy, which I consider the apex of my career in the volunteer industry. That and the New York State Volunteer Generation Campaign grant secured in 2011 which named LIVC a NYS Regional Volunteer Center, putting LIVC squarely on the map.

While I stayed on as the Treasurer and a board member, retiring from day-to-day in the trenches with a purposeful view of advancing the human condition was very hard on me. For all those 20 years, I did the work as a volunteer.

My paid position was Office Manager to my husband Peter's busy medical practice, a job I started in 1995, with a nine-year break when my sister took on the position—she gave it back in 2004. The practice was acquired by a local hospital effective February 1, 2018. I was asked to stay on to help with the transition but was advised, due to conflict of interest, that no wives could work in the same practice (this was shared during the negotiations, but it didn't fully register with either of us the full consequences from that directive). So, not only no more "mom and pop shop"—no more "mom." The intensity of the transition, while exhilarating, ended abruptly on April 30, 2018, my last day associated with my husband's life work. I felt totally heartbroken with a sense of loss that I couldn't shake. Not only had my volunteer job gone away, but I was also relieved of duties by the state to support my literal "work husband." It was a double whammy in a four-month period. My comfort zones were completely abandoned.

What to do next? I threw myself into projects at home—organizing, decluttering, redecorating. Next, I caught up on unread books, joined the local Rotary, volunteered at the Junior League Thrift Shop, traveled multiple times to my mother's Pennsylvania home to help her downsize for an upcoming move to senior housing/assisted living, and signed up for Hofstra University's adult education program which met four times a week. Then the coup de gras happened when all the newfound frenetic busyness came to a grinding halt – on August 1st, I fractured my wrist while ice skating on a cruise ship. Thank goodness I was wearing a helmet, or this could have been a much worse situation.

Surgery that required plate/pins and something that looks like a gardening tool installed to hold the wrist together was needed. You cannot believe what you cannot do with this kind of injury. The details are a bit humbling, so I'll spare the reader. Suffice to say I was brought to my knees and the "pity party" continued in earnest with occupational therapy three times a week. It didn't take long to realize, though, that all I really needed was downtime—to relax, renew, rejuvenate and embrace the day with whatever it brought. The healing has been slow, but the self-introspection was necessary. Intention, gratitude, and hope have replaced the nostalgic sadness and uncertainties about the future which plagued me daily. Maria Shriver's book "I've Been Thinking" also became a remedied source of inspiration.

There is a silver lining to this story which shows the interconnectedness of life circumstances. At a Rotary meeting in the fall that my husband and I attended, he introduced me to a doctor from the local hospital who was there to give a talk about programs and activities. I explained my background and that I was interested in finding another position in health care. He paved the way to reach a placement specialist in Human Resources who sized me up and immediately sent me over for an interview with the hospital welcome center (the person who was going to take a job there declined over the weekend right before I walked in at 10 am that Monday). The next day I was offered the job. What interested them in me was not just the time spent in medical practice, but also the years spent in the human service industry! I started there January 7, 2019, and now I help connect the dots from the public to the hospital by getting individuals to needed programs and services to improve their quality of life. The office also organizes and runs supports groups that bring people together to bond and to heal. What a great fit for me! My new manager asked each staff member to select a word to reflect on throughout the new year that would be a goal to work toward. I chose "mindfulness."

Theodore Roosevelt said, "Far and away the best prize that life offers is the chance to work hard at work worth doing." I was so blessed to have had such rewarding professional life opportunities at both the LIVC and my husband's office. The people I encountered along the way (like Joan Imhof, Lana Gluck, Anna Lyons, Anne Sprotte, Patricia Moynihan, Patricia Sands, Simone Leo, Patricia Force, and Valentina Janek to name a few) made me a better person, and the experiences from both settings yielded indelible memory markers. It was a particular honor to support Gwen O'Shea (who then led the Health & Welfare Council of Long Island) ramp up to meet the needs from Superstorm Sandy—that work brought out the best in all of us. We felt the kind of sympathy that means, "I suffer with you." If I had to pick my one word for this region's response to Superstorm Sandy, it would be "community", how we unselfishly came together to help those in deep distress by pooling our strength and sharing the work and the responsibility. I have never witnessed or experienced anything like it —manifestations of true camaraderie and genuine human kindness. It was the greatest privilege of my life to have a front-row seat at the LIVOAD (Long Island Voluntary Organizations Active in Disaster)

Volunteer Recovery Center seeing all the myriad organizations easing human suffering together on such a grand scale.

The knowledge that being a volunteer doesn't depend on what we do, what matters is that the exchange has been one of reaching out to be a partner in the human condition, in making that connection where you know something profound has happened. It's not an ideal or intangible objective, it's real life and certainly embodies the adage, "Volunteerism is not what you give, it's not even what you get, it's what you become."

I have just a handful of learnings to pass on:

The way you get meaning into your life is to devote yourself to loving others, devote yourself to your community around you, and devote yourself to creating something that gives you purpose and meaning.

Find that intersection of passion and purpose and live it out on purpose.

Faced with apathy, act.

Faced with conflict, seek common ground.

Faced with adversity, persevere.

Surround yourself with positive, thoughtful people.

Be kind.

Be grateful.

Find the good in goodbye.

Diana O'Neill

LACING UP THOSE COMBAT BOOTS

I have learned a thing or two about interviewing. First of all don't cave, don't give up. Keep calling or emailing or networking. Establish yourself as a person with goals and ambitions. Take the time to connect with people and surround yourself with others you can learn from who are in similar circumstances. Don't be a jerk and think that you are the only one in the situation you are in. Keep searching and keep mingling. Treat your downtime as a life experience. If you decide that you are bummed out, take a little break from interviewing and searching, and do something that you have never done before.

It will be stimulating and give you the energy you need to dust yourself off and start over again. Don't sell yourself short. Know your strengths. Believe that experience and maturity are contributory when you speak. Never give up or give in.

At some point in her life or career, a woman has to share her challenges with other women who have experienced some type of loss. She has to be a role model for others when she really didn't know she was, but listened attentively to other women who were reaching out for the same guidance as herself. The change that happens to women experiencing job loss in midlife begins with understanding and good old fashioned girl talk.

The rest became history for me! I decided to write these experiences not so much for me, but to try to inspire other women who are maybe not so different from me and have experienced a major change in their work life.

Girls, leave your combat boots on and keep plowing for your dreams.

As the old song goes, "Fairy tales can come true, it can happen to you, if you're young at heart!"

Believe it.

I was hopeful by the time I self published this book, I would be employed. Two years and six months counting since my downsize, I landed a position in the nonprofit sector, helping others. One year later, I changed careers once again, working in the financial industry reaching out to others, ironically enough, and cultivated the Long Island Breakfast Club as an entity on Long Island. It has been a wild and crazy ride with a lot of ups and downs, and at times I still feel like I am on a cyclone.

Continue to enjoy your ride, buckle up and take the ride. You won't be sorry.

Wait a minute. Did I stop? Hell no! The passion I experienced since my job loss kicked the extra adrenaline that was asleep in my psyche. I am looking forward to the next chapter.

Losing a job can be hazardous to your health. Don't let that happen to you. Make it a ride. Think about what you love, and do what you love. If you do what you love, you will always be successful.

Take a part time job doing what you love, while you still look for that career. Think I can! Make your age work for you. Stay positive! Laugh! Cry! Time is not on our side, so as boomers we need to enjoy every day! Be flexible! Let your personality shine through and show your stuff. Be your own advocate for sure.

Go back to basics and recycle those old thoughts that Mama used to tell you. Remember with age comes a wealth of knowledge, experience and history. Don't forget it. People start over every day. If it starts to feel right, keep moving along. What matters most is to keep moving, even if it's a frightening change. I don't know if I will ever reach the end of this ride, and may go up and down for another time in my life screaming, laughing, and getting bumped around, but hold on tight as each time you learn something new. It's a challenge. Do something you haven't done. This will make you strong!

Valentina

ACKNOWLEDGMENTS

Having published this book on January 18, 2019 which was the anniversary of my husband Ronald Janek's death, I am hopeful that he is looking down saying, *"Well Teeeen, You did it!"* Teeeen was an annoying nickname Ronnie always bellowed out to me at many times during the day. Sadly stated, your life was filled with many ups and downs in the past two years, but in the end I know you were ready to hang your hat with the rest of the family up in the pearly gates above.

I am eternally grateful to my publisher, Stephanie Larkin, for her insight, and ongoing support in bringing my stories to life. It is because of her efforts and encouragement that I have been able to make *From Fired to Freedom* a very special part of my past and future history. Stephanie, You taught me so many things, you stood by me and mentored me with the encouragement and expertise to make this book a reality. Having completed this project which started a few years ago, working together made me realize how my experiences have and can enhance a person's visibility and career no matter what profession you choose.

A very special thanks to all my contributors who embraced their story submissions with zest, honesty, and positivity. You have all made a significant impact to me and have made your experiences truly special.

I am sure these experiences will be very helpful to many jobseekers, and professionals in act two of their life who are thinking about changing their future or have experienced a big bad boot unexpectedly, a trauma or a funny experience. Having worked with each of you either on the phone, in a coaching session, at a networking event or club meeting, I say "Thank you! Thank you for bringing your stories to life with honesty and certitude."

First and foremost, I would like to say thanks to my wonderful circle of family and very close friends for having the patience with me to encourage and support yet another challenge which meant the world to me in completing *From Fired to Freedom: Life After the Big Bad Boot Gave me Wings*.

Throughout the process of writing this book, many individuals from my entire family, very close friends, and the members of the Long Island Breakfast Club in the community have taken time to meet with me and discuss some relative topics which resulted in

Philotimo !
Experience Impacts
The World Beyond Imagination
www.longislandbreakfastclub.org

my goal to complete this to be published on January 18th, the date of my husband's passing.

Most importantly, my daughter Jennifer and her partner Jenn have been on my side the past two years supporting my ideas and inspirational projects during a critical change in my life. My grandchildren Kaitlyn and Kyle are a big part of my current and future life as I continue in the third act in my personal and professional life. They make me feel wonderful when I spend time with them, while always encouraging me with their personalities, wisdom and wit.

ABOUT THE AUTHOR

Valentina Janek has held a variety of corporate, community, human resources, recruiting, and consulting positions in the financial marketing, media-public relations, publishing, technology, human resources, fundraising and events industries. Currently, Ms. Janek works as a Marketing Consultant, Career Coach, and a Mid-Life Advocate, and educates many individuals and organizations through her unique training as a business development officer with QS2 Training & Consulting.

Previously she spent two years at the County of Nassau Housing Unit developing the Employment Assistance Resource Network. She also worked as a marketing professional in the financial industry. Valentina's spent over ten years at CMP Media as an Administrative Operations Manager. It was during her tenure that her aspirations to be an author began, working along with such a skilled editorial team. Prior to CMP, Valentina worked in corporate management at Compaq Computer-Hewlett Packard. Her career spans over decades starting with Vernitron Corporation, as a representative for investor relations.

Valentina Janek is the President & Founder of the Long Island Breakfast Club, an organization providing referrals for small, medium, and large business owners, positivity, advocacy, support, career counseling for middle-income midlife jobseekers, business networking, social-preneuring, and advocacy tips. She also enjoys spending time with high school students as a mentor, teaching them about how giving back to communities through volunteering is important and rewarding.

Valentina is a social-preneur, networker, leader and media professional promoting paying it forward on Long Island, working on different and unique projects. A very powerful and strong woman who believes in the good old-fashioned back to basic principles of life. Her big world includes a plethora of wonderful family, a committed circle of friends, dedicated members of the Long Island Breakfast Club and many writers who contributed their stories to this book. Valentina stays motivated by getting involved with many communities. As a member of The Sons of Italy Women's Division Lodge 2344A in Lynbrook, she continues to be a vibrant member of the Italian culture.

Ms. Janek is frequently called upon with regard to her community outreach experience on Long Island. Janek was a featured guest on The Anderson Cooper Show on CNN Series, CBS News, Channel 12 News, the God Squad, Jobline, Cablevision's "Our Town" Series, Hometown and several local radio stations discussing the current turbulent times for professionals during their careers.

Valentina is sought out as a facilitator and inspirational speaker at schools, universities, community organizations and professional businesses.

Made in the USA
Middletown, DE
21 February 2019